Discovering Language

PERSPECTIVES ON THE ENGLISH LANGUAGE
Series Editor: Lesley Jeffries

Siobhan Chapman Thinking About Language: Theories of English
Urszula Clark Studying Language: English in Action
Lesley Jeffries Discovering Language: The Structure of Modern English

---

Perspectives on the English Language Series
Series Standing Order
ISBN 0-333-96146-3 hardback
ISBN 0-333-96147-1 paperback
(*outside North America only*)

You can receive future titles in this series as they are published by placing a standing order. Please contact your bookseller or, in the case of difficulty, write to us at the address below with your name and address, the title of the series and one of the ISBNs quoted above.

Customer Services Department, Macmillan Distribution Ltd,
Houndmills, Basingstoke, Hampshire RG21 6XS, England

Discovering Language

The Structure of Modern English

Lesley Jeffries

palgrave
macmillan

First published 2006 by
PALGRAVE MACMILLAN
Houndmills, Basingstoke, Hampshire RG21 6XS and
175 Fifth Avenue, New York, N.Y. 10010
Companies and representatives throughout the world

PALGRAVE MACMILLAN is the global academic imprint of the Palgrave Macmillan division of St. Martin's Press, LLC and of Palgrave Macmillan Ltd. Macmillan® is a registered trademark in the United States, United Kingdom and other countries. Palgrave is a registered trademark in the European Union and other countries.

ISBN-13: 978–1–4039–1261–9 hardback
ISBN-10: 1–4039–1261–0 hardback
ISBN-13: 978–1–4039–1262–6 paperback
ISBN-10: 1–4039–1262–9 paperback

This book is printed on paper suitable for recycling and made from fully managed and sustained forest sources.

A catalogue record for this book is available from the British Library.

Library of Congress Cataloging-in-Publication Data
Jeffries, Lesley 1956–.
Discovering language : the structure of modern English / Lesley Jeffries.
p. cm. – (Perspectives on the English language)
Includes bibliographical references and index.
ISBN 1-4039-1261-0 – ISBN 1-4039-1262-9 (pbk.)
1. English language–Grammar. 2. English language–Phonology. 3. English language–Syntax. I. Title. II. Series.

PE1106.J44 2006
425–dc22 2006044297

10 9 8 7 6 5 4 3 2 1
15 14 13 12 11 10 09 08 07 06

Transferred to Digital Printing in 2009

For Dave

Contents

List of Figures

List of Tables

Series Preface

This series has been a twinkle in my eye for a number of years. I am delighted to be able to launch it with the three 'core' books, *Discovering Language, Studying Language* and *Thinking about Language,* which together make a broad introduction to language study in general and the study of English in particular. An explanation of why I felt these books were needed is probably useful here, and it will also serve as an explanation of the series as a whole.

The first thing to note is that English language study is growing in Britain and elsewhere, to some extent at the expense of general linguistics. As a linguistics graduate myself I both regret this and also celebrate the numbers of students wanting to study English language. These students may be studying English language as part of a more general degree course, or as a single subject. All such students need tools of analysis. They need to be able to say what is going on in a text, whether that be a literary or non-literary text, spoken or written. *Discovering Language: The Structure of Modern English* aims to provide just these tools at the level required by undergraduates and their teachers.

Whilst there are many other introductory books on the market, and some of them are very good in different ways, none of them does exactly what *I* want as a teacher of English language undergraduates. I want to be able to teach them the tools of analysis and gain expertise in using them separately from the question of where they come from and whether the theory behind them is consistent or eclectic. We have therefore separated out the contextual and theoretical issues, making sure that all the basic tools are in one volume, *Discovering Language: The Structure of Modern English,* while the issues of context are collected together in *Studying Language: English in Action,* and the basic theories of language which inform all of these approaches are discussed in *Thinking about Language: Theories of English.*

The aim of the second volume, then, *Studying Language: English in Action*, is to put into practice some of the analytical techniques learnt in *Discovering Language*, and to add to these skills by learning about the techniques and problems of studying real language data, either spoken or written, from different points of view, whether social, geographical or even historical. The third book, *Thinking about Language: Theories of English*, enables the student to take a step back from the detail of description and research in order to consider what the underlying views of human language may be. It is likely that students will use these three books at different points in their studies, depending on the kind of course they are taking and the uses their tutors wish to make of them.

The first three books in the series have a logical relationship (description, research and theory), but they can be used in flexible and inventive ways by tutors who find that the individual books do not fit exactly into the modules or course structures they are working to. The series will be developed from here with a 'second wave' of higher-level textbooks, each of which will cover the kind of topic that might be introduced in final-year optional modules or on Masters' courses. These books are currently being commissioned, and the list is not final, but we hope to have titles on English Pragmatics, Conversation Analysis, Critical Discourse Analysis, Literary Stylistics and History of English. They will build upon the core texts by emphasising the three strands of these books: descriptive tools, underlying theories and the methodological issues relating to each topic. They will be written by scholars at the cutting edge of research, and will include both an overview and the latest developments in the field concerned.

LESLEY JEFFRIES

Acknowledgements

I would like to thank Urszula Clark and Siobhan Chapman, the authors of the other two companion books in this series, whose enthusiasm and efficiency in our joint project has helped me to write this book. The support of Kate Wallis, our 'in-house' editor, was also invaluable, and her belief in the project was infectious.

The many students I have encountered at the University of Huddersfield over the years have taught me how *not* to explain the basics of English description. I am grateful for this, and hope that this book shows that I have learnt at least some of their lessons. The remaining problems of exposition remain mine, of course.

I am also indebted to colleagues at the University of Huddersfield and elsewhere for their support and intellectual stimulation which has informed some of this thinking for this book, though they will acknowledge that I do not always take their advice! The anonymous readers, in particular, made some very helpful suggestions, some of which I was able to take up.

Finally, I would like to thank Jane Gaffikin, whose design and computing skills have ensured that the figures help to inform as well as looking just right.

LESLEY JEFFRIES

Introduction

This book is one of three companion books in the series *Perspectives on the English Language*. The others are *Studying Language: English in Action* by Urszula Clark and *Thinking about Language: Theories of English* by Siobhan Chapman. Together these three books provide the student of English with the foundation in descriptive apparatus, theoretical background and research skills needed at the undergraduate level.

The current volume provides tools of analysis that students can use in their own linguistic studies in English, and sets aside (to the other volumes) the question of how one actually goes about studying 'real' language data (see Clark, 2006) and of the theory underpinning these tools (see Chapman, 2006).

This book introduces the **levels** model of language, which enables students to learn about the smallest linguistic items (sounds) and work through the subsequent levels (morphology and syntax) until the sentence is reached. Many introductory books address the structural issues considered here, but they also usually include contextual and theoretical discussions that are dealt with in the other volumes in this series. As a result there is enough room to include a chapter on the basic lexical semantics without which the rest of the levels of language would not work.

Students of the English language should find this book useful, whether they are taking a single honours degree in English Language, a linguistics degree or a combined degree that includes some element of the English language. It can stand alone as a wide-ranging guide to describing English or serve as the foundation for more advanced work on the linguistic features of English. It also combines effectively with the books by Clark and Chapman to provide a rounded education in the study and description of the English language.

After many years of teaching undergraduates I have come to the conclusion that development of their understanding and knowledge often reflects the development of linguistics itself. It is therefore feasible to learn the formal description of language, as described here, and then progress to considering the ways in which the theory underlying this description may be flawed, and from there move to the higher reaches of phonological, grammatical and semantic theory. It is not so easy to start from problems of description and complications of theory as students can quickly become disillusioned with tools that appear not to work well. What they need first is something practical they can use (this book), together with advice on how to apply it to real data (Clark, 2006) and stimulating discussions about the basis of the tools they are using and that might lead them into other models and tools (Chapman, 2006).

The aim of our main approach to language description and the analytical tools we shall introduce is to help the reader to develop strategies for describing English texts in linguistic terms. It is important to note that the word **'text'** will be used throughout this book to mean linguistic data of any kind, whether spoken or written, prepared or impromptu. Thus the text that we study could be a conversation in our kitchen over breakfast, a poem or a political speech. It is worth noting that in some disciplines the word text is taken still further to include communications that are largely visual in nature, such as advertisements, photographs and films. While this extension of the term is an interesting development it is largely irrelevant to this book, which aims to develop the ability to describe only linguistic texts. The final chapter introduces the more contextual aspects of linguistics, leading towards a more integrated analysis of texts that may be both visual and linguistic in their form. For now we shall stay with the linguistic.

In order to be in a position to describe language data, the analyst needs 'tools' that can be shared with other analysts, so that they have a common vocabulary to compare their findings and debate issues of real concern about language and how it is used. Not all theories of language use the same tools, and some theories contradict each other. They may produce models that explain different aspects of the data.

Human language is a very complex phenomenon and it is unlikely that a single theory, producing a single model, will be able to describe language comprehensively and in ways that are useful for all purposes. This book is written with the student of English language and/or linguistics in mind, and its purpose is to enable such students to describe English texts from a variety of angles with a degree of accuracy and clarity, so that they can progress to discussing the English language in wider contexts using the kind of technical knowledge that enhances the quality of such discussions.

The theory underlying the book is largely **a structuralist theory** of language, though it is also informed in various places by the work of **function-**

al linguistics and the **transformational-generative theory** of language. This eclectic use of theory is practical, for the reasons given above: the reader requires a manageable and accessible set of tools for describing English. It is also theoretically sound, for reasons that are beyond the scope of this volume to explain.

One of the fundamental aspects of structuralism, which no other theory has explicitly denied or contradicted, is that language is an arbitrary system of communication. We shall discuss arbitrariness in Chapter 7, but let us consider the concept of **systematicness** here as one of the more influential ideas coming from structuralist theory. The basic idea is that linguistic items (for example words) have meaning not because they refer to something in the world, but because they contrast with other units in the language. So the meaning of a word such as *dog* is not the sum of all possible dogs in the world, but the fact that it contrasts with all the other animal words in English; it is not the same as *cat, horse, bird* and so on.

This concept of a **language system** led to linguists spending half a century or more looking almost entirely at the units and structures of language, and trying to work out how they related to each other, often without much reference to **language use** in real contexts. Though this has since changed, and many linguists now work mainly with real language data in real contexts, the idea that linguistic items and structures are defined largely in terms of each other remains a radical departure from the earlier common-sense notion that human language is basically a way of labelling some pre-existing reality. Linguistic activities in the twentieth century also produced very detailed and comprehensive descriptions of languages, particularly English, as did the other two main theories of language that arose during that period: transformational-generative theory and functional theory. We do not have sufficient space to consider these theories in depth, but they are all drawn upon in this book in places where they have the most to contribute to our declared purpose: to provide a workable toolkit for students of the English language.

Before embarking upon a detailed description of the sounds, units and structures of English it is helpful to have a mental 'map' of the territory we shall be covering. It has become almost unavoidable in all linguistic descriptions to divide the description into sections that deal with different sizes of unit, often called the levels of language. This is a convenient way of coping with the complexity of language, and it also reflects the theoretical understanding that language is indeed organised on a number of levels.

Note, incidentally, that the levels model of language is a metaphorical device that enables us to visualise the relationship between different sizes of unit as though they were physically separate, when in fact they all occur in the same stream of speech. Many scientific models, including linguistic ones, have a metaphorical basis of a similar kind.

If we begin with the smallest unit of language and proceed through the higher levels, the result is a structure like that in Table I.1.

The three levels of language that received the most attention in the past were **phonology**, **morphology** and **syntax**. In recent decades the linguistic context of sentences and utterances has received more attention in the sub-disciplines of discourse analysis, conversation analysis, stylistics and pragmatics. The two outer 'levels' are not really levels at all, but the 'reality sandwich' in between which language exists.

Phonetics is concerned with the production and reception of speech sounds, and in some ways is closer to the natural sciences (biology and physics) than to linguistics. Note also that although a great deal of phonetics is concerned with small speech sounds, there are other aspects of the physical production of language that are not made up of such small units. These include stress, including word-stress, and intonation. At the other extreme there is the study of exactly what happens when language is actually used, how the situation and the participants affect and are affected by what is said, and so on. This area of study has grown a great deal in recent years, and discourse study, pragmatics and other fields of linguistics have embraced the wider context as well as the individual context (including the speaker's brain) when looking at cognitive aspects of language. These studies, which also include cognitive stylistics, language pathology and language acquisition, border on the social sciences, particularly sociology and social psychology, and draw on many of their methods and theories.

This book starts with phonetics and then works through the levels presented in Table I.1, though with only a cursory glance at the **text** structure and **context** levels. These two levels have produced so much descriptive apparatus and methodological guidance in recent years that they are given broader treatment in *Studying Language* (Clark, 2006) and later books in this series.

No linguistic model can comprehensively represent and structure the data of language, and one of the problems arising from the levels model is that it sets meaning aside and places structure at the centre of the description. Meaning is not entirely ignored, of course, because **phonology**, **morphology** and **syntax** all have a contribution to make to meaning (see Jeffries, 1998). However the

Table I.1 The levels of language

Phonetics	The physical properties of speech
Phonology	The study of linguistic sounds
Morphology	The study of word structure
Syntax	The study of utterance/sentence structure
Text/discourse structure	The study of higher-level structures
Context and use	The influence of situation, participants and functions

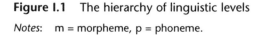

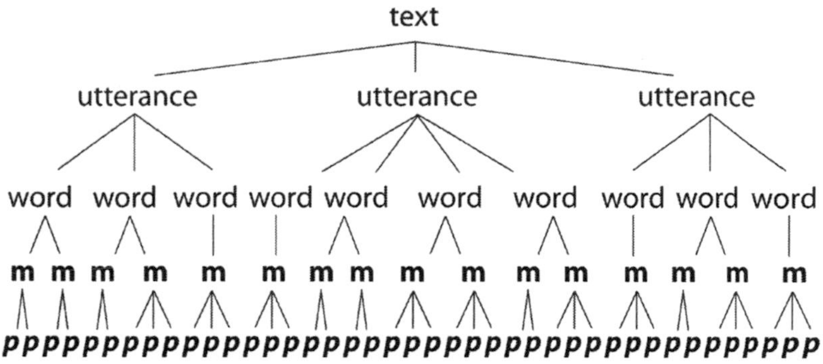

Figure I.1 The hierarchy of linguistic levels

Notes: m = morpheme, p = phoneme.

meaning of words, known as **lexical semantics**, has no clear place amongst the levels and is therefore covered in a separate chapter of this book.

The apparent anomaly of the place of **semantics** in the levels model may appear less peculiar if we consider the way in which language is structured. Whilst the levels model gives us an idea of how big the units are, and that they combine into larger units, the notion of levels on its own does not tell us in any detail how they combine and what rules or restrictions are in place to prevent any combinations being possible.

We can see that the levels combine sounds to make **morphemes** (see Chapter 3), and morphemes to make words, and words to make phrases and clauses, and so on, but the levels model on its own does not tell us not to produce English words such as **blinch* or **fqhcn* or that we cannot put words together to make phrases such as **my no spring will sky* or **blue spiders talk best*. Nor does it tell us that **blinch*, though non-existent, is more like English than **fqhcn* or that **blue spiders talk best* is more acceptable than **my no spring will sky*. The use of asterisks before the examples in this paragraph reflect common practice in linguistics, where an asterisk preceding a linguistic example indicates that it is not an acceptable form in the language concerned.

At each of the levels, as we shall see, we need to define and describe both the relevant units and the combinations or structures into which they can enter. This is an important distinction, and one that can be confusing for students who know a little bit about grammar already but may conflate, for example, the grammatical subject with the **noun phrase**. The subject is a position and role within a structure, and the noun phrase is a unit that can be placed into that role but is independent of it.

Another term for this distinction is the more pleasingly alliterative **'form and function'**, where 'form' is the unit and its particular shape or internal structure, and 'function' is how it operates within higher levels of structure. We shall return to these terms in later chapters.

The term **hierarchy** can be helpful in the description of language. It might be clear already that the levels model is itself a kind of hierarchy, though Table I.1 does not emphasise this way of looking at it. Figure I.1, however, uses a different visual representation to do so.

The way in which the word hierarchy is used in linguistics differs from the popular use of the word to indicate importance, as it does in many organisations and institutions that acknowledge those at the top of the hierarchy by conferring both material rewards and status. The linguistic notion of hierarchy, on the contrary, depicts the higher levels as simply representative of a larger body of language than the lower levels, or as more inclusive rather than more important. We shall consider other examples of hierarchy in later chapters.

The structure of this book is as follows. Chapters 1 and 2 introduce students to the study of speech sounds via articulatory phonetics and phonology: the description of sounds in terms of their physical production in the mouth and throat. There is nothing difficult about describing sounds by this method, and much to find intriguing, particularly for students who have not come across such descriptions before. Your tongue never feels quite the same in your mouth once you have discovered what it is capable of.

Chapter 3 looks at the structure of words by introducing the smallest building blocks of grammar: morphemes. It then investigates the range of word classes to which English words belong, and defines the membership of these classes by formal and functional criteria.

Chapter 4 takes the study of structure to the level above the word: the phrase. Each of the major phrase classes of English is introduced and its internal structure explained and illustrated.

Chapter 5 finishes the discussion of grammar by introducing clause structure and demonstrating the complexity of sentence structures when more than one clause is involved.

Chapter 6 provides a short introduction to lexical semantics: the meaning of words in English. It allows students to develop a vocabulary for discussing words they come across in the texts they are studying, and demonstrates the interface between the language system and language use.

Finally, Chapter 7 takes the reader just 'over the border' into the realm of text structure, discourse and linguistic theory. There are more details on some of these topics in this book's companion volumes (Clark, 2006, and Chapman, 2006), and later volumes in the series will be devoted to such topics. However in order to bring the student to the threshold of English language fieldwork and research, this chapter touches upon the patterning that can be found at these higher levels of structure.

Although this is a textbook I have endeavoured to give it the feel of a 'real' academic book. It is of great importance that students learn to read texts that deal with difficult subjects in their chosen field of study. Without over-complicating the topics, this volume also aims to treat students with respect as intelligent readers. For similar reasons, the exercises and questions are placed at the end of the book, though there are suggestions in the text for experiments that could be carried out by readers alone or in classes, and that aim to inculcate a spirit of enquiry. The only real way to understand how language works is to get your hands dirty and pull it to pieces. This book will help you to make a start.

CHAPTER

1 Phonetics

1.1 Introduction: human speech sounds

In the Introduction we saw that phonetics lies at one extreme of the linguistic levels model. It is placed there on the assumption that it is concerned with the smallest units of language: sounds. **Phonetics** is indeed the study of the sounds that human beings use to communicate through language, and it is mostly concerned with individual speech sounds that follow each other in a linear fashion, just as letters do in the written language Thus the word *cat* is made up of three letters when written (c-a-t) and three sounds when spoken [k-æ-t]. You will be introduced to the transcription system later in this chapter and in Chapter 3. However, we shall see towards the end of this chapter that some phonetic considerations go beyond the smallest units of sound. Stress patterns, for example, are phonetic in English.

This chapter introduces the broad range of possible speech sounds for human beings, and then Chapter 2 will narrow the focus to the phonology of English, which means that instead of looking at the articulatory detail of all possible human speech sounds we shall investigate the range of *significant* speech sounds in a single language; English. The significance of a speech sound concerns its ability to change meaning, a topic that phonetics does not generally consider.

Although there are differences in the range of sounds used in different human languages, the mechanisms and physical resources in the human vocal tract are basically the same, irrespective of whether the language being spoken is English, Urdu, Swahili or Swedish. This chapter will guide the reader through the basic mechanisms by which human beings make speech sounds. An understanding of articulatory phonetics is essential to grasping how the particular sounds of spoken English function in the language, although what will be considered in this chapter is not strictly limited to English. Before embarking on an exploration of the vocal organs and their functions, we need to be clear about which aspects of phonetics are covered in this book.

There are two subfields of phonetics that will not be explored here, despite being fascinating in their own right. These are 'acoustic' and 'auditory' phonetics. **Acoustic phonetics** is concerned with investigating how the sounds of speech are transmitted through the air between speaker and hearer, and **auditory phonetics** is concerned with how hearers receive the sounds of speech and decode (that is, understand) them. Both these subfields draw on the theories and methods of physics, and are outside the scope of this book. Here we shall concentrate on **articulatory phonetics** or the production end of the process – how the speaker creates the sounds. Unlike the other subfields it is closer to the biological than to the physical sciences.

In order to understand the conventions used in this and other linguistic books the reader needs to know that square brackets are generally used for the phonetic 'raw' material of human speech; that is, **transcriptions** of sounds as they are uttered, as exactly as possible in a written form: for example [kʰæt]. Slashes are used to enclose transcriptions that represent the sounds of a particular language, its phonology, usually in slightly less detail, but demonstrating the patterning of sounds in that language: for example /kæt/. Thus the word *that* may be pronounced [ðæʔ] by English speakers who pronounce the final /t/ as a glottal stop. The **glottal stop** is described in more detail later, but it sounds as though a /t/ is missing because the mouth remains open and the consonant is pronounced at the back of the mouth instead of the front. Despite the rather large difference in sound from the more recognisable pronounciation of /t/, this word is represented phonologically as /ðæt/ when the analyst is looking at the speech sounds of English in particular, because the glottal stop has no significance in terms of changed meaning. This is because the glottal stop is only a variant of /t/ in English, and not an independent speech sound in its own right.

Although this chapter is concerned with articulatory phonetics in general, which could in other contexts be applied to any human language, in fact almost all of the examples given will be from the English language. In addition, unless otherwise stated the examples will be taken from **Received Pronunciation** of southern British English, though there will also be many examples from other British and American accents. Received Pronunciation (RP) is the name given to the prestigious accent of the British upper classes, and though the value judgement that RP is a 'better' accent is thoroughly rejected, some form of RP remains a focal point for those describing English phonology.

1.2 Vocal apparatus

The production of human speech originates in the lungs as most human speech sounds are articulated on an outgoing breath. This process is known as the **egressive pulmonary airstream mechanism**. In other words the speech sounds of most human languages are made as we breathe out. Once the air has left the lungs it travels up the **trachea** (Figure 1.1) and leaves the body through the mouth, and sometimes also through the nose. On the way it may be modified by a number of the vocal organs that are the subject of this section. These modifications are responsible for making the egressive airstream sound differently, depending on where the airflow is restricted and by how much.

In addition to their linguistic function, the vocal organs have primary functions, that are related to the basic survival of human beings, such as breathing, eating and drinking. The linguistic functions are very specialised now but they evolved much later than the survival functions and are therefore secondary features.

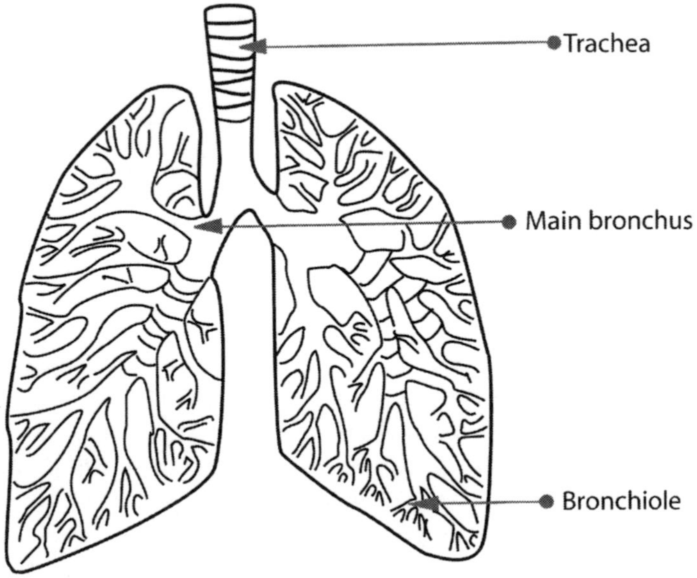

Figure 1.1 The lungs and trachea

1.2.1 Lungs to larynx

The vocal organs include the lower parts of what is primarily a breathing apparatus. The lungs take in air, release oxygen into the bloodstream and expel what is left, mainly carbon dioxide. This expelling of what is effectively waste material is the **egressive pulmonary airstream** mentioned above. The potential for these waste gases to be made into speech sounds as they leave the body has been exploited by the human race in a range of ways, as later sections of this chapter will demonstrate.

Before the expelled gases leave the body through the mouth and nose they pass through the **larynx** (Figure 1.2). This is a 'box' made of cartilage that contains two folds of flesh known as the **vocal folds.** The latter are joined together at the front of the larynx, at the point where the cartilage walls meet. This intersection of the sides of the larynx is visible on the outside of the throat as the Adam's apple.

Towards the rear of the larynx the vocal folds are attached by muscles to the **arytenoid cartilage**, and this mechanism can pull them close together (for example when straining to lift a heavy box) or keep them apart, as in quiet breathing (Figure 1.3). The vocal folds also have more specialised linguistic and musical functions, such as voicing and, related to this, the ability to change pitch when singing and to add intonation to speech.

At the top of the trachea there is a flap of cartilage called the **epiglottis**, which deflects food down the **oesophagus** and into the intestine. This prevents us from choking, except when small particles of food go 'down the wrong way' – that is, escape the epiglottis and enter the trachea. The combined apparatus of the vocal folds and the arytenoid cartilages and muscles is

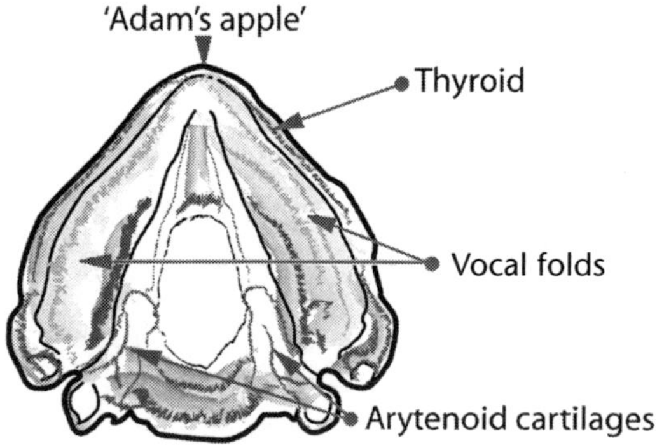

Figure 1.2 Structure of the larynx and vocal folds

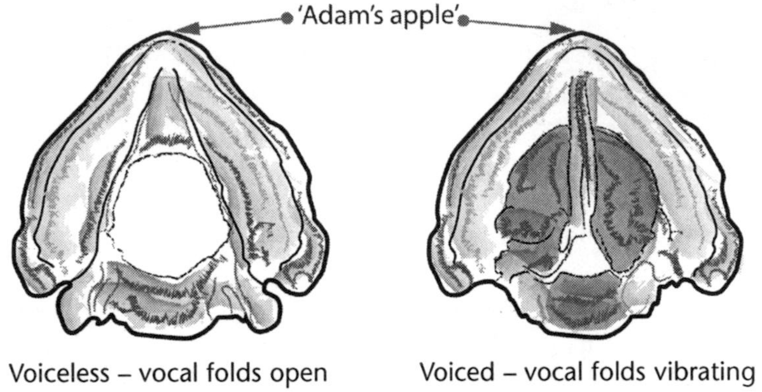

Figure 1.3 The vocal folds during quiet breathing and voicing

known as the **glottis**. This gives its name to one of the most notorious of English speech sounds, the glottal stop. This sound is sometimes mistakenly thought to reflect laziness, since it replaces a /t/ sound in some urban accents of British English, and because it is much further back in the mouth than a stereotypical /t/ it is viewed as a missing sound rather than an equivalent one. The most common place for a glottal stop is at the end of words (for example *ca***t**), but it also quite frequently occurs in the middle of words (for example *bu***tt***er*).

1.2.2 The oral and nasal cavities

Above the larynx there is a muscular tube known as the **pharynx**, which leads to the back of the mouth. The pharynx is able to contract, thus 'squeezing' the airflow and causing a class of sounds known as **pharyngeals**. These occur in Arabic and other languages, but not in English. Once past the pharynx the egressive airstream has a choice of direction. From here the air can escape through the mouth or the nasal cavity (Figure 1.4). When the sounds to be made are not nasal in tone the **velum** or **soft palate** is pulled back to make contact with the back of the pharynx, thus cutting off the nasal cavity route.

Some speech sounds exploit the resonance of the cavity behind the nose to make them distinctive. Some people have a quite nasal tone of voice, and people affected by a cold may temporarily have this vocal tone. No further modifications of the airstream are possible within the **nasal cavity**, which operates merely as a large resonating chamber.

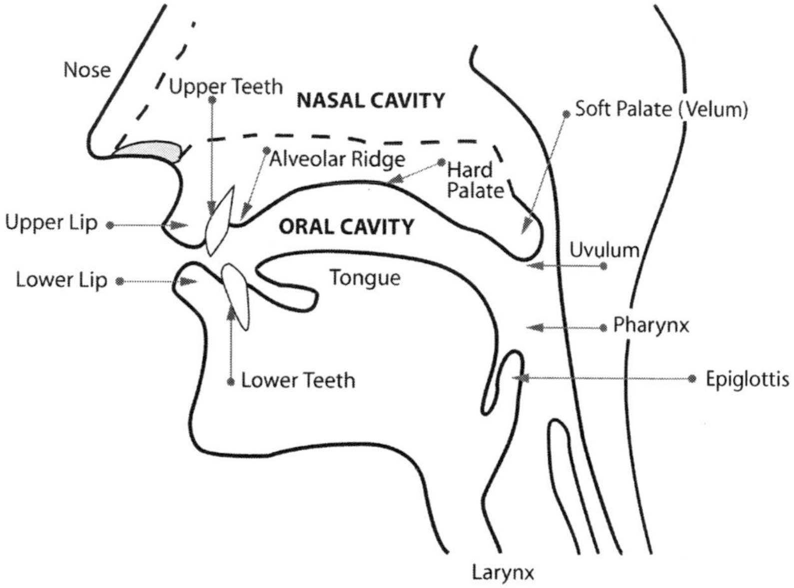

Figure 1.4 The oral and nasal cavities

If the velum cuts off the nasal escape route the air has to leave through the mouth. A number of parts of the mouth are used to modify the sound of the passage of air: the uvulum, velum, palate, alveolum, teeth, lips and tongue (Figure 1.4). We shall consider how sounds are produced by these articulators in Sections 1.4 and 1.5; here we shall simply outline the range of effects they can have on the airflow through the mouth.

As already mentioned the pharynx does not play a part in English sounds, though its capacity to contract does feature in Arabic. The sound made is difficult to emulate by native speakers of English, who are not used to having conscious control over the muscles of the pharynx.

The **uvulum** is a fleshy protuberance hanging from the back of the velum. It is often confused with the epiglottis. There are no uvular sounds in English, though in other languages it causes a sound by vibrating as the air leaves the glottis, as with the French 'r'.

The **velum** can be raised or lowered to cut off air or allow it to flow freely through the nasal cavity. It is lowered in the production of English nasal sounds such as /m/ and /n/, and is also used in a number of non-nasal English sounds, including /k/ and /g/. It is situated at the point at which the back of the tongue makes contact with the roof of the mouth. The **velum** is sometimes also known as the **soft palate** and you can find yours by running the tip of your tongue back from the teeth and across the hard palate until you feel the bone give way while the flesh continues. The fleshy 'dome' with no bone behind it is the velum.

In front of the velum is the **hard palate**, which is a bony structure and therefore has no independent capacity for movement or flexing. However its role in speech production is very important as the body of the tongue can press up into the palate, constricting the airflow as it does so. The palate is significant in English sounds such as /j/, which is usually spelt as a 'y' (as in *yacht*), and /ʃ/, which is spelt as 'sh' (as in ***sh**ower*).

The front of the palate dips down towards the teeth and forms a platform known as the **alveolar ridge**. Like the palate, being a bony structure it cannot move or flex on its own, but it is the place where the blade of the tongue makes many of the most common sounds of English, including /t/, /d/, /s/ and /z/.

The tongue, as already noted, can be used in a number of ways to make contact with other articulators. It has four significant areas that can be placed against the upper parts of the **oral cavity**. These areas are the tip, blade, body and root of the tongue (Figure 1.5).

The tip of the tongue is protruded between the teeth to produce the **interdental** 'th' sounds in English (as in ***th**is* and ***th**igh*). It can also make contact

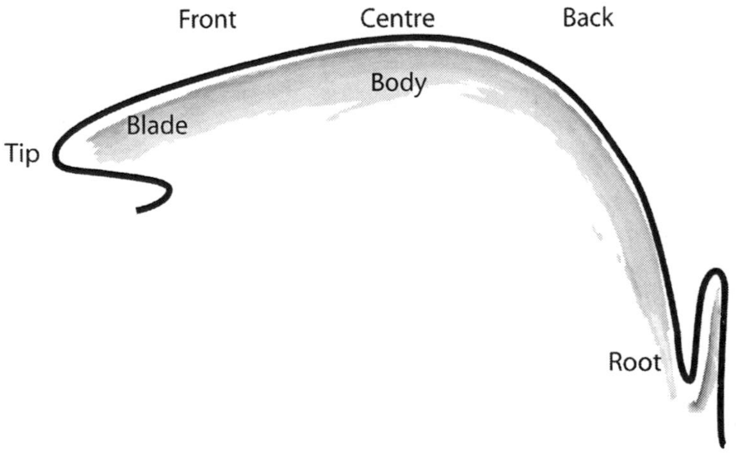

Figure 1.5 The tongue and its parts

with the back of the teeth to produce the Italian /t/ and /d/ sounds, which are described as **dental** and are subtly different from their English equivalents. Moreover it can 'tap' the alveolar ridge to form a rolled 'r' sound of the kind common in Spanish. In addition there is a set of speech sounds (not used in English) known as **retroflex**, where the tip of the tongue is curled back to tap the back of the alveolum. These sounds are found in most of the languages of India, and thus also in Indian accents of English.

Other parts of the tongue are used to make speech sounds in different ways. The **blade** of the tongue can be raised to meet the alveolar ridge and produce a great many English consonant sounds, including /t/, /d/, /s/ and /z/. The body and root of the tongue can be raised towards the palate and the velum respectively, to form either a complete closure or a partial closure.

All movements of the articulators described in this section have the effect of squeezing the airflow in some way, and this results in a range of acoustic effects that we describe as consonants.

1.3 Segments of sound

This chapter has so far used the convention of talking about individual speech sounds as though we divide speech into a series of separate sounds that are articulated one after the other and have no effect on each other, and clear boundaries between them – just like the letters of the written language. In fact speech is made up of a continuous stream of sound, which we divide into letters for convenience when writing but which has overlapping features of articulation when we are speaking. Take for example the phrase *strong man's sister*, which when transcribed phonologically looks like this: /strɒŋmænzsɪstə/

We shall look at the symbols of transcription in Sections (1.4 and 1.5), though it will help to know that /ŋ/ represents the 'ng' sound in *strong*. For now, just note that strictly speaking we should not put gaps between words in transcription as there are no real-time gaps when speaking. Also note that although we have identified individual points along the stream of speech as representing separate sounds, in fact the features of those sounds often carry over from one sound to another. Thus three sections of this phrase are longer than a single sound. These are articulated at the alveolar ridge and underlined in the following version /strɒŋmænzsɪstə/

There is also one section that is longer than a single sound and is nasal, and therefore has a lowered velum: /strɒŋmænzsɪstə/. Try saying this phrase very slowly, focusing first on the alveolar sections and then on the nasal section, and you may be able to feel the blade of the tongue positioned at the alveolar ridge and the velum drawn away from the pharynx for relatively long periods.

We shall return to this topic in the next chapter, but for now it is important to note that the cutting of a continuous stream of sound into segments is partly a convenient fiction that helps us to make sense of the data we are studying. It is also worth noting that there are important features of speech that are clearly not segmented in this way. These include **intonation** contours, which add expression and emotion to the words we articulate. However in general alphabetic human writing systems were originally phonetically based, and they usually represented sounds as individual units of about the length of what we call consonants and vowels. This provides some support for dividing the speech stream into sections, as phonetics and phonology do.

1.3.1 Consonants versus vowels

Most literate speakers of a language are aware that we divide speech sounds into two types: **consonants** and **vowels**. They may even be aware that vowels tend to occur between consonants, and that there are no words without vowels (or at least not in the spoken language), though there may be some without consonants.

What, then, is the phonetic difference between these categories? We have already seen how speech is produced by modifying the outgoing air from a speaker's breath. The qualitative difference between consonants and vowels is due to the different kinds of modification the two categories of sound make to this airstream. Whilst consonants squeeze and constrict the airflow, to the extent of sometimes stopping it altogether, vowels allow free passage of air through the mouth (and nose), but with a variable shaped cavity in which the sound resonates differently, causing the different sounds of the vowels.

You can test this difference yourself by saying a long vowel (such as *aaaah* or *eeeee*) and noting that, once in position, the mouth does not change shape, but simply allows the air to resonate around the resulting cavity shape. If you contrast this with any of the consonants (try /d/ and /s/ to start with), you will notice that, when pronouncing a consonant, your articulators need both to place themselves in position and to move away from that position, usually towards a vowel shape.

As is usual with linguistic categories, the boundary between vowels and consonants is not absolutely clear. There is a set of consonants that are less extreme in their constriction of the airflow than the typical consonants, and as a result are sometimes called semivowels. These sounds involve movement of the articulators, but not so much as to disturb the flow of air significantly. They include /w/, /r/ and /j/ (spelt 'y' in English). There is also a set of vowels known as **diphthongs**, which, unlike the pure vowels, require some movement from one vowel position to another. For example in many accents of English the vowel in *house* is a diphthong, though this is not universal.

Scots English speakers, for instance, may say it with a long close back vowel, /huːs/, and speakers from the southern United States with a long open front vowel, /hæːs/. With diphthongs the effect of the movement from one vowel position to another is that it sometimes sounds almost consonant-like, rather like a semivowel, and this audible squeezing of the air is known as a **glide**.

Because readers of this book will have a range of different accents you may find it useful at this stage to locate a diphthong in your accent, and to make sure that you have understood the general point about vowels being either **pure** or diphthongs. Try the words *fair, fire* and *fear* – one or more may have diphthongs in your accent. These will be /fɜə/, /faɪə/ and /fɪə/ in RP and other southern British English accents. If your articulators move once you have left the /f/ behind, then it is probably not a **pure** vowel. Contrast *four, fur* and *far*, which in many British and American accents will have a pure vowel; /fɔː/, /fɜː/, /fɑː/. Note that the transcriptions here reflect what is known as a **non-rhotic** accent. This refers to those accents, such as RP and some accents of American English, in which 'r' is not pronounced when it follows a vowel. In the case of some prestigious east coast accents in the United States, as well as Scots English and some West Country dialects in England, these 'r' sounds are pronounced. Try the words for yourself, and work out whether you speak with a rhotic or a non-rhotic accent.

1.4 Consonants

We established in the previous section that consonants involve some kind of movement into position, a constriction (or complete blockage) of the airflow, and then a movement away from that position, possibly towards a vowel position or another consonant.

The way in which we describe consonants in phonetic terms is according to where they take place, how they are articulated ('manner') and whether the vocal folds are vibrating ('voice'). This three-way description of consonants is often known as the **VPM** (voice-place-manner) description, and it can be used to describe consonants in any human language. There are other features of articulation that may also be relevant in particular cases (for example aspiration), but in general the **VPM** description is sufficient to characterise the different consonants of a language.

The transcription symbols currently used by phoneticians were developed in the 1880s by English and French language teachers who were members of the **International Phonetic Association (IPA)**. The first version of the international phonetic alphabet, produced by the IPA, was published in 1888. Though it has been revised and extended a number of times, the basic principles of description have remained the same since the first version. In the case of consonants, this means that the VPM description takes priority and forms the basis of the consonant 'grid' (Figure 1.6), whilst other features (for example **nasalisation** and aspiration) are indicated by **diacritics**, which are small additions to the basic symbol. Thus, for example, a **velarised 'l'** is indicated by the addition of a diacritic that looks like a curvy line cutting through the normal symbol for 'l': [ɫ]. This sound is distinctive in Russian, but can also be heard at the end of English words such as *pool*. If you say this word and stop still on the final consonant you may be able to feel that the back of your tongue is raised, rather than the blade. If you compare it with the position of your tongue when getting ready to say a word such as *light* you may feel that there are two kinds of /l/ in your accent.

Figure 1.6 shows the full version of the current IPA consonant chart. There are no diacritics, though the official **IPA chart** has a list of diacritics appended to it. Note that the place and manner distinctions take priority, being on the horizontal and vertical axis respectively. The third distinction, voice, is represented as a split within the boxes on the grid. Thus a box containing [p b], for example, indicates a third axis, which cannot easily be shown on two-dimensional diagrams, with the voiceless sound on the left-hand side, and its voiced counterpart on the right-hand side.

1.4.1 Place of articulation

All consonant speech sounds are articulated between the lips and the larynx, the area of the mouth where a significant obstruction of the airflow takes place. The places of articulation are shown in Figure 1.7.

Starting from the front of the mouth, **bilabial** sounds involve both lips and include /m/, as in *music*, and /w/, as in *weird*. As in all the places of articulation, bilabial consonants constrict the airflow to a greater or lesser extent. **Labiodental** articulation involves the top teeth and bottom lip, and produces sounds such as /f/, as in *fine*, and /v/, as in *vine*. You may wish to experiment with these sounds before reading on, so that you are confident of the reason for their description as either bilabial or labiodental. One exercise that can be helpful here is to prepare to say a word beginning with the relevant sound but stopping before pronouncing it. Whilst keeping your articulators in place you will increasingly feel the nerves of your tongue, lips and so on, and in future you will be more aware of this consonantal placing.

THE INTERNATIONAL PHONETIC ALPHABET (revised to 1993, updated 1996)

CONSONANTS (PULMONIC)

	Bilabial	Labiodental	Dental	Alveolar	Postalveolar	Retroflex	Palatal	Velar	Uvular	Pharyngeal	Glottal
Plosive	p b			t d		ʈ ɖ	c ɟ	k ɡ	q ɢ		ʔ
Nasal	m	ɱ		n		ɳ	ɲ	ŋ	ɴ		
Trill	ʙ			r					ʀ		
Tap or Flap				ɾ		ɽ					
Fricative	ɸ β	f v	θ ð	s z	ʃ ʒ	ʂ ʐ	ç ʝ	x ɣ	χ ʁ	ħ ʕ	h ɦ
Lateral fricative				ɬ ɮ							
Approximant		ʋ		ɹ		ɻ	j	ɰ			
Lateral approximant				l		ɭ	ʎ	ʟ			

Where symbols appear in pairs, the one to the right represents a voiced consonant. Shaded areas denote articulations judged impossible.

CONSONANTS (NON-PULMONIC)

Clicks		Voiced implosives		Ejectives	
ʘ	Bilabial	ɓ	Bilabial	ʼ	Examples:
ǀ	Dental	ɗ	Dental/alveolar	pʼ	Bilabial
ǃ	(Post)alveolar	ʄ	Palatal	tʼ	Dental/alveolar
ǂ	Palatoalveolar	ɠ	Velar	kʼ	Velar
ǁ	Alveolar lateral	ʛ	Uvular	sʼ	Alveolar fricative

VOWELS

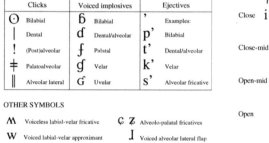

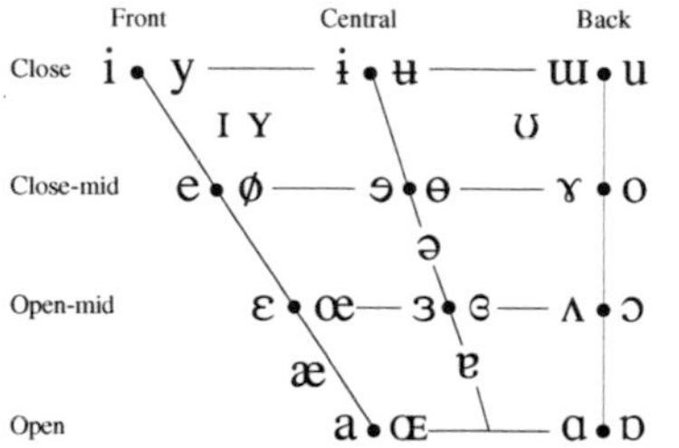

Where symbols appear in pairs, the one to the right represents a rounded vowel.

OTHER SYMBOLS

- ʍ Voiceless labial-velar fricative
- w Voiced labial-velar approximant
- ɥ Voiced labial-palatal approximant
- ʜ Voiceless epiglottal fricative
- ʢ Voiced epiglottal fricative
- ʡ Epiglottal plosive
- ɕ ʑ Alveolo-palatal fricatives
- ɺ Voiced alveolar lateral flap
- ɧ Simultaneous ʃ and x

Affricates and double articulations can be represented by two symbols joined by a tie bar if necessary. k͡p t͡s

SUPRASEGMENTALS

- ˈ Primary stress
- ˌ Secondary stress ˌfoʊnəˈtɪʃən
- ː Long eː
- ˑ Half-long eˑ
- ̆ Extra-short ĕ
- | Minor (foot) group
- ‖ Major (intonation) group
- . Syllable break ɹi.ækt
- ‿ Linking (absence of a break)

DIACRITICS Diacritics may be placed above a symbol with a descender, e.g. ŋ̊

̥	Voiceless	n̥ d̥	̤	Breathy voiced	b̤ a̤	̪	Dental	t̪ d̪
̬	Voiced	s̬ t̬	̰	Creaky voiced	b̰ a̰	̺	Apical	t̺ d̺
ʰ	Aspirated	tʰ dʰ	̼	Linguolabial	t̼ d̼	̻	Laminal	t̻ d̻
̹	More rounded	ɔ̹	ʷ	Labialized	tʷ dʷ	̃	Nasalized	ẽ
̜	Less rounded	ɔ̜	ʲ	Palatalized	tʲ dʲ	ⁿ	Nasal release	dⁿ
̟	Advanced	u̟	ˠ	Velarized	tˠ dˠ	ˡ	Lateral release	dˡ
̠	Retracted	e̠	ˤ	Pharyngealized	tˤ dˤ	̚	No audible release	d̚
̈	Centralized	ë	̴	Velarized or pharyngealized	ɫ			
̽	Mid-centralized	e̽	̝	Raised	e̝ (ɹ̝ = voiced alveolar fricative)			
̩	Syllabic	n̩	̞	Lowered	e̞ (β̞ = voiced bilabial approximant)			
̯	Non-syllabic	e̯	̘	Advanced Tongue Root	e̘			
˞	Rhoticity	ɚ a˞	̙	Retracted Tongue Root	e̙			

TONES AND WORD ACCENTS

LEVEL			CONTOUR		
e̋ or	˥	Extra high	ě or	˩˥	Rising
é	˦	High	ê	˥˩	Falling
ē	˧	Mid	e᷄	˦˥	High rising
è	˨	Low	e᷅	˩˨	Low rising
ȅ	˩	Extra low	e᷈	˧˦˧	Rising-falling
ꜜ		Downstep	↗		Global rise
ꜛ		Upstep	↘		Global fall

Figure 1.6 The IPA consonant chart

Acknowledgement: grateful thanks to the International Phonetic Association, copyright owner of the International Phonetic Alphabet and the IPA charts. See www.arts.gla.ac.uk

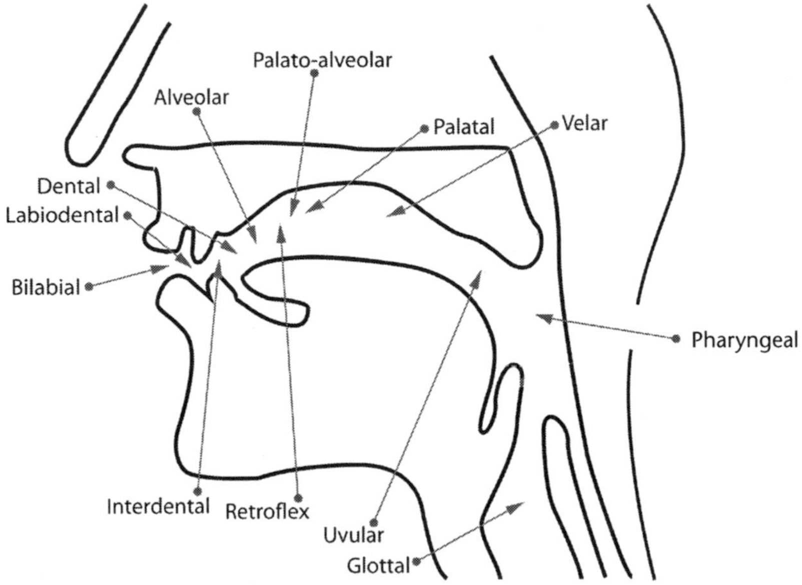

Figure 1.7 The places of articulation

The teeth are the site of a number of speech sounds. The tongue may protrude between them to create **'interdental'** sounds, which are those spelt as 'th' in English: /θ/ as in ***think*** and /ð/ as in ***though***. In some languages, though not usually in English, a number of **dental sounds**, are produced when the tongue creates a blockage against the back of the teeth. These sounds seem similar to /t/ and /d/ to the English speaker's ear, though English /t/ and /d/ are normally articulated with the blade of the tongue and further back in the mouth than the dental [t̪] and [d̪] in Italian and French. That is. they are alveolar rather than dental.

Alveolar sounds occur when the blade of the tongue is placed against the alveolar ridge, a bony platform just behind the teeth. It is the place of articulation for a number of English sounds: /t/, /d/, /s/, /z/, /l/, /r/, /n/ are all alveolar.

Further back, some sounds are produced halfway between the alveolar ridge and the hard palate. These are known as **post-alveolar** sounds and involve the body of the tongue being raised towards the front of the palate. They include the English sounds /ʃ/ and /ʒ/ , which are spelt 'sh' and 's' respectively and occur, for example, in **sh**ame and lei**s**ure. Further back still, there are the **palatal** sounds, where the body of the tongue rises towards the most domed section of the palate. English only has one **palatal** sound, the 'y' sound, which is represented as /j/ phonologically and is found in *yes*.

Behind the palate is the velum, or soft palate. **Velar** sounds involve the back of the tongue moving towards or making contact with the soft palate. There are three velar sounds in English: /k/ as in ***king***, /g/ as in *goat* and /ŋ/, which only occurs at the end of syllables, is spelt 'ng' and occurs twice in ***singing***. Further back still there are the uvular and pharyngeal places of articulation, but as already pointed out there are no sounds in English that come from these places of articulation. Sounds that are produced here include the French rolled 'r', which is is **uvular** and involves repeated oscillation of the uvulum, with only a slight raising of the back of the tongue, and Arabic pharyngeal sounds that are produced by constricting the root of the tongue and the wall of the pharynx, and are recognisable by their 'throaty' sound. Both sounds are very difficult to produce by non-native speakers of these languages. The final place of articulation is the glottis, where a number of sounds are theoretically possible. The only pressure that can be put upon the airflow in the glottis is by pivoting and closing the vocal folds. English has two glottal sounds: the glottal stop, which replaces /t/ in some accents, and the voiceless **glottal fricative**, /h/, which is an 'h' sound, as in ***house***.

1.4.2 Manner of articulation

Having considered all the places of articulation we shall now look at the other main axis of the consonant chart: **manner of articulation**. We shall spend most time looking at the manners of articulation used in English, but in order to give the English sounds a little context, others will be touched upon.

The most consonantal of the manners of articulation is the **plosive**, where there is a complete closure of the vocal tract at one of the places of articulation. The pressure builds up from below, with the egressive airstream being pushed out of the lungs and into the oral cavity. Eventually this pushes the articulators (for example the tongue and alveolar ridge) apart, resulting in a small explosive sound. The plosive sounds in English are /p/, /t/, /k/, /b/, /d/ and /g/. The English consonant sounds and their transcription symbols will be discussed in Section 1.4.4. It is important to understand the mechanism by which plosive sounds are produced, and to make sure of this you can experiment by pronouncing words beginning with these sounds, such as *pick, top, count, buy, day* and *give*. If you make the closure for the first sound and then delay the onset of the vowel, you should find that the build-up of pressure behind the closure eventually forces the articulators apart.

The **nasal** consonants share a common feature with plosives in that they involve a complete closure at some point along the vocal tract. The term that is used for this is **stop**, and in some phonetic descriptions the nasals and plosives are designated as a single group of 'stop' consonants. The difference in the case of nasals is that the velum is lowered away from the back wall of the pharynx and the air escapes through the nose at the same time as entering the closed-off oral cavity. This means that there is no pressure build-up and therefore no (ex)plosion as the air streams out steadily through the nostrils. It is worth noting a qualitative effect of nasal consonants, which in English are all voiced: they can be prolonged for as long as the speaker has breath to exhale, and since they are voiced they can also hold a pitch. This makes nasal sounds ideal for humming. The English nasals are /m/, /n/ and /ŋ/, the latter being the sound usually spelt as 'ng' in English orthography. To get a sense of the difference between plosive and nasal consonants, try saying a word beginning with /m/, such as *mine*, and lengthen the first consonant. You will find this much easier than with the plosives. Extend the /m/ for as long as you wish, and you ought to be able to hum a note too!

Before we consider the next major manner of articulation of English sounds, it should be noted that many languages use a range of **flaps** and **trills** to enlarge their consonant range. The flap is a single, fast movement of the tip/blade of the tongue, usually against the alveolar ridge, which makes the 'r' sound found in Spanish and in some accents of British English, notably in Scotland. The double 'rr' in Spanish and other languages is known as a trill. It is produced at the front of the mouth, with the tongue blade vibrating in response to the outgoing breath. Other trills are produced further back in the mouth, as in the French uvular 'r', which as we have already noted involves vibration of the uvulum.

If we take the stop consonants (both plosives and nasals) to be stereotypical consonants because of their complete obstruction of the airflow, then **fricatives** can be seen as consonantal but with less obstruction of the airflow. The fricative consonants involve the articulators (tongue, teeth, alveolar ridge and so on) coming into close contact, but without a complete closure. This enables the outgoing airstream to escape through the small space left between the articulators. The result is a 'messy' sound, rather like the sound made by wind whistling through a draughty window, or the hissing of steam leaving a small opening in a kettle or saucepan lid. The resulting friction of the air passing through these narrow gaps provides us with the name of this group of sounds. Like the nasal consonants, because there is no complete obstruction of the air these sounds can be extended as long as the speaker has breath available. The English fricatives are /f/, /v/, /θ/, /ð/, /s/, /z/, /ʃ/, /ʒ/ and /h/. You could test your lung capacity by breathing in fully and pronouncing a fricative – say /s/ – for as long as you are able without taking in another breath. This could be done competitively in class, using the convenient stop watches that are usually found on mobile phones these days.

Though the fricatives form a single class of manner of articulation, a subset of these consonants have a distinctive sound and are sometimes behave in similar ways to each other. These are known as **sibilants:** /s/, /z/, /ʃ/ and /ʒ/. They are so-named because of their slight 'whistling' sound, and they are articulated by producing a 'groove' in the centre of the tongue, down which the air flows. The groove is slightly wider for the post-alveolar /ʃ/ and /ʒ/ than for the alveolar /s/ and /z/. These sibilant sounds differ from the other fricatives in terms of the focus of the sound, which is clearer than the more 'messy' sounds of /f/ and /v/. The non-sibilant fricatives have a wider gap than the sibilants, which tend to be produced in a smaller, circular hole between the groove of the tongue and the upper parts of the mouth. Breathing in quickly whilst holding a /s/ or /ʃ/ position can help you to identify the nature of these sounds and contrast the grooved shape of the tongue with its flat position in other fricatives.

Still less consonantal, though still not quite vocalic (vowel-like), are the **approximants** or **semivowels.** These sounds are produced by the articulators moving towards closure but not getting close enough to cause either friction or a plosive build-up of pressure. The English approximants include /w/, /r/ and /j/ (the latter being spelt 'y' in English) and the **lateral** approximant, /l/. If you pronounce words beginning with these sounds very slowly you may be able to feel that the 'swooping' movement is similar in each case, and it is this that distinguishes them from the more definitely consonantal fricatives and stops. Try pronouncing words that are otherwise identical in sound, such as *what, rot, lot* and *yacht.* The lateral, /l/, is one of a number of possible lateral speech sounds produced when the tongue touches the alveolar ridge but the sides of the tongue are lowered to allow the air to escape freely.

In the range of consonants between plosive and fricative sounds there are two consonants in English that are known as **affricates.** They are not always recognised as separate consonants by phoneticians because they appear to be made up of two consonants. However it is the normal convention in English phonology to treat them as individual sounds. Like the plosives they begin with a complete closure, but instead of the air building up and causing an explosive release, it is released slowly, with the effect that there is a short fricative phase when the articulators separate but before they move completely apart. The affricates are transcribed as /tʃ/ and /dʒ/ and occur twice in the words ***church*** and ***judge*** respectively. If you say these two words very slowly indeed you should be able to feel the complete closure of the plosive phase, followed by a gradual release with frication.

1.4.3 Voicing

The larynx and vocal folds were described in an earlier section. Here we shall consider the third of the VPM consonant descriptors, **voicing,** which is an effect of the airstream flowing out of the lungs and through the larynx, causing the vocal folds to vibrate. This vibration only happens when the vocal folds are pulled fairly close together but not clamped shut (see Figure 1.3).

Once the vocal folds are vibrating the **voice** can take on a pitched note (resulting from the frequency of the vibrations). This gives intonation to speech and is the basis of the singing voice. When a violin player moves his or her finger from side to side on a string it is known as 'vibrato', and the sound produced can be much louder than the same notes played without vibrato. Similarly the voiced sound is much louder than voiceless sounds, as evidenced by the fact that when we wish to be quiet we whisper, which involves the **devoicing** (that is, getting rid of the voicing) of all speech sounds.

If the vocal folds are clamped tight together, this produces the plosive sound known as the **glottal stop**. As we shall see in Chapter 2, this occurs as a speech sound in English, particularly as one of the variants of /t/. It is also evident when we strain hard – for example when moving or lifting heavy objects. In this case it is simply a physical consequence of an activity, and not a strictly linguistic unit of sound, though it may incidentally communicate to bystanders that we need help! Try lifting or moving a heavy object, and notice how difficult it is to do so without making a noise. This noise is most likely to be a glottal stop.

The only other use of the vocal folds in English is as the place of articulation for the glottal fricative, /h/, which is a sound that results from the vocal folds being placed close together, though not close enough to vibrate, as in voiced sounds. It is therefore a voiceless sound, despite being articulated by bringing together the vocal folds.

Returning to voicing itself, we can now begin to see that the vibration of the vocal folds is independent, in most cases, of the placing and manner of the consonant articulation. Thus we may have a bilabial plosive, such as /p/, which is voiceless, and a completely identical counterpart, /b/, which is voiced. Many of the English consonants occur in such pairs, and in the IPA chart (Figure 1.6) they are placed in the same place/manner box, but with the voiceless variant always to the left of the voiced one.

In order for you fully to recognise the difference between voiced and voiceless sounds it is worth experimenting a little with these sounds. Try alternating a very long voiceless /ssssssssss/ with a long voiced /zzzzzzzzzzz/. If you touch the side of your throat lightly whilst alternating these otherwise identical sounds you will be able to feel the voicing switching on and off. It is harder to produce this feeling with plosives because they are so short, and the nasals, though they have the potential to be long, do not have voiceless counterparts in English. The fricatives are therefore ideal, and you may wish to try the same effect with /ffffffff/ and /vvvvvvvv/, where the 'switching' is much more marked and less smooth than with /s/ and /z/.

1.4.4 English consonants

We now have all the terminology and tools that we need to describe the consonants of English. This section will draw together the different articulatory features explored in Sections 1.4.1 to 1.4.3 in order to arrive at a complete list of the English consonants, their features and some examples.

There are surprisingly few variations of the number or basic features of English consonants in the world's English accents. This is not to say that there are no differences – we have already noted that for some Scots accents the 'r' sound is labelled a flap rather than an approximant. There are also many variants of basic sounds that depend on the positioning of the consonant in the speech stream. These issues will be explored in Chapter 3, where the phonology of English is described.

For now we simply need to note that English generally has the 24 basic consonant sounds shown in Table 1.1, and that these could be described in a great deal more phonetic detail if we wished to do so (for example, for the sake of charting particular accents, speech disorders and so on). Detailed transcriptions of speech sounds of this kind rely on the diacritics in the full IPA system, and allow the phonetician to make minute distinctions between different sounds. For example if a voiced plosive is devoiced in certain contexts, this can be indicated by the addition of a small circle beneath the usual symbol – [d̥] – and plosives that have extra exhalation, known as **aspiration**, may have a superscript 'h' added: [tʰ]. A very detailed transcription that makes use of the full range of diacritics is known as a **'narrow' transcription**. In this book we shall limit ourselves to a **'broad' transcription** system, which reflects only meaningful differences in pronunciation and is therefore closer to a phonological than a phonetic record of what is being articulated.

There are three voiceless/voiced pairs of plosives, and they occur in the same three places of articulation as the three nasals, all of which are voiced (see Table 1.2).

These sounds are quite straightforward and can mostly be worked out from the letters of the alphabet that are used to represent them. Whilst not all alphabetic letters in English have a consistent sound, those used in Table 1.2 are reasonably consistent. Note that the velar nasal, /ŋ/, which is usually spelt 'ng', only occurs at the end of syllables in English:

> pill /pɪl/, bill /bɪl/, till /tɪl/, dill /dɪl/, kill /kɪl/, ghyll* /gɪl/
> mill /mɪl/, nil /nɪl/, king /kɪŋ/,
>
> *A 'ghyll' is a Yorkshire dialect word for gorge.

Apart from /h/, which is articulated in the glottis, the fricative sounds of English are produced forward in the mouth (Table 1.3)

Table 1.1 The consonants of English

	Bilabial	Labio-dental	Inter-dental	Alveolar	Post-alveolar	Palatal	Velar	Glottal
Plosive	p b			t d			k g	
Nasal	m			n			ŋ	
Affricate					tʃ dʒ			
Fricative		f v	θ ð	s z	ʃ ʒ			h
Approximant	w			r		j		
Lateral				l				

Table 1.2 Plosive and nasal consonants in English

	Bilabial	Alveolar	Velar
plosive	p b	t d	k g
nasal	m	n	ŋ

Table 1.3 Fricative consonants in English

	Labio-dental	Inter-dental	Alveolar	Post-alveolar	Glottal
fricative	f v	θ ð	s z	ʃ ʒ	h

The normal alphabetic letters represent their common English values, although the letter 's' can just as soon represent /z/ as /s/ phonetically (see the examples below). The Greek characters /θ/ and /ð/ represent the 'th' sounds in *thankyou* (voiceless) and *these* (voiced) respectively. Try putting your tongue between your teeth and alternating the voicing, as you did earlier (Section 1.4.3). The characters /ʃ/ and /ʒ/ are similarly related, with /ʃ/ representing 'sh', as in *sheep* or *shower*, and /ʒ/ being the voiced equivalent, occurring only in the final position in syllables, as in the 'French-influenced' pronunciation of *garage*: /gærɑːʒ/.

> half /hɑːf/, halve /hɑːv/, bath /bɑːθ/, bathe /beɪð/, peace /piːs/, peas /piːz/, pressure /prɛʃə/, leisure /lɛʒə/

The least consonantal sounds, the approximants or semivowels, are represented by the expected letters, /w/, /r/ and /l/, with the exception of the palatal approximant, which is represented by /j/, though it is often spelt as 'y' in English.

Table 1.4 The approximants in English

	Bilabial	Alveolar	Palatal
Approximant	w	r	j
Lateral		l	

The bilabial /w/ is close in position to /b/ and /p/, but not being a plosive there is no sharp explosion of escaping air. Instead there is a constricting of the airflow as the lips purse together and release again, as in *wheel* /wi:l/. The alveolar approximant, /r/, is a little further back in the mouth, but quite similar in other ways to /w/. The difference between /r/ and /l/ is that the lateral has an additional feature; the blade of the tongue makes full contact with the alveolar ridge but the sides of the tongue are lowered, so that the airflow is not completely blocked. The approximant is articulated with the sides of the tongue moving into and out of position and causing a distortion of the airflow, which is what gives it a distinctive sound.

In order to feel the shape of the tongue during articulation of an /l/, put your mouth into the right position by pretending you are about to say *lion*, and then breathe in sharply without moving your tongue. You will find that the cold air moving in across your tongue makes you aware of its shape, and you should feel the air particularly at the sides, where the air is entering.

The palatal consonant, /j/, is harder to feel as there are far fewer nerve endings in the body of the tongue than in the tip and blade. It therefore takes a little effort to feel what is going on when we make the first sound in words such as *yes* and *yellow*. However, if you start to say them and then stop on the /j/, pressing the tongue really hard up against the palate, you will be able to work out the main articulatory feature of the sound; that is, the body of the tongue rises up towards and then comes away from the hard palate.

Typical occurrences of the English approximants are as follows:

wham/wæm/, ram/ræm/, lamb/læm/, yam/jæm/

You can see from these examples that the spelling of words in English is not an accurate predictor of their pronunciation. Here we have *wham* with a letter 'h' and *lamb* with a letter 'b', neither of which are pronounced in most accents of English (though there are still a few RP speakers who pronounce 'wh' as [hw].

Before we move on to look at vowels it is worth noting that as well as describing consonants according to their VPM descriptions, there are times when it is useful to group them in other ways. We have already seen, for example, that there is a subset of fricatives known as sibilants, and that plosives and nasals can be grouped together as stops. In addition to these, there are two major groups of consonants known as **sonorants** and **obstruents**, anf these are significant in the construction of English syllables. The sonorants include the nasals and approximants, and as the name suggests they have a more resonant sound than the obstruents, which is a term covering both fricative and plosive consonants where the main sound effect results from the obstruction of the airflow.

1.5 Vowels

Unlike consonants, vowels do not involve any serious constriction of the airflow from the lungs. Instead they exploit the shape of the oral cavity, which can be made different sizes and shapes by raising and lowering different sections of the tongue. The air flowing through the glottis is voiced by the vocal folds, and then resonates in the cavity made by the tongue and palate. The different **frequencies** and **amplitudes** of the resulting soundwaves are enough to give us an enormous range of vowel sounds; approximately 21 in English. Frequency is the number of vibrations per second, and relates to the perceived pitch of the sound. Amplitude is the extent of the vibration of the air from the 'centre', and relates indirectly to the perceived loudness of the sound.

1.5.1 The vowel chart

We cannot give vowels the same kind of VPM description as consonants because vowels are all voiced in English, so this is not a distinguishing factor. They are also all formed with only the tongue and the palate, rather than the range of articulators used for consonants, so place of articulation is not really an issue and the manner of articulation is always the same – the formation of a resonating chamber. Thus the challenge for early phoneticians was to find a precise way of describing what seemed like a very vague range of movements.

This challenge was tackled by Daniel Jones (1956), who proposed that we should map out the vowels that were most different from each other as reference points for the actual vowels of human languages. The extremes of the tongue's movements were thus used to form a **vowel chart**, upon which linguists would be able to map the variations in the positioning of the tongue relative to these 'cardinal' points of reference (Figure 1.8).

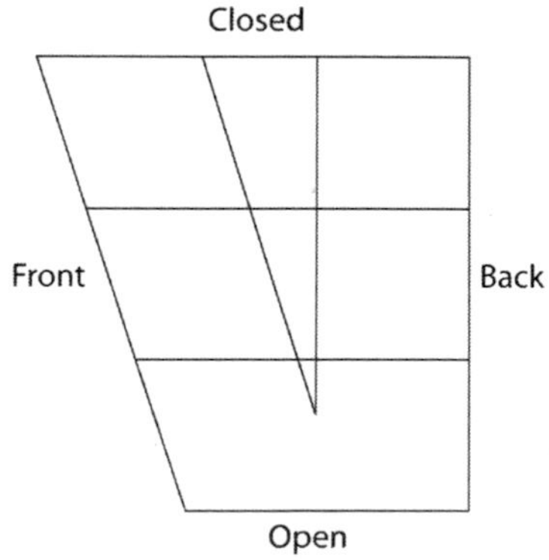

Figure 1.8 Daniel Jones' vowel chart

The shape of the chart reflects the shape of the resonating cavity that produces the different vowel sounds. It is not intended to reflect the shape of the mouth itself, and this can be confusing for some users of the chart. The two main dimensions of the chart are the front–back and **closed–open** dimensions, and these reflect the positioning of the resonating chamber – either towards the front or the back of the tongue, and with the tongue raised quite high, leaving a small cavity (closed), or with the tongue lowered, leaving a larger resonating chamber (open). There are also vowels that are produced near the centre of both dimensions. In order to begin to understand the vowel chart, try making a very long and closed *eeeee* sound – think carefully about the positioning of your tongue and about the space that is left for the sound to resonate. There should be quite a small resonating chamber near the front and top of your mouth. As a contrast, try the same thing with *aaaaaah* and then *oooooooo*, and note the different places and sizes of the space left by the tongue.

Apart from positioning the vowels in relation to the height and front–back dimensions, we need to take into account two other features that can be used to differentiate otherwise similar vowels: **lip-rounding** and **length**. You can try out the effect of lip-rounding by pronouncing just the vowel in the word *peace*, and then try it again, but this time pushing your lips together and forward. If you're familiar with French vowel sounds you may recognise that what you have just pronounced is a very accurate French vowel, to be found in the word *tu* (you, familiar). Many English speakers of French mistakenly think that the 'u' in *tu* is a /u/ sound, which is a back vowel with lip-rounding. But a much more accurate accent is obtained by using the tongue position for /iː/ (as in *peace*) and adding lip-rounding, which is not present in the English version of the vowel.

The other feature that can distinguishes vowels is length. The difference, for example, between the vowels in *sheep* and *ship* is partly a difference in length, with *sheep* being longer. There are other slight differences in height and frontness too, but the length is particularly salient to speakers. Despite its audibility, vowel length is not considered to be particularly significant in English because there are no pairs of vowels that differ only in length.

Figure 1.9 shows the vowels, as charted by Daniel Jones. As mentioned above, Jones thought that if some 'ideal' vowels were charted, showing the most extreme shapes of the oral cavity, the real vowels that people pronounce could be plotted against these ideal ones. He called them **cardinal vowels**, and the complete set of **primary and secondary vowels** in his chart is more complex than we require for describing the basic vowel sounds in English. It is included it here to give you an idea of the principles behind the description of vowel sounds, should you wish to carry out a more detailed study of phonetics in the future. It should also help you to understand the basis of English vowel distinctions.

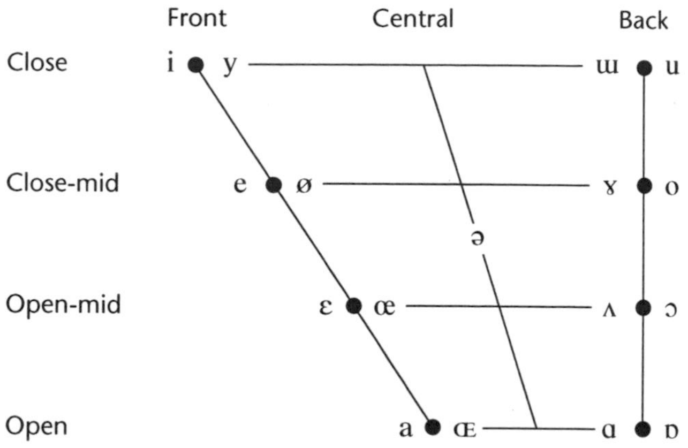

Note: Where symbols appear in pairs, the one on the right represents a rounded vowel.
Source: Adapted from Jones (1956).

Figure 1.9 Chart showing primary and secondary cardinal vowels

The primary cardinal vowels are those listed around the outer edge of the chart, and they represent idealised forms of the most common vowels in human languages. The secondary cardinal vowels are listed just within the perimeter of the chart and are less in evidence in the world's languages, though we have already met one of them (y) in the French word *tu*. Apart from the central vowels, most English vowels relate to the primary set of cardinal vowels.

The cardinal vowels are **'pure' vowels**, which means that they do not involve a slide from one vowel position to another. These pure vowels are not always easily recognised by English speakers because many of the vowels in English, including the names of the letters 'A', 'I', 'O', are actually diphthongs, which are made up of two vowels and the movement between them. Try saying these letters and decide whether or not there is a diphthong. If a letter is a diphthong your jaws will move during the pronunciation. A pure vowel will cause the mouth to take up a position initially, but it will not move after that. It is worth practising pure vowels, and in particular working out how to say the cardinal vowels, which Daniel Jones was recorded pronouncing in the early twentieth century. There are a number of websites where you can hear these recordings. The most reliable source of much phonetic information is University College London's phonetics website (www.phon.ucl.ac.uk).

In the remainder of this section we shall investigate the articulatory features of the English vowels. The vowel chart in Figure 1.10 shows the placing of the so-called pure vowels in southern (RP) accents of British English. Note that some of the symbols are followed by /ː/. This indicates that the vowel is a long one, roughly twice as long as the short vowels. In English, length is not

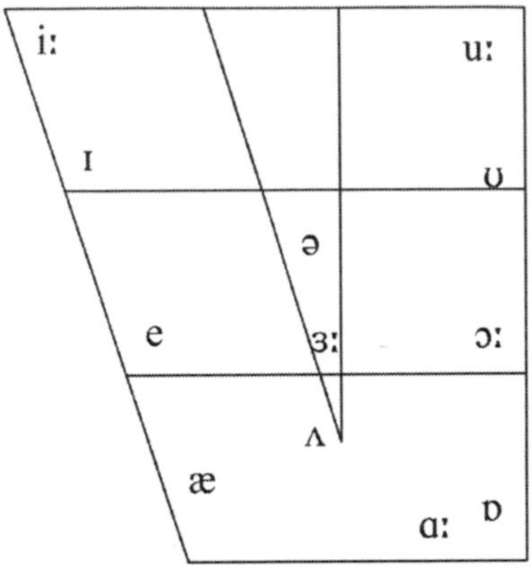

Figure 1.10 The pure vowels in English

normally the only difference between vowels, but it is easily heard and the symbols mark its presence.

1.5.2 Front vowels

There are four **front vowels** in RP accents of English, three of which are short and one long. The most closed front vowel is /iː/, which is long and close to Jones' 'cardinal 1'; that is, the most closed and most front vowel there is. Try saying a long *eeeeee* without moving your tongue, and feel how small a cavity the air has to resonate in. Also note how your lips are spread, which is the opposite of lip-rounding and is particularly marked in this vowel.

Now, starting from the /iː/ position, very slightly open your mouth and let your tongue lower with the movement of your jaw. If you articulate a short vowel in this position it should be something close to the /ɪ/ in words such as *bit* and *lip*. This vowel is half way between the closed and half-closed positions in the front of the mouth. Many foreign learners of English make the mistake of articulating them both at the same (closed) position and using only the length to distinguish them. This may work in terms of differentiating the meaning, but it does result in a marked 'foreign' accent.

The next vowel is more than **half-open**, and therefore lower in the mouth than cardinal 2, which is close to an Italian 'e'. Try out a stereotypical Italian accent – you will find yourself making an [e] sound that is more closed than the English /ɛ/ in *bed* and *wet*. Do not be confused by one of the diphthongs in English, /eɪ/, which starts in the cardinal [e] position but then moves to a position close to /ɪ/. This diphthong is found in words such as *say* and *fame* and in the name of the letter A. It also varies a lot, so if you are from London or Essex, for example, you might start with a much more open mouth, resulting in a sound much closer to /faɪm/; and if you live in the North of England you might not produce a diphthong at all (/feːm/). Note whether your jaw and tongue move during the pronunciation of these words; with an Italian /e/ they would be static.

The final front vowel in the English accent is /æ/, which is almost completely open and is close to cardinal 4, but not quite so far forward in the mouth. If you try saying only the vowel in words such as *cat* and *sad* you should be able to feel that the cavity, though concentrated in the front of the mouth, also has some space in the centre.

Now that we have introduced all the front vowels, it would be useful for you to practise saying them in turn, starting with the close vowels, in order to become familiar with the way in which the jaw and the tongue gradually open further for each vowel: /iː/, /e/, /ɛ/, /æ/.

1.5.3 Back vowels

There are more **back vowels** than front vowels in English: three long and three short. However, as with the front vowels there are no cases of two vowels being distinguished by length alone. Instead they are also differentiated by the height of the tongue; in this case the back of the tongue.

Beginning with the most open back vowel, /ɑː/ is at the opposite extreme from /iː/, and for obvious reasons it is traditionally the vowel your doctor asks you to say when she or he looks down your throat! Try saying it, and feel how there is no contact between the tongue and the palate. The mouth is wide open and the lips are spread, as you can tell if you choose to purse them instead when saying /ɑː/.

The next most open vowel is one that occurs in southern British English and some Australian accents, but not in the north of Britain or in many other global accents of English. However, as it is a significant feature of southern British accents, and RP in particular, all phoneticians of English need to recognise it. The vowel concerned is /ʌ/, which is slightly less open than /ɑː/ and also slightly less far back, and short. This means that speakers who are not accustomed to hearing the /ʌ/ sound may try to mimic southern British speakers by using the nearest available short open vowel: the front vowel, /æ/, as in *cat*. Thus in words where RP speakers and other southerners use /ʌ/ when saying *cup*, the mimic might say *cap*.

The remainder of the back vowels involve lip-rounding, and this distinguishes them from the front vowels, which do not. The next most open back vowel is /ɒ/, which occurs in words such as *box*, *sausage* and *rob*. Note that in most British English accents these words have the short /ɒ/ sound, but in some American accents the vowel is long. Try alternating the two vowels, /ɑː/ and /ɒ/, and note whether your jaw closes a little for the /ɒ/ sound and your lips push forward into a rounded position. If you try saying the following words, one after the other, you will be able to establish whether you are sounding four different vowels, or whether your accent is one that merges two or more together: *cot, caught, cart, cat*. In RP these will be /kɒt/, /kɔːt/, /kɑːt/ and /kæt/, but in some accents different pairs of these words will sound the same. In certain North American accents the merging of the two vowels in *cot* and *caught* is a recognised phenomenon and has been mapped by the Telsur Project team at Pennsylvania University, producers of *The Atlas of North American English* (Labov *et al.*, 2005). This project has produced detailed linguistic and geographical information on the phonology of American English.

Moving up to the **half-closed** position on the vowel chart, the next vowel is /ɔː/, which is long and involves lip-rounding. In RP it is found in words such as *for, paw* and *storm*. Try running through the whole list of back vowels (missing out /ʌ/ if it's not in your normal repertoire) and note the gradually closing position of the jaw, and therefore the raising of the tongue against the palate. This closing process continues as you move to the final two back vowels: /ʊ/ as in *book* and /uː/ as in *food*. A little like the front pair, /iː/ and /ɪ/, these two are differentiated both by the height of the tongue, with /ʊ/ being slightly more open than /uː/, and by length, with the most extreme back closed vowel, /uː/, also being a long vowel.

1.5.4 Central vowels

Though most of the English pure vowels are positioned around the edges of the vowel chart, indicating a clear front–back divide, there are also two **central vowels**, that have an identical tongue position but differ in length. These are transcribed as /ə/ and /ɜː/ and sound like the 'er' sound we make when hesitating or thinking in the middle of speaking. With these vowels the tongue is half closed, but leaving a small resonating cavity in the centre of the mouth, under the highest part of the hard palate. These vowels are easily spoken when the mouth is in a relaxed state, and they lie mid-way between the furthest back and the furthest forward sounds, both of which may be reasons why they are used for hesitation in English, since speakers are not sure what sound they will articulate next, and a central vowel provides the best chance of getting to the next required tongue position.

The short vowel /ə/ is the only phonetic sound with its own name: **schwa**. It is important in English because it occurs in many **unstressed syllables** and never carries a stress in an English word. It therefore occurs in grammatical words such as *the* and *a*, when they are spoken naturally and without extra emphasis, and in the unstressed syllables of multisyllable words such as *about, father* and ***per**haps*.

The longer central vowel, /ɜː/, is a normal stressed vowel which behaves unlike schwa and more like all the other vowels we have encountered. It can be found in many English words such as *bird, first, birth* and *worse.*

1.5.5 Diphthongs

As we have already seen, diphthongs are a combination of two different positions of the tongue, with an audible 'glide' from one to the other. Figure 1.11 shows how the tongue moves in English (RP) diphthongs.

If for convenience we divide them up according to the final vowel of the diphthong, then we have three groups of diphthongs in RP English: those ending with schwa, /ə/, those ending with /ɪ/ and those ending with /ʊ/.

The first group are **'centralising' diphthongs** because they move from the periphery of the mouth towards a central vowel. There are three of them, two moving from the front of the mouth: /ɪə/, as in fear and /ɛə/ as in *fair*; and one moving from the back of the mouth: /ʊə/ as in *poor*. Note that not all southern British speakers use /ʊə/ consistently, or even at all, though it is still common in northern Britain and amongst traditional RP speakers, such as the royal family and other upper-class speakers. Many southern speakers have replaced it with /ɔː/ in at least some words, resulting in the identical pronunciation of words such as *moor* and *more*, which northern British speakers distinguish as /mʊə/ and /mɔː/. Other accents of English around the world vary in similar ways. In many Australian accents of English, for example, the pure vowel and the diphthong remain distinct, while in some American accents they have merged.

The second group of diphthongs involve a movement towards the front, closed position of /ɪ/. In two cases the starting position is a more open front position: /eɪ/ as in *say* and /aɪ/ as in *sigh*. In the third case the diphthong

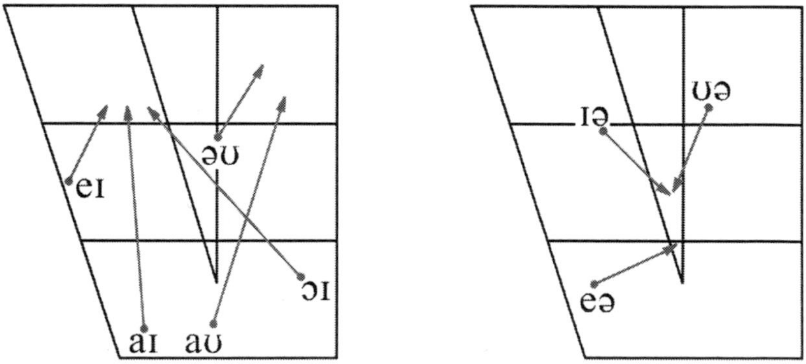

Figure 1.11 English diphthongs

moves from a half-open back vowel: /ɔɪ/ as in *boy*. In northern accents of British English and many US accents the /eɪ/ diphthong is replaced by a pure vowel that is more closed than the /ɛ/ in *bed* and longer too, more like a lengthened cardinal 2: [eː]. Try pronouncing *say* with both a diphthong and a pure vowel to see whether you can detect the different accents inherent in these pronunciations. In order to pronounce a pure vowel, start to say the word *say*, but stop immediately after the /s/ sound, stopping on the first part of the diphthong. If this comes naturally to you, then try the diphthong instead, and having said the word, try to raise your tongue towards an /ɪ/ sound.

The final pair of English diphthongs end at the half-closed back vowel, /ʊ/, in one case from an open front vowel, /aʊ/, as in *house*, and in the other from a half-open back vowel, /oʊ/, as in *boat*. In northern accents, and particularly in some broad Scottish accents of British English, these diphthongs are replaced by pure long vowels, so that *house* is pronounced /huːs/ and *boat* is pronounced /bɔːt/. Also, in some southern British accents there is an increasing move away from the use of a rounded back vowel in /oʊ/ and towards schwa, resulting in /əʊ/.

1.5.6 Summary of English vowel sounds

As stated in Section 1.5.1, there are more diphthongs in English than in some other European languages, and it has more vowel sounds in its range than many other languages. Vowels and diphthongs are the main distinguishing features of the many different accents of English throughout the English-speaking world. For this reason it is difficult to capture a single set of vowels that account for English vowels in the same way as it is possible for consonants.

However, in order to enable you to investigate the accents you encounter (including your own), a range of possible vowel sets are presented in Tables 1.5 and 1.6. Firstly, in Table 1.5 we have the recognised set of RP vowels spoken by certain southern and upper-class speakers of British English.

In order to make comparisons easier across accents, Table 1.6 lists vowels sets for other British accents, and one American accent, often called **general American**. Australian accents tend to have a similar number of vowels to British accents, although the pronunciation may differ in some cases.

Note that vowels 8 and 20 are the same in southern British accents, and vowels 9 and 12 are the same in northern British accents. This means that these accents each have 20 different vowel sounds. General American accents, by contrast, have only 16 different vowel sounds, numbers 6 and 7 being the same and numbers 17 to 20 being repeats of earlier vowels in the list. The diphthongs (numbers 17 to 20) that end with a schwa (/ə/) in British English occur in non-rhotic accents, whereas in **rhotic accents**, such as gen-

Table 1.5 Summary of RP English vowel sounds

	Symbol	Word	Transcription	Notes
Pure Vowels:	iː	bead	/biːd/	
	ɪ	bid	/bɪd/	
	ɛ	bed	/bɛd/	Sometimes transcribed as /e/
	æ	bad	/bad/	Sometimes transcribed as /a/
	ɑː	bard	/bɑːd/	Not present in many northern British accents
	ɒ	cot	/kɒt/	
	ɔː	caught	/kɔːt/	
	ʊ	cooked	/kʊkt/	Replaces /ʌ/ in most northern British accents
	uː	coot	/kuːt/	
	ɜː	curt	/kɜːt/	
	ʌ	cut	/kʌt/	Southern British accents only
	ə	about	/əbaʊt/	Unstressed vowel called 'schwa'
	Symbol	**Word**	**Transcription**	**Notes**
Diphthongs:	eɪ	bay	beɪ	Northern British accents would use a long /eː/ here
	aɪ	buy	baɪ	
	ɔɪ	boy	bɔɪ	
	oʊ	boat	boʊt	In southern British accents this diphthong is /əʊ/
	aʊ	bout	baʊt	
	ɪə	mere	mɪə	
	ɛə	mare	mɛə	
	ʊə	moor	mʊə	Often replaced by ɔː in southern British accents

eral American, the pure vowels are instead followed by the /r/ sound. Thus an American pronunciation of *mare* would be /mɛr/, whereas a British (non-rhotic) pronunciation of the same word would be /mɛə/.

1.6 Larger units

As we shall see in the remainder of this book, the larger units of language have more and more to do with meaning as well as structure. Phonetics, which focuses mainly on the articulatory/acoustic/auditory structures of lan-

Table 1.6 Summary of differences between major accents of English

	Word	Southern British	Northern British	American English
1	bead	iː	iː	iː
2	bid	ɪ	ɪ	ɪ
3	bay	eɪ	eː	eɪ
4	bed	ɛ	ɛ	ɛ
5	bad	æ	æ	æ
6	bard	ɑː	æː	ɑː
7	cot	ɒ	ɒ	ɑː
8	caught	ɔː	ɔː	ɔː
9	cooked	ʊ	ʊ	ʊ
10	boat	əʊ	oʊ	oʊ
11	coot	uː	uː	uː
12	cut	ʌ	ʊ	ʌ
13	curt	ɜː	ɜː	ɜː
14	buy	aɪ	aɪ	aɪ
15	bout	aʊ	aʊ	aʊ
16	boy	ɔɪ	ɔɪ	ɔɪ
17	mere	ɪə	ɪə	ɪ
18	mare	ɛə	ɛə	ɛ
19	mire	aɪə	aɪə	aɪ
20	moor	ɔː	ʊə	ʊ
21	about	ə	ə	ə

guage, has also traditionally focused on the smaller units of human language, such as the consonants and vowels we have been discussing.

However it is also clear that, in addition to the individual sounds of language, there are features of the sound of speech that extend beyond these units. Although connected in intricate ways with the meaningful aspects of language, there are some things that we can investigate on a purely phonetic basis in order to find out what patterns are evident in human language in general and, for the purposes of this book, in English in particular.

1.6.1 Syllables in English

One feature of all human languages is the way that consonants and vowels work as groups to form **syllables**. Because vowels are formed by a shape of the mouth and consonants by a constriction of the airflow from the mouth, vowels tend to be more resonant and thus more salient to hearers than consonants. It is almost as though vowels are the fabric of the language, and they are bordered, cut up or delineated by the harder lines of the consonantal sounds. You can easily speak a sentence pronouncing only the vowels, but a hearer will find it difficult to decipher and work out where the individual sounds end. If, on the other hand, you try to articulate the same sentence with only the consonants, the task will be almost impossible and you will find little vowels creeping in between the consonants to make it feasible. Try these two experiments with the following sentence: *No one could think of the answer to the question.*

So it seems to be the case that vowels are the centre of linguistic syllables, and indeed the English syllable is, at its simplest, made up of a single vowel, as in the word *eye* or *oh* and many syllables in longer words, particularly unstressed syllables, as in ***a**fraid* .

One of the distinguishing features of different human languages is their syllable structure, and it is the number and range of consonants that can occur before and/or after the vowel that makes this distinction. A very common pattern of syllable in the world's languages is the simple 'open' syllable, which has a single consonant before the vowel, as in English words such as *my, car* and *who.* This CV (consonant-plus-vowel) format is also the early syllabic form learnt by children when they acquire their first language.

Initial **consonant clusters** in English have a minimum of zero and a maximum of three consonants, and final consonant clusters have a minimum of zero and a maximum of four consonants. The structure of the English syllable is often represented as follows: $C^{(0\text{-}3)}VC^{(0\text{-}4)}$

Thus the smallest syllable can be made up of a single vowel (V), and in theory the largest syllable could be made up of seven consonants and a vowel (CCCVCCCC), though in fact the most complex initial and final consonant clusters never occur in the *same* syllable. In the next section we shall investigate the combinations of consonants to be found in syllable-initial and syllable-final positions.

Another common way of presenting the structure of the syllable is to refer to the different sections as **onset, nucleus** and **coda**, and to represent them as having the relationship shown in Figure 1.12.

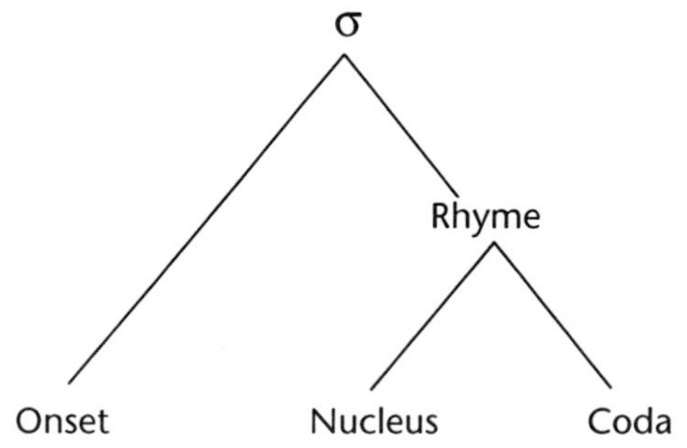

Figure 1.12 Syllable structure

The onset, is the initial consonant cluster, and the rhyme (which is the section of the syllable that needs to be identical for full rhyme) is made up of the vowel (the nucleus) and the coda (the final consonant cluster). Note that on occasion in English a sonorant consonant – a nasal /m/, /n/ or /ŋ/) or an approximant /w/, /r/, /l/ or /j/ – may take the place of a vowel as the nucleus of the syllable. These 'syllabic' consonants will be explored in Chapter 3.

1.6.2 Consonant clusters

The possible consonant combinations in a language is sometimes known as **phonotactics**. In English, as we have already seen, there are a maximum of three consonants before the vowel and four after. In fact the occurrence of four consonants is very rare indeed. Even when there is a possibility of pronouncing four consonants together the processes of assimilation and elision, which involve sounds changing to be more like their neighbours or being missed out altogether, usually ensure that this number is reduced. Take for example the word *sixths*, which theoretically could be pronounced /sɪksθs/. Most speakers would pronounce it /sɪkθs/, with the middle /s/ missing. Try saying this word, or the word *twelfths* (/twɛlfθs/), and see how hard it is to pronounce all four of the final consonants. See Chapter 2, Section 2.3, for more on these processes.

The onset of English syllables may be empty (no consonant), but when there is a single consonant any of the English consonants may occur, except /ŋ/ and /ʒ/. When there are two initial consonants, the first one cannot be /h/, an affricate (/tʃ/or /dʒ/) or a sonorant. This leaves the two 'obstruent' classes: the plosives and the fricatives (though note that /h/ is excluded, despite being a fricative).

The initial CC syllable cluster in English is made up of obstruents followed by sonorants such as /pl/, /kr/, /tw/ and so on, as in ***plane***, ***crisis*** and ***tweed***. You will notice that the spelling (and also the transcription) of these CC consonant clusters shows only voiceless obstruents in the initial position. The reason for this is that the difference between voiced and voiceless obstruents is neutralised in this context. Try saying an invented word such as *blane*, *grisis* or *dweed* and you will see that they are too similar to ***plane***, ***crisis*** and ***tweed*** to be useful as independent English words.

The only additional consonant that can be added to this pattern in the onset of English syllables is /s/, which can be added to the beginning of CC clusters, as in /skr/, /str/, /spl/ and so on. Thus we have ***sprain***, ***strain*** and ***spleen***, amongst others.

The coda is left unfilled more often than the onset. When it has a single consonant this can be any consonant except /w/, /j/ and /h/. When the cluster has two consonants, in theory any consonant can be followed by an obstruent, for example /pt/, /ʃt/ or /ŋk/, as in *apt, fished* and *ink*. In Chapter 2 we shall see that this is not the whole story, as consonants can affect other consonants adjacent to them. In principle, however, the rule holds.

The final part of the syllable, the final consonant in a CCC coda, is the mirror image of the initial cluster, with /s/ being the only consonant allowed to occupy this position. Examples include /ŋks/ and /fts/, as in *sinks* and *lifts*.

To summarise, in English the syllable is made up of the following elements (with optional parts in brackets):

> (/s/) + (obstruent) + (sonorant) + verb + (any consonant [except for /w/, /j/ and /h/]) + (obstruent) + (/s/)

Whilst this structure describes all the combinations that *do* occur, there are some that it allows for but do *not* occur. These include initial consonant clusters such as /sr/, which can be articulated by English speakers but happen not to occur in any known English words.

1.6.3 Word stress

Another feature of the sound pattern of human language is what is known as 'stress'. This comes in different forms, some of them more meaningful and structural than others. In English, **word stress** is usually phonetic in that it does not contribute to meaning and is not connected to the structure of the words in any evident way.

Although speakers are aware of some differences in stress in their speech they are not always clear about what makes a syllable prominent. Whilst we may assume that it is likely to be loudness (intensity or amplitude) that has this effect, acoustic phonetic investigations have shown that pitch change (frequency) and duration can be just as important in making syllables stand out, and in some cases more so.

In comparison with some languages English has free stress, which means that it does not occur regularly in the same place in the word, although there is a preference for stress not to be placed on the first syllable of **multisyllabic** words. Other languages have regular stress patterns, such as putting the stress on the penultimate syllable (for example Spanish), but the stresses in English words have neither this regularity nor any meaningful significance, except when they are used for emphasis or contrast.

If you take a range of multisyllabic words, almost any positioning of the main stress is apparently possible, with little or no connection to grammatical class or meaning. In the following list there are two-, three- and four-syllable words, with stresses (underlined) in most of the possible positions:

Two syllable: *hopeful* *persuade*

Three syllable: *culpable* *fantastic* *undermine*

Four syllable: *terrorism* *enormity* *superstition*

Although there is no consistent pattern of stresses that match either grammar or meaning, there are a few cases where the phonology of two words is identical except for the stress pattern and some noun–verb pairs where the stress is what indicates the word class. So the words *below* and *billow* are differentiated in many English accents by the stress placement alone:

/bɪləʊ/ (*below*) /bɪləʊ/ (*billow*)

There is also a growing tendency (particularly, but not only, in American English) to make noun–verb pairs conform to the following stress difference:

/kɒntrɑːst/ (*contrast*, n.) /kəntrɑːst/ (*contrast*, v.)

Thus a change is currently taking place with words such as *address*, which is traditionally stressed on the second syllable in British English but is increasingly being regularised to the distinctive pattern because of the influence of American pronunciations:

/ædrɛs/ (*address*, n.) /ədrɛs/ (*address*, v.)

Note that there is a tendency for the unstressed vowel to be reduced to schwa, though not in all cases.

In longer English words there is often thought to be more than one stressed syllable. Some phoneticians identify three and four levels of stress, and generative phonologists have been known to theorise an infinite number of different stress levels, though these are not necessarily able to be heard by the naked ear. What is clear is that there is always one main stress, and sometimes other syllables also appear to have some degree of prominence. In five-syllable words the main stress (underlined) and other stresses (highlighted) are usually separated from the main stress by an unstressed syllable, causing the kind of **iambic rhythm** (unstressed syllable followed by stressed) that is not only typical of Shakespeare but is also claimed to be typical of English in general. In the following notation above the transcription of the word *possibility* the oblique stroke represents stressed syllables, and ˘ , represents unstressed syllables:

/ ˘ / ˘ /
pɒ sɪ bɪ lɪ tiː

1.7 Further reading

It can be helpful to read more than one description of the same phenomenon, particularly when the concepts are difficult to grasp. Slightly greater detail and depth on basic articulatory phonetics can be found in Roach (2001), which is related specifically to English and would be useful for students working only with the English language.

For readers who wish to pursue the study of phonetics beyond the basic introduction given here the two volumes by Ladefoged (1993, 2000) provide accessible and lively introductions to the subject. Although acoustic and auditory phonetics are not considered here, readers who wish to learn about the subject should read Johnson (1997); Ladefoged (2000) also discusses the acoustic features of human speech. For readers who are interested in the more theoretical aspects of the study of speech sounds, Laver (1994) is a good place to begin.

There are many websites that provide explanations and illustrations of articulatory phonetics. These vary in quality, but those associated with University courses are often helpful. The website of University College London's Phonetics and Linguistics Department (www.phon.ucl.ac.uk) is a reliable and interesting place to begin, and it has many tutorials and exercises on recognition of sounds and practice in transcription. Another useful website for general support on these topics is that of Washington University (faculty.washington.edu/dillon/PhonResources/vowels.html), which has George Dillon's comparisons of British and American vowels, amongst other things. Macquarie University website considers the speech sounds of Australian English (www.ling.mq.edu.au/speech/phonetics/topics.html), and this site also has a useful explanation of the difference between broad and narrow transcription (www.ling.mq.edu.au/speech/phonetics/transcription/broad_transcription/broad_transcription.html). Although we have treated American English as though there were a single accent, in reality there is considerable variation, particularly in the case of vowels. The *Atlas of North American English* (Labov *et al.*, 2005) is based on work carried out at the University of Pennsylvania and its website is very informative on the range of sounds in different American accents (www.ling.upenn.edu/phono_atlas/home.html).

CHAPTER

2 Phonology

2.1 Introduction: English speech sounds

Phonology is the study of the sound system of particular human languages, including **dialects** and other language **varieties**. At this level of study it may seem to be similar to the study of phonetics because the transcription systems used are quite similar, but you should remember that the principle behind the discussion in this chapter is quite different from that in Chapter 1, which considered how human beings use their vocal apparatus to produce speech sounds in general. Here we are concerned with the range and type of sounds made in English in particular, and we shall look at how sounds translate into meaningful speech.

As with all aspects of linguistic study there are a number of ways of approaching the study of phonology, and these are based on different theoretical positions and their related models of how language works. Here we shall mainly follow the structuralist approach to the phonology of English, although other theories and models will be touched upon. The reason for this choice of approach is that it provides the most workable system of description for relative newcomers to linguistics. Many researchers in phonology use at least a modified version of the structuralist model, and some use a largely generative model, but these are not easily assimilated and in general do not provide a useable transcription system, which is one of the great strengths of the structuralist model.

One of the principles of the structuralist model of language is that the meaning-potential of units in the language (sounds, words, phrases and so on) is based on their relationship with each other rather than, for example, their relationship with the world they describe. This is true in phonology, where the focus on individual speech sounds is not concerned with detailed differences of sound, as is the case with phonetics. Instead, what phonologists are interested in is how sounds differentiate meaning, and therefore how many sounds are needed to produce all the different combinations a language requires.

Let us look at a couple of examples where phonetics and phonology treat the same material differently. Say out loud the words *lake* and *kill*, in as natural a way as possible. If you listen very carefully you may notice that the two 'l' sounds and the two 'k' sounds are rather different. In the case of 'l', the one that appears at the beginning of the word is pronounced further forward in the mouth than the one appearing at the end of the word. This is not necessarily true of all languages, but is generally true of many accents of English. We call the first kind of 'l' 'clear' and the second kind 'dark'. These will be explored in more detail in later sections of this chapter. As far as the 'k' sound is concerned, you ought to have noticed that the initial occurrence in *kill* produces more audible breathiness than the one occurring at the end of a word. This is called aspiration. If you pronounced the word *lake* too carefully, this difference might not have been noticeable, but if you now put another word after it you may find the /k/ sounds less aspirated. Try *lakeside* to see if that works.

Although we can perceive these differences in pronunciation, English does not treat the two 'l' and 'k' sounds as different units because they do not significantly alter meaning. Try swapping the sounds round, so that you pronounce the initial /k/ without aspiration (it is difficult to do) and the final /k/ with aspiration – or initial /l/ as dark and final /l/ as clear. Whilst there may be a slight strangeness in the resulting pronunciations the words remain essentially the same; that is, they are the same English words but pronounced a little oddly.

Phonology is interested in regular variants of this kind, but its initial task is to consider the significant meaning-changing speech sounds of the language, leading to what is known as a broad transcription system; that is, one that does not include detailed differences in pronunciation but only differentiates between meaning-changing sounds.

If you look at the letter A in a number of different people's handwriting you will see an enormous variation in the precise shape and size of the letters, but you will still recognise them as letter A, unless the handwriting is so bad that you can not decipher it (Figure 2.1).

This situation, whereby the 'concept' of a letter is idealised but we learn to recognise all sorts of variants as belonging to the same form, is analogous to the situation with phonemes, which are similarly idealised as a concept but are realised rather differently in different accents of English. Compare, for example, the /ɑː/ vowel in the word *car* when it is spoken by a Southern British English speaker and by a person from Leeds or the United States. The

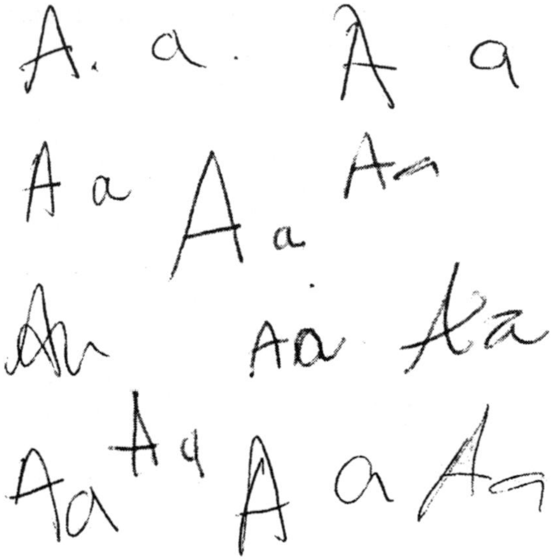

Figure 2.1 Different handwritten versions of the letter A

Southern British English version will be the standard cardinal five vowel in Daniel Jones' (1956) chart, [ɑː], whereas the Leeds version, and many American versions, will be more fronted, and thus strictly speaking nearer to cardinal four, [aː]. Another example is the more aspirated /t/ in the Liverpool accent, which at times is also fricative in nature, almost like [ts]. This does not mean that there is a different number of phonemes in the Liverpudlian accent, just that their precise variant is different from that of others.

To sum up, the difference between phonetics and phonology is that phonetics tries to get as close as possible to describing exactly what is going on in the mouth, whereas phonology is only interested in the extent to which sounds are contrastive in the language; that is, cause meaning change. This difference is analogous to the difference between studying an alphabet system and analysing handwriting styles or fonts.

2.2 Phonemes

The meaning-changing sounds of any language are called **phonemes** in many phonological descriptions, and it is a useful term to describe the concept of abstract sound segments that have the function of changing meaning in a particular language and also tend to have a core of phonetic features that identify them. In English the phonemes have slight regional variations, but in most cases there is approximately the same number of phonemes, even if the pronunciation of some of them varies.

There is a sense in which the notion of the phoneme is artificial, as the stream of speech is usually continuous and the division between the individual sounds is therefore non-existent. Our ability to cut up this stream into segments, then, is partly based on perceptual properties of the sounds themselves (for example the resonance of vowels) and partly a convenient 'fiction' that analysts have been able to exploit to further the study of speech. It is probably the case that our familiarity with alphabetic writing systems has influenced the evolution of phonemic analysis, but it should be noted that the alphabetic writing system itself probably evolved in response to the human ability to discriminate focal points in a continuous stream of sound, and to identify them consistently.

2.2.1 Minimal pairs

Although this book does not require you to find out for yourself what the list of English phonemes is, you may understand the sound system better if you are told a little about how the list was arrived at in the first place. The way in which early linguists (of the twentieth century) set about working out the phonemes of any language (including those which had never been written down) was to transcribe as closely as possible a number of simple words in the language, and then work out, with the use of **minimal pairs**, where a single change of consonant or vowel made a difference to the meaning. In the case of English this was easy to do, as the investigators were English speakers. However the **discovery procedure**, as it was called, was also used to record a great number of unwritten native languages in places where anthropologists had to ask local people whether two apparently quite similar utterances were identical or different in meaning, in order to work out not just the grammar and vocabulary of the language but also its phonology.

Minimal pairs are sets of words (often, but not only, pairs) that differ phonetically, but only in one way at a time. For example the following English words differ in only their initial consonant:

pot, tot, cot, hot

This set of words provides evidence that the sounds /p/, /t/, /k/ and /h/ are phonemes of English, because it makes a difference which one you say in the identical context of the vowel /ɒ/ followed by a /t/. The similarity in their pronunciation is evident in the spelling as well as the transcription, but more complex words do not have straightforward spellings in English and transcriptions are needed to show that the words are indeed minimally different.

Table 2.1 Minimal pairs/sets demonstrating English phonemes

Minimal	Pairs . . .	or . . .	Sets	Phonemes
pot/pɒt/	tot/tɒt/	cot/kɒt/	hot/hɒt/	/p t k h/
big/bɪg/	dig/dɪg/	gig/gɪg/		/b d/
me/miː/	knee/niː/			/m n/
rim/rɪm/	ring/rɪŋ/			/m ŋ/
fast/fɑːst/	vast/vɑːst/			/f v/
thigh/θaɪ/	thy/ðaɪ/			/θ ð/
Sue/suː/	zoo/zuː/	shoe/ʃuː/		/s z ʃ/
leisure/lɛʒə/	letter/lɛtə/			/ʒ t/
church/tʃɜːtʃ/	lurch/lɜːtʃ/			/tʃ l/
yes/jɛs/	less/lɛs/			/j l/
white/waɪt/	right/raɪt/			/w r/
jeep/dʒiːp/	seep/siːp/			/dʒ s/

Table 2.1 contains a group of word sets and pairs that between them demonstrate the meaning-making potential of all the consonants in English (at the end of each line is a list of the phonemes that have been introduced by each set of words).

Note that most of the transcriptions are identical except for the initial sound, though some of the spellings are not so similar. The only pairs that have a difference in the middle or end of the word are *leisure/letter* and *rim/ring* because the palatal fricative, /ʒ/, and the velar nasal, /ŋ/, do not occur at the beginning of words in English.

If you look back at section 1.5.6 you will see that the illustrative words given to show the vowels in English are also in minimal sets/pairs. In the following example they are again, but a single addition (see if you can spot it) and set out differently to emphasise the minimal sets.

bead/biːd/, *bid*/bɪd/, *bed*/bɛd/, *bad*/bad/, *bard*/bɑːd/ (/iː ɪ ɛ æ ɑː/)

cot/kɒt/, *caught*/kɔːt/ (/ɒ ɔː/)

cooked/kʊkt/, *caked*/keɪkt/ (/ʊ eɪ/)

coot/kuːt/, *curt*/kɜːt/, *cut*/kʌt/ (/uː ɜː ʌ/)

bay/beɪ/, *buy*/baɪ/, *boy*/bɔɪ/ (/eɪ aɪ ɔɪ/)

boat/boʊt/, *bout*/baʊt/ (/oʊ aʊ/)

mere/mɪə/, *mare*/mɛə/, *moor*/mʊə/ (/ɪə ɛə ʊə/)

The only vowel that cannot be put into a minimal pair is schwa, /ə/. This is because it only occurs in English as an unstressed vowel, and by their nature the other vowels will not appear in the same context as they are usually stressed. Some phonologists argue that schwa is not really a phoneme at all because it does not make a meaningful difference. This question will be considered in the next section. In the meantime think of some words that could contain schwa (for example *the* or *of*) and consider whether it makes a difference to use schwa or the so-called 'full' vowel. Can we say *the* as both /ðə/ and /ðiː/ and *of* as both /əv/ and /ɒv/, and does it make any difference to the meaning?

2.2.2 Allophones

Once phonologists have identified the set of phonemes that make up a language it is useful to work out the range of variation of each phoneme, and whether and to what extent these variable pronunciations occur in a patterned way. The variants of phonemes are known as **allophones**. These are usually phonetically similar to each other and have what is known as a **complementary distribution**. This means that the different allophones occur in distinct places in the syllable structure and therefore are not strictly interchangeable, although as we saw earlier they can be exchanged with no loss of meaning and only a little strangeness of sound. Thus if aspirated /p/ (phonetically [p^h]) occurs only at the beginning of syllables in English and unaspirated /p/ only at the end, they are likely to be considered two 'realisations' of a single phoneme, /p/. If this is so, you should be able to replace one by the other without any damage to the sense, though it may sound a little odd. If you say the words *pie* and *keep* with an aspirated and unaspirated /p/ in each position, this point should be evident in the odd but recognisable pronunciations of these words.

The aspiration of initial voiceless plosives in English is one example of a similar patterning of allophones across different phonemes. Thus /p/, /t/ and /k/ are all aspirated in the syllable-initial position and are usually unaspirated or even **unexploded** at the end of syllables. The unexploded version consists of a simple closure of the articulators, with no subsequent escape of air. If you are having trouble recognising the aspiration it can be made visible by holding a small piece of paper to the tip of your nose and letting it hang down in front of your mouth. Aspirated sounds will make the paper jump considerably more than unaspirated ones.

The phoneme /t/ is a special case amongst the voiceless plosives as it frequently has a number of other allophones, depending to some extent on the accent of the speaker. Thus in the syllable-final position, as well as in the unaspirated version, in many cases /t/ transfers its place of articulation to the glottis, and this results in a glottal stop. Try saying *but, pit,* and *sat* to establish whether you use a glottal stop or simply an unexploded plosive version of /t/. You may find that you do both – that your tongue is clamped tightly against the alveolar ridge but there is also a tightness in the glottis, producing a glottal stop as a secondary feature of the sound. Some speakers also use the glottal stop in internal positions in the word, as in *butter, matter* or *bottle,* though this variant is not always consistent within a single speaker's accent and can vary according to the formality of the situation and the of constraint the speaker is under to speak formally.

Another regular variation in English phonemes is the case of /l/, which has already been described as having **clear** (alveolar) and **dark** (velar) allophones. The alveolar allophone occurs initially (for example in words such as *linger* or *lounge*) and the velar version occurs after vowels (for example in words such as *feel* or *cool*). Note that for some speakers, such as those with urban accents in the south-east of England, the dark /l/ has become even less like a consonant and is often described as being **vocalised** because there is no contact between the articulators. In fact it almost becomes the same as a /w/, though since most /w/ phonemes are not pronounced at all in the word-final position we cannot argue that the two phonemes have merged into one. Try saying the words *fuel* /fjuːl/ and *few* /fjuː/ and note that the second one involves no discernible movement of the articulators, which would indicate the presence of a consonant, though the first does have the 'swoop' that is typical of approximants. Although the difference between the alveolar and velar lateral approximant, /l/, is not significant in English, this *is* a phonemic distinction in Russian, which effectively has two /l/ phonemes.

2.2.3 Free variation

The allophones introduced in the previous section have complementary distribution – that is, they occur in different contexts (for example syllable initial or final). There are some variants of phonemes that are less patterned than this, and vary according to the accent of the speaker and the context in which she or he is speaking. This is known as **free variation**. The glottal stop, introduced as an allophone of /t/ in the previous section, is both patterned by context (that is, it occurs most often at the end of syllables, less often between vowels and almost never at the beginning of words) and also varies in these positions, even in the case of individual speakers. But some variants are not restricted to positioning, and vary according to the speaker's accent and the extent to which he or she is trying to 'speak properly'.

For example, /θ/ and /ð/ are realised as /f/ and /v/ in some accents, particularly working-class London accents (see the BBC soap opera, *Eastenders,* for some examples). For some accents of English, /l/ is always 'dark' (velar). This is particularly true of some Glaswegian accents. In Liverpool some Scouse speakers have a /t/ phoneme that is so highly aspirated it is almost fricative, and unlike in other accents this is consistent wherever it occurs, not only in syllable initial positions:

take [tˢeɪk], *right* [raɪtˢ], *water* [wɔːtˢə]

Note that although allophones are part of the phonology (the sound system) of language, they sometimes require a more narrow transcription than a phonemic one in order to capture some of the phonetic detail of the variants of phonemes as they are actually spoken. In this case the /t/ phoneme is accompanied by a superscript diacritic, indicating that although the sound starts out with a closure typical of a plosive sound, the release of the closure is less explosive than is normally the case, and the more gradual opening of the articulators allows for some friction to occur before the sound is complete. It is articulated in a similar way to the affricates /tʃ/ and /dʒ/, though it takes place a little further forward than these.

Table 2.2 summarises the English phonemes in groups according to their manner of articulation (consonants) and their front or back position in the mouth (vowels). Other aspects of their phonetic description, and examples of words in which they are found, can be revised by rereading Chapter 1.

Table 2.2 Summary of English phonemes

	Symbols
Consonants:	
Plosives (voiceless)	/p t k/
Plosives (voiced)	/b d g/
Nasals	/m n ŋ/
Fricatives (voiceless)	/f θ s ʃ h/
Fricatives (voiced)	/v ð z ʒ/
Affricates	/tʃ dʒ/
Approximants (semivowels)	/w r l j/
Vowels:	
Simple vowels (front)	/iː ɪ ɛ æ/
Simple vowels (back)	/ɑː ʌ ɒ ɔː ʊ uː/
Simple vowels (centre)	/ə ɜː/
Diphthongs (fronting)	/eɪ aɪ ɔɪ/
Diphthongs (centralising)	/ɪə ɛə ʊə/
Diphthongs (backing)	/oʊ aʊ/

2.3 Connected speech

So far we have treated phonemes as separate segments of the stream of speech, but many modifications occur when these segments are put together in connected speech, particularly when the speech is fast and informal, and precise articulation or consciousness of accent are not priorities. You may be able to think of occasions when you are very careful about your articulation, such as when reading something aloud on the phone for another person to write down, or when trying to make a good impression at an interview for a job where your speaking voice would matter, for example as a telephone receptionist. On such occasions we do tend to place one phoneme after another, with individual phonemes having no interaction with or effect upon each other.

The following example is an extract from a children's book (Henderson, 1995), transcribed as it might very carefully be read to, or by, a young child.

> sæm ən ðə bɪg məʃiːnz
> sæm ðə smɔːl laɪkd bɪg məʃiːnz hiː laɪkd ðəm bɛtə ðən wɒtʃɪŋ tiː viː ɔː wɔːlks ɪn ðə pɑːk ɔː frɛndz həʊm fə tiː hɪz feɪvrɪt weɪ tə spɛnd ə deɪ wəz wɒtʃɪŋ træktəz ən dɪgəz θʌmpəz ən dʌmpəz bʊldəʊzəz rəʊdroʊləz paɪldraɪvəz pʌmps

It is good practice for you to read phonemic transcriptions of this kind in order to get into the habit of seeing the sounds of language, rather than their spelling. If you find it a struggle to understand any of this passage it is reproduced below, but please do not look at it until you have tried to decipher the transcribed version. The best way is to read out the sounds as they appear, and you will hear yourself utter words that you were not able to read off the page.

> *Sam and the Big Machines*
> *Sam the small liked big machines. He liked them better than watching TV or walks in the park or friends home for tea. His favourite way to spend a day was watching tractors and diggers, thumpers and dumpers, bulldozers, roadrollers, piledrivers, pumps* (Henderson, 1995, pp. 1–4).

Note that the transcription mostly shows words in the form they would take if they were quoted alone, for example in a list of unrelated items. There are a few exceptions; even in a careful rendering of this passage the word *for* would probably be articulated not as /fɔː/ but as /fə/, with the unstressed vowel being reduced to a schwa. Similarly the word *the* is almost always pronounced as /ðə/ rather than /ðiː/. These words are grammatical items that do not carry the semantic content of the text, and therefore do not usually carry any stress in context.

You will also see that the transcription has no gaps between words, no punctuation and no upper-case letters. This is because phonemic transcription is trying to replicate the effect of connected speech, and not the conventions of the written language. When we are speaking, particularly informally, we very rarely speak in complete sentences of the kind that are typical in the written language. This does not mean we are using the language badly; it just means that the grammar of the spoken language is different from that of the written language. The book by Carter and McCarthy (2005) is a complete grammar of the spoken language, based on a corpus of recorded speech. It treats the grammar of speech as a complete language system in its own right, instead of a pale and inadequate reflection of the written language, as it has often been treated.

The features of connected speech fall into two categories. There are those features which result in the adaptation of the segments (phonemes) to their surroundings. These are discussed in the rest of this section. The second category consists of features of sound that are not **segmental** but are spread over a number of phonemes and introduce meanings that are additional to the meanings of the words themselves, as well as additional to the combination of meanings made by the grammatical arrangements of the words. These are known as **suprasegmental** aspects of the phonology of English because they are overlaid upon the segments and include intonation and stress, which will be introduced in Section 2.4 below.

2.3.1 Assimilation

One consequence of putting phonemes together in close proximity is that they sometimes become more like each other than they would be in isolation. This is mainly because it is easier to articulate quickly if the sounds are close together in the mouth, or similar in manner of articulation. The forms of **assimilation** in English can either be **anticipatory** (also called **regressive**) or **retrospective** (also called **progressive**); in other words a sound might become more like the subsequent sound (anticipatory) or more like the preceding sound (retrospective). We shall consider examples of both kinds of assimilation below.

As well as the direction of assimilation, we also need to consider the type of merging that is happening. You will remember that consonants are defined by a VPM (voice, place, manner) description. Each of these features can be the basis of an assimilation, though some are more common than others. Thus a consonant may be voiced or devoiced to match the preceding or subsequent consonant, it may change its place of articulation to be closer to or at the same place as the preceding or subsequent consonant, or it may change its manner of articulation to match the preceding or subsequent consonant.

Let us consider some short phrases in English where assimilation may happen in fast connected speech. Table 2.3 provides examples of anticipatory (or regressive) assimilation.

The assimilations in the table are all consequences of putting words together, and of the end of the first word anticipating some aspect of the beginning of the second one. The assimilation occurring in *bad man* is very common, with many word-final plosives assimilating to a following plosive or nasal, particularly towards the bilabial place of articulation or the velar position, as in *fine candles* /faɪŋkændəlz/. You may be able to think of other examples, such as *right place* /raɪppleɪs/, *hard bread* /hɑːbbrɛd/ and *wrong colour* /rɒŋkʌlə/. Note that in some cases the assimilation technically makes two apparently different English words sound the same. Take *right* and *ripe*, for example. In the sentence *Get me the right [ripe] mangoes* it can be very difficult to distinguish them: /gɛpmiːðəraɪpmæŋgoʊz/. What speakers usually do in such situations is to use the context and semantics to work out the most likely word, which in this case is probably *ripe*, though one could imagine a situation (a fruit wholesaler perhaps) in which *right* could be the correct meaning. Of course when there is genuine confusion the speaker has the option of repeating the sentence with a clear break between the words, in which case the assimilation is not likely to happen. It is also likely that, in an effort to make absolutely clear which plosive is occurring, the final consonant will be aspirated, though in general this is not the normal allophone for final positions.

Incidentally there are a number of other assimilations in the transcribed sentence: /gɛpmiːðəraɪpmæŋgoʊz/. The word *get* assimilates to the manner

Table 2.3 Anticipatory assimilation in English phrases

Orthographic version	Careful pronunciation	Assimilation	Type of assimilation
Bad man	bædmæn	bæbmæn	Place – alveolar to bilabial
Good times	gʊdtaɪmz	gʊttaɪmz	Voice – devoicing
Good night	gʊdnaɪt	gʊnnaɪt	Manner – plosive to nasal
Fine candles	faɪnkændəlz	faɪŋkændəlz	Place – alveolar to velar
Give me	gɪvmiː	gɪmmiː	Place/manner – labiodental to bilabial and fricative to nasal

of articulation of the subsequent bilabial nasal in /gɛpmiː/, and there is assimilation within the word *mangoes*, where the nasal consonant assimilates to the subsequent velar plosive, becoming /ŋ/ rather than an alveolar /n/.

The examples of assimilation of voicing (*good times*), manner (*good night*) and place/manner (*give me*) all result in a double-length consonant of an identical kind: /gʊttaɪmz/ and /gʊnnaɪt/. The double consonant is qualitatively different from the single one, and therefore cannot be seen as a 'missing' consonant. They are like the double consonants of Italian, where instead of two separate closures followed by two releases, there is one extra long closure phase followed by a normal release, whether plosive or nasal in nature. These examples are less widespread than the place assimilation discussed above. They tend to be used more by some speakers than others, and only in the most informal and fast speech. You may find that you do not recognise these features in your own speech, but if you try saying them with the assimilation you may be able to hear that they are familiar to you from others' speech. The earlier examples of place assimilation are very common indeed, and if you are convinced that you do not use them it is probably because you are being overly influenced by the spelling. Try to say them fast and listen carefully to the sounds being made. Note that common examples can be given an **orthographic** form that occasionally becomes the standard way to indicate this pronunciation: *gimme* is an example of this.

Progressive assimilation, where the first of two adjacent consonants affects the second one, is common in grammatical contexts, particularly between parts of a word but not so frequently between words themselves. To start with the common morphological assimilations, let us look at the plural of nouns, the third-person present tense of verbs and the **possessive** suffix in English (Table 2.4). In each case the grammatical morphemes (that is, suffixes) appear in the spelling as an 's', and in each case the pronunciation depends on the preceding consonant.

What happens in each case with these grammatical additions to the word is that the morpheme is pronounced /z/ to match the voicing of all preceding voiced consonants and vowels, except for sibilants. It is pronounced /s/ to match the voicelessness of all voiceless preceding consonants, except sibilants. And because sibilant sounds are too similar to the morpheme itself to be heard clearly, an additional vowel is inserted in these examples, making the pronunciation of the morpheme in each case /ɪz/.

These assimilations between morphemes are, in a sense, part of the system of English and it is not possible to articulate a 'careful' version where they do not happen. However the process is very similar to the assimilation between words. Progressive assimilations between words often include the phoneme /ð/ as the first consonant of the second word, and it is usually assimilated to the place and manner of articulation of the preceding consonant, resulting in

Table 2.4 Progressive assimilation in English words

Preceding consonant	plural nouns	Third person singular present tense	Possessive
Voiced (including vowels but not sibilants)	Dogs /dɒgz/	Plays /pleɪz/	John's /dʒɒnz/
Voiceless (not sibilants)	cats /kæts/	Fights /faɪts/	Kate's /keɪts/
Sibilants (voiced and voiceless)	Horses /hɔːsɪz/	Kisses /kɪsɪz/	James's /dʒeɪmzɪz/

a double consonant of the kind we saw earlier. Table 2.5 shows some examples of this kind of progressive assimilation.

The words affected by this kind of assimilation are mostly grammatical words, which are less likely to carry sentence stress and are therefore more susceptible to change than the lexical words preceding them.

Progressive assimilation of voicing is not as common between words as within words where initial consonant clusters often have a devoiced second consonant. Try saying the following words but stop before the vowel in each case:

small, slap, slush, trap, class, crush.

You should find that the /m/, /l/ and /r/ phonemes are effectively voiceless, as a result of following the voiceless /s/ consonant. What is happening here is that phonemes that are regularly voiced in English (there is no such thing as a voiceless nasal, for example) are being pronounced as voiceless. This makes no difference to the understanding of the words as they are effective-

Table 2.5 Progressive assimilation in English phrases

Orthographic version	Careful pronunciation	Assimilation	Type of assimilation
Who's this?	huːzðɪs	huːzzɪs	Place: interdental to alveolar
In that car	ɪnðætkɑː	ɪnnækkɑː	Place/manner: interdental plosive to alveolar nasal
Save them	seɪvðəm	seɪvvəm	Place: interdental to labiodental

ly allophones of the voiced phoneme and are only devoiced depending on their context. Though the phonemic (broad) transcription cannot show devoiced consonants of this kind, the phonetic (narrow) transcription can use a diacritic of a small circle underneath the consonant to show devoicing:

small/smɔːl/ (broad transcription), [sm̥ ɔːl] (narrow transcription)

There are also a few common phrases where progressive devoicing also happens regularly, to the extent that they are not often pronounced in any other way. These include:

have to /hæftə/ *and used to* /juːsttə/

A final type of assimilation is known as **'fusion'**, because, rather than one segment becoming more like another, the two segments both assimilate towards each other, usually ending with an affricate as the resulting merged sound:

caught you /kɔːtʃuː/, *would you* /wʊdʒuː/

In both cases the alveolar plosive /t/ or /d/ followed by a palatal /j/ sound is replaced by the voiced or voiceless affricate, making the place of articulation somewhere between the alveolar ridge for the original plosives and the palate for the approximant /j/; in other words they occur in the post-alveolar place of articulation of English affricates.

2.3.2 Elision

Another process that takes place in connected speech is **elision**, which involves the loss of a sound that would be articulated in a careful pronunciation. The most frequently elided consonants in English are /t/ and /d/, particularly when they occur between other consonants, as in the examples in Table 2.6.

The loss of the alveolar plosive in these cases does not cause confusion since there are no words that are otherwise identical to them, but lack the alveolar consonants. Note that in some cases the elision causes two consonants to be adjacent and this might also lead to an assimilation taking place. In the case of *windmill*, for example, once the /d/ is elided the conjunction of an alveolar and then a bilabial nasal /nm/ may well change further to a double /mm/ sound, making the pronunciation easier and thus more rapid, with /wɪmmɪl/ as the resulting pronunciation. Two further examples of this combination of elision and assimilation are:

thousand points/θaʊzəmpɔɪnts/ and *handbag*/hæmbæg/

Table 2.6 Elision of consonants in English words

Orthographic version	Careful pronunciation	Elided version
handsome	/hændsəm/	/hænsəm/
windmill	/wɪndmɪl/	/wɪnmɪl/
mostly	/moʊstliː/	/moʊsliː/
kindness	/kaɪndnɛs/	/kaɪnnəs/
attempts	/ətɛmpts/	/ətɛmps/

Although it is extremely uncommon, these words can in fact be pronounced with all of the missing consonants included and assimilations avoided, though it would sound odd in normal conversation. There is a famous example from Oscar Wilde's play *The Importance of Being Earnest*, in which one of the characters, Lady Bracknell, is told that the protagonist had been found as a baby in a handbag. She reiterates this shocking fact in her usual exaggerated manner, 'A Handbag?', with every vowel and consonant pronounced in its fullest version; thus what would be /əhæmbæg/ in casual speech is emphasised by being pronounced /eɪhændbæg/.

Although it is less common than elision of consonants, vowels may also be elided. These elisions tend to be regular and conventional, and in some cases have an associated spelling (Table 2.7).

Note that the full version of *she's* (*she is*) will probably have an inserted /j/ consonant between the vowels because the transition from /iː/ to /ɪ/ does not result in a normal English diphthong. The modal and other auxiliary verbs are also unusual in that in a number of cases the elision of a vowel also has an effect on the previous syllable, a phenomenon that seems to be restricted to the following verbs: *shan't, can't, won't* and *don't.*

In some cases the loss of a vowel results in a consonant (usually /l/ or /n/) becoming **'syllabic'**, which means that the consonant has to take the place

Table 2.7 Elision of vowels in English words

Orthographic version	Careful pronunciation	Elided version
She's	ʃiːɪz	ʃiːz
Don't	duːnɒt	doʊnt
Geography	dʒiːɒgrəfiː	dʒɒgrəfiː
Police	pəliːs	pliːs
Bottle	bɒtəl	bɒtl
Hidden	hɪdən	hɪdn

of the vowel as the nucleus of the syllable, and therefore has a separate audible 'beat' or 'pulse'. The words *bottle* and *hidden* are two-syllable words, whether they include the schwa in the second syllable or not. It is often difficult to be sure whether the schwa is entirely elided, though there is a slight difference in sound quality when the syllabic consonants are used, as the previous plosive tends to be released through the place of articulation of the syllabic consonant. Thus in *bottle* the /t/ has **lateral release** with lowered sides of the tongue anticipating the /l/, and in *hidden* the /d/ is released through the nasal cavity and can sound rather like a snort. The phonetic transcription diacritic for syllabic consonants is a small vertical line under the consonant concerned, as shown below:

bottle [bɒtl̩] *hidden* [hɪdn̩]

To hear and feel the effect of the lateral and **nasal release**, try saying those words very slowly, making sure you go directly from the /t/ or /d/ to the /l/ or /n/ without an intervening vowel.

2.3.3 Insertion

To aid the flow of speech, consonants and vowels are sometimes added to words in a casual style when they would not be pronounced if the word was said on its own. This is known as **insertion**. The most common examples occur when the first word ends in a vowel and the second begins with a vowel. The inserted consonants are usually approximants, /r/, /j/ and /w/, because they are less consonant-like than the other consonants and detract less obviously from the vowels in the two words. In some cases these consonants are indicated in the spelling. The /r/ sound, of course, is pronounced by some speakers of English, but is left unpronounced by many others, except before another vowel, as in the examples in Table 2.8.

This use of approximants to make an easier transition from vowel to vowel is not restricted to words such as these, where the spelling already anticipates

Table 2.8 Insertion reflected in the English spelling

Orthographic version	Careful pronunciation	Version with insertion
My aunt	maɪɑːnt	maɪjɑːnt
Your uncle	jɔːʊŋkl	jɔːrʌŋkl
Their in-laws	ðɛəɪnlɔːz	ðɛərɪnlɔːz
Four antiques	fɔːæntiːks	fɔːræntiːks
How awful	haʊɔːfʊl	haʊwɔːfʊl

Table 2.9 Insertions not reflected in the English spelling

Orthographic version	Careful pronunciation	version with insertion
I understand	aɪʌndəstænd	aɪjʌndəstænd
go under	goʊʌndə	gowʊʌndə
to others	tuːʌðəz	tuːwʌðəz
be optimistic	biːɒptɪmɪstɪk	biːjɒptɪmɪstɪk

the process and also reflects an earlier historical pronunciation. There are also examples of the approximant being added when there is no hint from the spelling of a likely insertion (Table 2.9).

Now study the following version of the passage from *Sam and the Big Machines* (Henderson, 1995) that we looked at earlier. Note the changes that have been made to demonstrate a possible rendering of this passage when reading to an older child at greater speed and more informally.

> sæm n̩ ðə bɪb məʃiːnz
> sæm ðə smɔːl laɪp bɪb məʃiːnz iː laɪt ðəm bɛtə ðn̩ wɒtʃɪn tiːviːj ɔː wɔːks ɪn nə pɑːk ɔː frɛnz əʊm fə tiː ɪz feɪvrɪp weɪ tə spɛnd ə deɪ wəz wɒtʃɪn træktəz n̩ dɪgəz θʌmpəz n̩ dʌmpəz bʊldoʊzəz roʊdroʊləz paɪldraɪvəz pʌmps

Here the assimilations are found in the phrases /laɪp bɪb məʃiːnz/, /iː laɪt ðəm/, /wɒtʃɪn tiːviː/, /feɪvrɪp weɪ/ and /wrtʃɪn træktəz/. These are all examples of assimilation to the place of articulation, and all are regressive. This is the most common form of assimilation in connected speech. The elisions are mostly of consonants: /iː/, /əʊm/ and /ɪz/ are all missing the /h/ phoneme and /frɛnz/ has a simplified final consonant cluster, with the /d/ elided. The only elided vowels are the /ə/ in *and* and *than*, which both result in a syllabic consonant: /n̩/ and /ðn̩/. There is one example of insertion: /tiːviː j ɔː wɔːks/. Here the positioning of two full vowels, /iː/ and /ɔː/, next to each other allows a semivowel insertion to ease the movement from front closed vowel to back half-open vowel.

2.4 Intonation and stress

Earlier we saw that words with more than one syllable may have a primary (and sometimes a secondary) stress, and unstressed syllables too. These word stresses are not generally meaningful, and were therefore discussed under the heading of phonetics, which is more concerned with the physical processes of speech production than with meaning.

In this section we shall consider another layer of stress that operates at a suprasegmental level and is known by different names, though here we shall call it **utterance stress**. This level of stress allows speakers to give particular emphasis to certain words, independently of the content or meaning (semantics, see Chapter 6) of the words themselves.

Another suprasegmental system that we shall investigate is **intonation**. This is related to utterance and word stress, because the stressed syllables of words and utterances carry the pitch levels and changes that make up intonation. However it is more complex than stress alone, and will be considered separately in the light of what we have already said on the topic of stress.

It is worth noting here that English does not use moving pitch as part of the phonology of individual words. Chinese and other 'tone' languages have words whose segments (phonemes) are identical, but when uttered with a rising or falling tone they mean something completely different. This is not true of English and many other European languages, which reserve moving pitch for more general meanings that apply to structures larger than the word.

2.4.1 Utterance stress

The first thing to recognise about utterance stress is that not every word stress in an utterance will carry it. English is known as a **'stress-timed' language**, which roughly means that the stressed syllables of utterances are spaced evenly in time, but unstressed syllables between them will be hurried past if there are many of them. The following sentences have a progressively larger number of unstressed syllables between the two (underlined) stressed syllables:

John wants a cake	(one unstressed syllable).
John does want a cake	(two unstressed syllables).
John doesn't want any cake	(four unstressed syllables).
John doesn't want any more cake	(five unstressed syllables).

Though the notion of stress-timing has not been proven as an absolute physical reality (in terms of measuring the exact time between stresses), it does roughly describe the tendency for English and other stress-timed languages to operate with this internal clock regulating the spacing of the stressed syllables, and speeding up the unstressed ones when there are many of them. Other languages, including Spanish, Italian and Russian, are known as **syllable-timed languages** and an approximately equal amount of time is allotted to each syllable, whether stressed or unstressed, giving them a rhythm that may sound unusual to the English speaker's ear.

The maximum number of utterance stresses that can occur in English matches the potential maximum number of word stresses. This is roughly equivalent to the number of lexical words, as opposed to grammatical words, in the utterance. However it would become very tedious if all lexical words were equally stressed, so there are normally fewer utterance stresses than this. In the following sentence, if all the lexical words were stressed (underlined here) the result would be odd, to say the least:

> *John Morris never walked into town without taking a large umbrella.*

Try saying this sentence aloud with all the underlined words emphasised, and then try saying it more naturally and see how few are likely to be given utterance-level stresses. Depending on the context, there may be two or three utterance stresses in a natural rendering of the sentence. We shall now investigate the most likely placing of significant utterance stress.

In order to understand fully the workings of utterance stress you may need to read some parts of Chapter 5, and refer to the glossary where necessary. Rather than repeating the grammatical information, the terms will be taken as understood here. We shall be taking the clause as the basic building block of utterances, but note that a range of different grammatical units can come into play when considering suprasegmental phonology.

English clauses have an information structure that places the **new** and therefore the most important **information** towards the end of the clause. Utterance stress, when used neutrally, is normally associated with the final clause element, and in particular its head (underlined):

> *The three men were wearing grey suits.*

What we mean by 'neutrally' is that the utterance stress does not make any significant changes to the interpretation of the sentence as conveyed by the words themselves. We are expected to understand the **'given' information** that there are three men, and the definite article is confirmation of this. The verb element (*were wearing*) is not normally seen as producing 'new' information, unless it is the final element in a clause (for example *Michael Jackson was ironing*). The final clause element, the object (*grey suits*), is the new information, and therefore takes the most prominent stress in this clause.

If this was all that could be said about utterance stress there would be no choice in its placement, and it would therefore be a meaningless addition to the phonetic features of the speech stream. In fact, because the main utterance stress can be moved into different positions with resulting meaning changes, it is part of the phonological system. When the utterance stress is moved to one of the other clause elements in a clause it is known as **contrastive stress**. This is because, unlike with the neutral placing of stress, the result indicates an implicit contrast with another possible version of reality. If, for example, we choose to stress the subject or the predicator in the sentence we discussed above, the results would be as follows (with the implicit contrast in brackets):

The three men were wearing grey suits (not the three women, children etc.).

The three men were wearing grey suits (not buying, selling, washing them).

Although the emphasis does not indicate which of the options it is rejecting, the point is that contrastive stress is rejecting *something*. Contrastive stress produces the implication that what is being rejected has either been specifically proposed in the conversation by another speaker, or is somehow implicit in the context of the conversation.

So far we have only looked at cases of the stress being moved onto the main (head) words of each clause element (subject and predicator). It is also possible to place it on subordinate words, such as adjectives in noun phrases, auxiliary verbs in verb phrases and even, though more rarely, grammatical words.

The three men were wearing grey suits (not the four, seven, only man).

The three men were wearing grey suits (though you/he claimed they were not).

The three men were wearing grey suits (not red, blue or pinstripe suits).

The three men were wearing grey suits (not just any three men).

If you read these variants out loud with exaggerated stress on the underlined words, it should become clear how contrastive stress works. You might like to try this out with a sentence of your own (or the one given below). It is even possible to emphasise individual morphemes in this way, but this implies a contrast with another unit of the same level (that is, another morpheme): *I said he was disinterested (not uninterested).* Note that the use of contrastive stress within a word in this way results in a change in the word stress, which would normally be on the second syllable in these words but here is moved to the first for contrast. The following is a sentence for you to use to experiment with contrastive stress:

I never thought you'd finish with him on New Year's Eve!

2.4.2 Tones

While stress is delivered by phonetic features such as intensity and duration, as well as pitch changes, intonation is more closely related to pitch alone, and in particular to pitch levels that slide upwards and downwards, rather than moving in steps. Although steps in pitch are also part of the intonation pattern of English, the major meaningful elements of intonation are the moving tones. It is important to stress that here the word 'tone' refers to additional meaning brought to English words and utterances by the movement of pitch. The same term is often used when discussing 'tone languages' such as Chinese, which uses moving pitch as an integral part of the phonology of individual words, just like phonemes themselves. For the remainder of this book, tone will be used only for its intonational meaning.

There are five major pitch patterns, or **tones**, in English, and these can be attached to a single syllable or a number of syllables. For the time being we shall consider them in relation to the single syllable word *yes*. Figure 2.2 shows the symbols used for the five major tones.

We shall discuss the meaning of the tones later, but in order to become familiar with their sounds and some of their potential meaning, it is a good idea for you to practice saying the word *Yes* (or *No* or other single words) with the different pitch changes. Start by extending the length of the vowel and exaggerating the pitch movements until you are familiar with them. Then speed up and ask your friends and family to help you by performing them too. When you are confident that you can hear the pitch changes at near normal speed, try listening to speakers on the radio and spotting individual tones in their speech. Do not forget that not every word has a pitch movement of this kind. Many words simply step up or down in pitch and do not slide in the way that tones do.

Figure 2.2 The tones of English

Once you have mastered the ability to recognise the five major tones you should spend some time considering what they would mean in the different contexts you might hear them. Note that you have been looking for, and producing, tones on single syllables. Many tones are spread over a number of syllables and you could try to identify these too. The spread of the tone begins on the most prominent (stressed) syllable of the tone group and then continues the pattern of movement over the remaining syllables. In the case of the standard clause-length tone group and the most neutral intonation pattern, the pitch movement will begin on the head of the final clause element and continue until the clause is finished:

The children were building ↘ sandcastles.

Note that the word *sandcastles* has three syllables, with the stress – and therefore the beginning of the pitch change – on the first. That leaves two syllables in the remainder of the clause to continue to carry the falling tone of the intonation pattern. The symbol that indicates a moving tone is usually placed just before the syllable where the movement begins. The tone pattern can continue over a number of words, as well as any remaining unstressed vowels, unless they are so significant as to warrant their own tone group. The first of the two sentences below has an extra clause element, *on it*, which is an adverbial prepositional phrase. This could form a separate tone group, but because it is so short, refers to old information and is made up of unstressed syllables it is more likely to continue the pitch movement that begins on the word *sand*. The second sentence, by contrast, has a longer adverbial and seems to be bringing new information into the utterance. It is therefore likely to have its own tone group, with another pitch movement beginning on the main lexical word, *beach*:

The children were building ↘ sandcastles on it.

The children were building ↘↗ sandcastles | on the ↗↘ beach.

If you read the sentence out loud you will hear how the second tone group (*on the beach*) steps back up in pitch, in order to allow for the falling tone on the final word. This stepping up (or down) of pitch between tone groups is common and may sometimes be confused with moving tones. It is mostly a question of practice to hear the distinction, but it is also important to understand the grammatical structures of utterances as these indicate the most likely placing of stresses and tones.

We shall look at a different approach to intonation in Section 2.4.4, but here it might be useful for us briefly to consider the contexts in which the fall, the rise and the level tones are used.

In very general terms, the **fall** and the **rise-fall** are associated with statements and utterances that are 'finished' in some way, such as agreement. **Rises** are associated with unfinished utterances or indecision, such as questions, and **fall-rises** particularly occur in conditional clauses that need a main declarative clause to resolve them. Note, however, that sentences with two clauses related in this way can have a range of different tones:

If you are going ↗ out, | make sure you lock the ↘ doors.

If you are going ↘ out, | make sure you lock the ↘↗ doors.

The detail does not show up in this system of notation, but it is worth trying to articulate these two patterns in a convincing way to hear how they sound. You should find that the first is more natural, and thus more neutral in tone, with the second clause carrying the important (that is new) information. The second version does not have contrastive stress but contrastive intonation because the conditional clause has an unexpected falling tone, and in order to make the sentence work the speaker would probably begin the second clause in a very low-pitched part of the voice, and then step up to the beginning of the fall-rise that ends it. The effect is to reverse the given and new information. Now the speaker appears to know that the addressee is going out and wishes to remind her or him of the need for security. In the first version, by contrast, the neutral reading of the sentence is that the first (conditional) clause has an unknown truth value, but that the second (main) clause is clearly the new information, in the form of a nagging reminder.

The **level** tone, although not technically a moving pitch, can still be used as the tone in a tone group, though it is fairly restricted in its use as it is non-committal in meaning and is generally used in situations where there is little grammatical connection between the different tone groups. For example one might expect a series of rising tones in a list, with a falling tone for the final item in a list:

Can you get ↗ carrots, | ↗ peas, | ↗ potatoes, | ↗ onions | and cour↘ gettes?

Though level tones could be used for the items in a list, it is less likely when the list occurs in a full grammatical context. However when a list is all that there is and there is no significance in its ending, the level tone is used as a kind of non-tone; one that has no meaning intrinsically. This can occur when a teacher is reading out a register, a list of symptoms and diseases are being read out to someone who is undergoing a health check or an insurance application, and so on.

→ *heart disease,* | *dia* →*betes,* | *hepatitis* → *B,* | → *liver disease . . .*

If the questioner were to use rising tones, she or he would sound almost too personally interested in the medical history of the person being questioned. The level tone allows for a degree of detachment on the part of the speaker, and the respondent may therefore be able to answer more comfortably when discussing his or her private health record with a complete stranger.

Note that when discussing lists we have moved away from treating the tone group as equal to a clause as the norm, and instead have phrases or even individual words as whole tone groups. This variation will be explored in more detail in the following section.

2.4.3 Tone groups

As explained earlier, intonation is another aspect of suprasegmental phonology that is laid over the phonemes and adds a different layer of meaning to utterances. It interacts in various ways with stress placement, as we saw in the previous section and shall see in this section and the ones that follow.

If for now we take the clause to be the basic unit of intonation (though this is not the whole story, of course), we can describe the most neutral intonation pattern of an **indicative clause or statement** (as opposed to a question, for example) as involving a falling pitch on the final main clause element. This is very similar to the placement of the utterance stress discussed in Section 2.4.1, and indeed the main pitch movement usually occurs on this same stressed syllable:

The child chased a ↘ *<u>ball</u>.*

The unit of intonation description is normally called a tone unit or **a tone group**, and includes the whole of the section from one end of a moving tone to the next. For convenience we are treating these tone groups as equal to clauses but as we shall see later in this section there is much variation from this norm.

The first syllable in the moving part of the pitch pattern is known as the **nucleus** or tonic syllable, and in the most neutral form of intonation pattern it will correspond to the last lexical item in the clause, or sometimes to the head of the last clause element. We saw examples of tonic syllables in tone groups in the previous section, the following ones are identifiable by immediately following the tone notation:

The elephant raised its ↘ *trunk.*

No-one knew what ↘ *time it was.*

At least the weather was ↘↗ *sunny.*

The tonic syllable ↘ *trunk* carries the whole of the pitch change in the first tone group. In the second sentence the tonic syllable ↘ *time* begins the falling tone, and it is completed across the remaining syllables, *it was*. Those syllables, which follow the tonic syllable and carry the pitch movement are known as the **'tail'** of the tone group. They may include stressed and unstressed syllables, and are usually limited in length, as a long tail is likely to be broken up to form further tone groups.

Although the tonic syllable and tail carry the most important intonational meaning, the other syllables in the tone group are also patterned in terms of their pitch. Any unstressed syllables before the first stressed syllable are known as the **pre-head** in this model of intonation, and those occurring between the first stressed syllable and the tonic syllable are known as the **head**. It is normal for pre-heads to be spoken at the same pitch, and for heads to be pitched in a range of ways according to the clause content. Whilst the detail of these pitch patterns is beyond the scope of this book, it is worth noting that some heads step upwards, or downwards in pitch, but in a distinctly different way from tones, which slide through the pitch range. Think about the head in the following tone group, and note the stressed syllables (underlined) that occur before the tonic syllable, and then try to say it with an increasingly high pitch till you reach the tonic syllable, when the pitch can fall downwards. The more you use the stepping up of the head, the more outraged your version will sound!

> *I never* (pre-head) *saw such a terrible shambles in my whole* (head) ↘ *life!* (tonic syllable)

It is perfectly possible to say the same sentence with a fairly low pre-head and head, and with a low fall on the final word. The difference is one of emotion. The stepped head will sound energetic and angry, the low pre-head, head and low fall will sound resigned, if not depressed.

Before we turn to a slightly different model of intonation and look more closely at its meaning, let us return to the mapping of tone groups onto utterances. Although we have been using the clause as the most typical length of a tone group for ease of presentation, in fact tone groups can be any length, and in normal connected speech you will often find that in phrases smaller than a clause, words and even morphemes can be coterminous with (that is, have the same end-points as) the tone group. The following sentence can be said with a number of different tone group patterns:

| *The Pope is visiting his native* ↘ *Germany.* |

| *The* ↘↗ *Pope* | *is visiting his native* ↘ *Germany.* |

| *The* ↘↗ *Pope* | *is* ↘↗ *visiting* | *his native* ↘ *Germany.* |

| ↗ *The* | ↗ *Pope* | ↗ *is* | ↗ *visiting* | ↗ *his* | ↗ *native* | ↘ *Germany.* |

Whilst the first is perhaps the most likely division of this sentence into tone groups, in theory all the others are possible. Interestingly they sound more patronising or frustrated as you add more tone groups, until the final version, where it seems to be a read-aloud version, either because the reader or the hearer requires a slow, word-by-word rendition.

2.4.4 Discourse intonation

The model of intonation introduced so far in this chapter has been phonologically based, though concerned also with the relationship between the structure of the utterance and its suprasegmental features. The difficulty for phonologists studying intonation is that there is a danger of describing ever more complex sound patterns, without always being able to pin down their relevance to meaning. This phonetic-oriented model of intonation has been supplemented (and in some cases supplanted) in recent years by a discourse-based model of intonation, which starts from the broadest of intonational distinctions and relates them to general discourse meanings, before considering more detailed questions of the potential meanings of the finer pitch distinctions in speech. This approach to intonation grew out of Hallidayan **functional linguistics** and was pioneered by Brazil and Coulthard (1980).

There were two reasons for this development. One was the desire to produce a simpler model that would be useable by teachers and students of English as a foreign or second language. The other, more theoretically based reason was that the meanings inherent in intonation seemed to be unlike those associated with morphemes and words. The meanings were more general and less referential in nature, often related to the emotions and attitudes of the speakers towards their subject matter, and thus similar to what had become known as 'discourse meaning'.

The first principle of the system of **discourse intonation** is that the moving tones fall into two categories, **proclaiming** and **referring** tones, which refer to tones ending on a falling and rising pitch respectively. The meaning of the tones is paramount here, and the fall and rise-fall tones are therefore seen as introducing new information, whereas the rise and fall-rise tones refer to meaning that is already shared or has already been negotiated in the conversation. The level tone, in this approach, is seen as signalling utterances that are not intended to be interpreted as a direct part of the ongoing discourse.

In addition to categorising tones on the basis of their meaning instead of their physical properties of pitch, discourse intonation also simplifies the other aspects of intonation by using a musical analogy, **key**, to refer to the general pitch 'envelope' within which each tone unit functions and that may cause it to be contrasted with neighbouring tone units. A speaker's choice to step up (or down) at the beginning of a tone unit can be used for a number of discourse purposes, including disagreement, taking the conversational 'turn' and so on.

2.5 Further reading

For a more detailed handbook on phonetics and English phonology, that is accessible to beginners, see Roach (2001). This book and its associated recorded material will help readers to understand the principles of both phonetics and phonology, and become proficient at transcribing phonologically. Those who wish to practice their transcription skills in particular may find Maidment and Garcia Lecumberri (2000) helpful. A more detailed treatment of English phonology is provided in Harris (1994). This book is aimed at advanced undergraduate levels, and will be useful for students who wish to use phonological analysis in their advanced studies.

The more detailed handbook by Roca and Johnson (1999) introduces advanced aspects of phonological theory and phonological features of English, and Carr (1993) specialises in generative phonology for those who wish to study this theoretical development. For more information on discourse intonation see Brazil (1992).

CHAPTER

Word 3

3.1 Introduction: word structures and classes

This chapter begins the study of grammar by looking at the structure of words in English (morphology) and considering the different classes or groups to which English words belong. In the following chapters we shall see how these word classes are used when putting together longer structures in English. There is no natural dividing line between the internal structure of words, the membership of word classes and the structuring of phrases, clauses and sentences, so readers should consider Chapters 3, 4 and 5 as together making up the grammar of English. In order to make sure that readers who use other books are not confused, we should point out here that the term **syntax** refers to the structuring of the language above the level of the word, thus including phrase, clause and sentence structure. The study of grammar as a whole consists of both morphology and syntax.

The study of **morphology** is the study of the structure of words in a language and it considers the individual parts of the word, commonly called **morphemes**, as the smallest unit of meaning in the language. Although it is not a familiar term outside linguistics, the morpheme is one of the most useful concepts introduced in twentieth-century linguistic theory, as it gives a generic name to those units of language that fall between phonology and syntax and were previously known only by different names (**prefix**, **suffix**, **base**, and so on) according to their behaviour.

In the following examples, the words have been divided up to show their morpheme structure:

sing-ing, bright-ly, de-motiv-ation, ice-rink

The word singing, for example, is made up of two morphemes: the verb *sing* and the suffix *-ing*. We shall investigate the different types of morpheme later, but for now we should note that some morphemes look quite acceptable on their own (for example *sing, bright, motive, ice, rink*) while others need to be attached to other morphemes in order to make sense (*-ing, -ly, de-, -ation*).

Unlike phonemes, which (with a few exceptions) do not have meaning of their own – just the capacity to change meaning – morphemes usually have an identifiable meaning. Thus *-like,* means 'being similar to', as in *childlike, birdlike* and *cloudlike.* However morphemes that are dependent on others for their existence are not always easy to paraphrase. The meanings of *-ing, -ly, de-* and *-ation,* for example, are difficult to pin down, though *-ing* is something to do with the length of time an action continues, *-ly* means 'in the manner of' (loudly), *de-* usually indicates the undoing of an action (*de-ice, decode*) and *-ation* indicates the product of an action (*consultation*).

So whilst morphemes are often said to be the 'smallest unit of meaning' in a language – and this is true in one sense, since you cannot easily define the meaning of a phoneme, such as /p/ – it is worth remembering that phonemes do change meaning, even though they do not seem to contain meaning (see the following section).

As for how morphemes operate in a language, it is theoretically possible at one extreme to have a language in which each word is a single morpheme. In such a case there would be no need to study morphology as all of the grammatical modifications would be syntactic; that is, they would happen by placing words/morphemes into structures with other words/morphemes. At the other extreme there could be a language in which no individual morphemes stood alone as a unit, but all morphemes always occurred in combination with other morphemes to make larger units – words. In fact all human languages operate somewhere between these extremes, usually having some words at their simplest containing only one morpheme but with many words containing two or more.

3.2 Morphology

The level of morphology lies between the levels of phonology and syntax. The reason for this is that the same feature of meaning may be delivered by the morphology of one language and the syntax of another. A good example of this is the verb phrase in English, which uses up to four auxiliary verbs to deliver aspects of meanings, such as in the verb phrase *will have been being served,* where the lexical verb is *served* and the other four are the auxiliary verbs adding modal, perfective, progressive, and passive meanings. In other languages these same meanings may be delivered partly or largely by the addition of morphemes to the end of the lexical verb. English speakers may find the endings of French verbs hard to learn, but French speakers often find the combination of the four English auxiliaries equally difficult.

3.2.1 Free and bound morphemes

There are two types of morpheme in all languages: **free and bound morphemes**. Free morphemes are essentially the words of the language with no additions, whereas bound morphemes are the **affixes** that are added to free morphemes to alter their grammatical effect in various ways. We shall explore this shortly. We have already seen examples of free morphemes (*sing, bright, motive, ice, rink*) and bound morphemes (*–ing, -ly, de-* and *–ation*) and it should be clear that bound morphemes cannot normally occur on their own, whilst free morphemes can, and often do.

In English all lexical morphemes and many grammatical ones are free – they can stand alone or be combined with bound morphemes. Some free grammatical morphemes in English are bound in other languages. Take for example the preposition class (for example *in, on, under, by, for*). In many languages (German, Latin, Russian) these concepts are attached to the noun by means of the **case system**. English has a relatively low number of bound morphemes, though there are some that are regularly attached to the main lexical word classes and are grouped under the heading 'inflection', as we shall see shortly. There are others that occur less regularly and are collectively known as 'derivational morphemes'. These different processes of affixation will be explored in Section 3.3 on word formation.

To illustrate free and bound morphemes in action, let us consider a simple passage from a teenage novel:

> *It was a mile wide: all the land between the main road and the sea. There was a grassy field below the road, then the lane with her house, then more fields, then a railway line, then another field and the sand dunes and the beach. To the right there was a parking area and a little shop, and a tiny caravan site that you couldn't see from the house; and to the left there was an estuary, where a little river, which only a few miles back in the hills was tumbling swiftly among rocks, spread itself out wide and slow through a tidal lagoon. Beyond that there were more dunes and, at the very edge of the horizon, an airfield from which tiny silver planes occasionally took off, to skim over the sea and vanish. Everything from the airfield to the caravan site, from the main road to the edge of the sea, was Ginny's* (Pullman, 1990, pp. 12–13).

There are 157 separate words in this passage, and the majority of them (129) are free morphemes. The 28 exceptions are as follows:

dunes (twice), *fields, hills, miles, planes, rocks*

Ginny's

spread, took, was (six times), *were*

tumbling, parking

Everything, itself, railway, airfield (twice)

grassy, tidal

occasionally, swiftly

Some of these words have clearer morpheme boundaries than others. The set in the first line set is made up of noun plurals, and the free morpheme in each case can clearly be seen with the additional *-s* of the plural morpheme added to the end: *dune-s, field-s* and so on. The second line, *Ginny's,* has the only example of a possessive morpheme, which is clearly separated from the free morpheme by the apostrophe.

The third line is not so evidently made up of complex words, as it has a range of past tenses that are marked not by the addition of a clear affix but by the changing of the base form of the word. So we have *take* becoming *took* in the past tense, and *is* (or *are*) becoming *was* (or *were*). In addition we have an example of an English verb that does not change in the past tense: *spread.* We shall explore the irregularities of English verb forms a little later, but it should be noted here that many past tenses in English are much more clearly morphological than these. A few examples are: *play-ed, start-ed, pour-ed, stay-ed.*

In the next line we have *tumbl-ing* and *park-ing,* both clearly made up of two morphemes and both looking like the progressive version of a lexical verb. We shall return to these examples later, as the context shows that they are slightly different, despite their superficial similarity.

The similarity between the members of the next line, *Every-thing, it-self, rail-way, air-field* is that they are made up of two free morphemes. This process is known as compounding and will be investigated in more detail in section 3.3.3.

The two examples that follow are superficially different but illustrate the same derivational process. They are both adjectives created by the addition of a bound morpheme to a base noun: *grass-y, tid-al.* The final two examples are similar to this, but a bound morpheme is added to an adjective to make an adverb: *occasional-ly, swift-ly.* Note that there is an additional morpheme in the case of *occasion-al-ly*, which has a free noun morpheme, *occasion*, as its basis, an *-al* added to make it into an adjective, and *-ly* added to make it an adverb. We shall see more such examples in the section on derivational morphology.

3.2.2 Allomorphs

Before we turn to the detail of English word formation, let us consider some of the issues that arise when describing the morphology of a language. The concept of the morpheme is based on that of the phoneme, from the theoretical perspective of structuralism, which is mainly concerned with finding patterned relationships between the units and structures of a language. The two units (phoneme and morpheme) are seen as parallel because they both have an abstract identity that is responsible for changing meaning in one case (phoneme) and carrying meaning in the other (morpheme), and the actual **realisation** of these units can vary quite considerably. We saw in Chapter 2 how the phoneme /t/ can vary from a glottal stop to an aspirated alveolar plosive. In the case of morphemes there is a similar phonological variation in their realisation. However there is also a more irregular variation that is only explicable by to the history of the language and appears anomalous in terms of regular patterning.

Analogous to the phoneme–allophone relationship, the term **allomorph** describes the different forms that a morpheme can take. As already noted, these forms may vary in more than just a phonological way, and so there has been some motivation to make the identity of the morpheme even more abstract than that of the phoneme; in other words, not to tie it to a particular set of sounds but to give it a symbol, such as {Pl} for the plural morpheme, and {Past} for the past morpheme. The curly brackets have been adopted to indicate morpheme status. Note that this abstract way of signifying morphemes is most useful for bound morphemes and is rarely used to represent free morphemes, though in principle there is no reason why, for example, a lexical item such as {bird} cannot be shown to be a free morpheme in this way.

We shall consider the full range of allomorphs of inflectional morphemes in Section 3.3.1. To complete our more general discussion of allomorphs in this section, let us consider the plural morpheme {Pl} in a little more detail. The examples of plurals in the above passage from a novel are all apparently regular, being formed as they are by the addition of an *-s*: *dunes, fields, hills, miles, planes, rocks*. If we consider their pronunciation the situation changes, as the morpheme now varies between the voiced version /z/ and the voiceless version /s/, depending on the voicing of the preceding sound:

/djuːnz/, /fɪəldz/, /hɪlz/, /maɪlz/, /pleɪnz/, /rɒks/

Whilst the first five words end in voiced sounds, and thus have a voiced plural morpheme, the final word has a voiceless ending and its plural morpheme is therefore also voiceless. What we do not have is an example of a sibilant ending (see Section 2.4.2), which would actually cause the allomorph to become /-ɪz/, as we saw in the discussion of assimilation in Section 2.3.1. One example is the noun *fox*, which phonologically is /fɒks/ and in the plural is /fɒksɪz/. These plurals are phonologically regular and explicable in terms of a general rule, but there are also nouns in English that have irregular plurals. These include those which change vowel(s) to indicate plurality (for example *man – men*; *woman – women*) and those which do not change in the plural (*sheep, fish*). These irregular forms can also be considered to be allomorphs of {Pl}, making the range of allomorphs rather an odd mix of accidental and phonologically determined forms.

3.3 Word formation

We can look at word formation from the point of view of free and bound morphemes and allomorphs, but it is also useful to distinguish three different processes of word formation in English: inflection, derivation and compounding.

Inflection is the process by which the main lexical word classes (noun, verb, adjective and adverb) in English acquire regular endings to form particular grammatical structures. Because English is not a highly inflected language (compare a case-heavy language such as Russian or Welsh) these are quite simple, as we shall see in Section 3.3.1.

Derivation is the process by which words have a morpheme added that changes their meaning and often their class too, in a way that is less regular or patterned than inflections. Thus a morpheme that can turn a verb or an adjective into a noun (for example *-ation*) will not be added to every noun, and will not change the meaning in exactly the same way every time, although it might translate roughly as 'process of (becoming)':

Mature – maturation; motivate – motivation; create – creation

Note that *maturation* is a process (of becoming mature), whilst *motivation* is usually more of a product than a process, and *creation* can be either a product or a process:

The *maturation* of the cheese takes place over a few weeks.

My *motivation* was the result of your encouragement.

The *creation* of designer clothes is a long process.

These *creations* by Dior are wonderful.

Compounding is the process whereby a word is formed from two equally free morphemes and becomes a compound word. The meaning of a compound word is always more specific than a phrase made up of the same two free forms would be, and this is emphasised in the fact that it will only have a single word stress:

blackboard, blackbird, paperback, shoehorn

The next three sections will go into more detail about the three main processes of word formation in English. It is worth remembering that what they have in common is that they operate at the level of the word, and all make use of the two basic kinds of morpheme: free and bound.

3.3.1 Inflection

The inflectional morphemes in English are all suffixes, that is, they are all bound morphemes added to the end of the base word. What characterises them is that they are fairly regular, in both form and meaning, and apply to all the members of a word class, but with some significant irregular exceptions. It is also important to note that the inflectional morphemes do not change the class of the word, but alter the grammatical form in ways that are relevant to the word class concerned.

The noun class, for example, has only four forms in English. These are the singular base form of the noun, which is a free morpheme (for example *sister*), the plural form (*sisters*) for countable nouns only, and the two possessive forms, where the possessive morpheme is added either to the singular form (*sister's*) or to the plural form (*sisters'*) to indicate the belongings of a single sister or more than one sister respectively. Note that the mass nouns in English have only two forms, singular and possessive (for example *water* and *water's*), though many also have specialised countable uses that have particular meanings (for example *to take the waters*).

Some nouns have unusual plural forms (*man – men, woman – women*) and some have no change in their plural form (*sheep, fish*) for historical reasons. These examples are simply irregular forms, and this is quite a common occurrence in all languages, particularly when, as with English, there have been a great many influences on the language at different times. Many of the English irregular forms are the oldest in the language, deriving from Anglo-Saxon origins rather than Latinate ones. They are also quite common words, and for this reason they are fairly resistant to change, though some may be pulled in the direction of regularity. The plural of *fish*, for example, in some contexts seems to vary, and may eventually become *fishes*, though at the moment this seems to be used mostly when discussing pond and ornamental fish, which are more likely to be seen as individuals, than when referring to cod stocks in the Atlantic.

The inflections of English verbs will be considered later when discussing the verb phrase, but we shall examine them here as examples of inflectional morphology. In English regular verbs have a base form, which is identical for the infinitive and the present tense (except for the third-person form):

sigh, promise, cut

This is the form that is normally listed in dictionaries and is treated as the identifying form, also called the **citation** form, of the lexeme (see Chapter 6) as a whole. Note that in some contexts, the infinitive form requires the presence of a preceding *to* (for example *to sigh, to promise, to cut*). This does not affect the morphology of the verb form itself, and the two are equivalent, the *to* being a necessary but essentially redundant addition.

Verbs also have a third person singular morpheme, *-s*, which has a similar range of phonological variations to the plural morpheme, depending on the sound that precedes the morpheme. The following transcriptions of the verbs *sighs, promises* and *cuts* demonstrate this variation:

/saɪz/, /prɒmɪsɪz/, /kʌts/

As we saw in Section 2.3.1, this pattern is a common phonological assimilation in English. The end of *sigh* is a vowel, which is voiced, and the morpheme is therefore realised as the voiced /z/. The verb *promise* ends in a sibilant, /s/, and the third person morpheme is therefore the /-ɪz/ form. The verb *cut* ends in a voiceless plosive, /t/, and the morpheme is therefore also voiceless, /-s/.

Regular verbs also occur with the regular {past} tense morpheme, which means adding either *-d* or *-ed* to the orthographic form. This morpheme has a similar range of phonological variations to the plural morpheme, which depends on the nature of the preceding sound. So the morpheme is pronounced in a voiced form /d/ when it follows a voiced sound (for example *praised*, /preɪzd/), is voiceless after voiceless consonants (for example *parked*, /pɑːkt/) and has an additional vowel before the alveolar plosive when the end of the verb is also alveolar (for example *patted*, /pætɪd). Note that these regular verbs have exactly the same ending in their **participle** form, which follows the perfective and passive auxiliaries (for example *have/was praised, have/was parked* and *have/was patted*). One reason why we cannot argue that the past tense (*she parked*) and the participle form (*she has parked*) are the same morpheme is that there is a small number of very common, but irregular, verbs, that do not have identical forms for these two functions. We can therefore suppose that there is in fact a distinct perfective/passive morpheme, which just happens to be identical to the past morpheme for regular verbs but often has the form *-en* in irregular verbs. One such verb is *break*, /breɪk/, which has an irregular past tense, *broke*, /brəʊk/ (involving a change of vowel) and the participle form *broken*, /brəʊkən/, which confirms that there is a theoretical difference between these two forms, even when they look and sound the same, as in *painted* and *started*. There is no easy way of tidying up an area of grammar that is intrinsically messy in this way, so it is best to choose such an explanation and allow for variants of the morpheme to be specified for individual verbs.

The final verb inflection we need to discuss is the progressive *-ing* form of the verb. All English verbs, however regular or irregular they may be, have this form. It is used in verb phrases following the progressive auxiliary (for example *was trying, should be arriving, has been arguing*) and also occurs as a non-finite verb form (see Chapter 5) in subordinate clauses (*after carrying all the suitcases, the hotel porter expected a tip*). They also occur as a premodifying adjective in noun phrases (*the singing policeman*) and as a derived head noun, in the position normally taken by nouns (*the dancing was wild and dangerous*).

In English **adjectives** only have **comparative** and **superlative** inflected forms, and even then not all adjectives are able to take these morphological additions:

nice, nicer, nicest

The regular form of the comparative morpheme is to add *-er* and for the superlative to add *-est*. However there are a few irregular forms, such as *good, better, best*, and some gradable adjectives that do not inflect but can be made comparative or superlative by the addition of a modifying adverb (*exciting, more exciting, most exciting*).

There is also a range of adjective subclasses that are not gradable, and therefore cannot occur in either type of comparative or superlative construction:

**African-er/African-est, *more African/*most African*

There are some contexts in which such forms are in fact possible, but the norm is for **non-gradable adjectives** not to inflect, even if they sometimes take a modifying adverb.

Adverbs have a similar set of inflections, comparative and superlative forms to gradable adjectives, though there are many, including the intensifiers (for example *very, so, really*), that cannot be inflected. In practice most adverbs, apart from the common *well, better* and *best*, are combined with intensifying adverbs for comparative and superlative forms:

slowly, more slowly, most slowly

Note, however, that there is an increasing tendency in the spoken language, particularly with comparative and superlative forms, to use the adjective in place of the adverb:

He did the work slower than I did.

Inflectional processes in English, then, do not occur as a very complex set of forms, do not change the word class of the word and tend to change the word's meaning in a consistent way. They usually apply to all regular words in a class, though the adjective and adverb classes are an exception to this. As we shall see, derivational morphology is a much less regular affair in English.

3.3.2 Derivation

With the exception of zero derivation (see below), derived forms normally have a morpheme added to the base form, and normally change the word class of the original, resulting in a corresponding change in meaning. Thus the *-ion* morpheme will turn a verb into a noun, and usually refers to the process or product of that verb (for example *react-ion, correct-ion, interrupt-ion*). Another morpheme, *-ance* or *-ence*, also turns verbs into nouns and refers to the process or product of the verb (*interfer-ence, disturb-ance, persever-ance*).

As we can see from these examples, derivation is less regular and less comprehensive than inflection. Some nouns have endings that turn them into adjectives (for example *bookish*), but this does not apply to all nouns (for example **table-ish*), and there are other derivational morphemes that turn nouns into adjectives (for example *jammy*). Although there may be historical reasons for the forms that exist, within a synchronic (contemporary or non-historical) description of English there is no apparent pattern to why *-ish* or *-y* morphemes might be added to a noun, why a verb might have *-ion* or *-ance* morphemes added to make it a noun, or why any individual word will or will not have particular derived forms.

As we have seen, there are a number of different forms that do the same kind of thing. The negative morpheme is a particular case in point, and is unusual in being a prefix rather than a suffix:

__de__mystify, __un__ravel, __a__moral, __in__complete, __dis__used, __mis__fit

The negative morpheme has the general meaning of 'the opposite of', though the precise meaning depends on the free morpheme to which it is attached. For example it may become a directional opposite, such as *demystify* (reverse the process of mystification), or a complementary opposite, such as *amoral*, (the mutually exclusive opposite of moral).

There are some words where a morpheme that was once free has changed meaning within the derived form and no longer seems to be free in its relevant meaning:

disgraceful, untoward, hardware, software

Although *graceful, toward, hard* and *soft* are free morphemes in their own right, in the context of the morphemes above their meaning is changed quite radically.

While derivational morphemes do not attach to words in a very regular way, there are some groups of words with shared semantic features that have similar derivations:

violinist, cellist, oboist, flautist, trombonist, percussionist, clarinettist

Here the morpheme *-ist* added to the name of the instrument to produce the player of the instrument. This works for many instruments, but not all of them. *Trumpeter* and *drummer* have different derivational forms, for no obvious reason. This is not restricted to terms for musicians, as we can see from the different derivational forms in the following list of occupations:

artist, scientist, engineer, dancer, footballer, cricketer, rugby player

Note that there are some words in groups of this kind that do not have a derived form. *Rugby player, viola player* and *double bass player*, all rely on a phrase to convey the same information conveyed by a derived form in other cases.

There is one kind of derivation in English where there is no affixation. This is known as **zero derivation** and is quite common. The derivational process simply changes the word class of the free morpheme, which leads to it being able to have the relevant inflectional morphemes added. This often happens between the noun and verb categories:

a play/to play, a hammer/to hammer, a drink/to drink

With zero derivation it can be difficult to tell which is the more basic form. Here it is likely that the noun *play* is derived from the verb *to play*, the noun *hammer* is derived from the verb *to hammer* and the noun *drink* is derived from the verb *to drink*. As a noun, *play* can be made plural (*plays*) and has a possessive form (*play's*), though these inflections are incidental to the derivation, which itself involves no additional morpheme. As with the other derived forms, zero derivation can occur in limited patterns in localised areas of vocabulary. Thus we have verbs derived from not only *hammer*, but also *chisel* and *saw*, where the derived form effectively means *to use the x*. Whilst this does not work for all tools, the pattern, once learned, can lead children to make mistakes in applying it, resulting in forms such as *I'm screwdrivering*.

3.3.3 Compounding

The combining of two free morphemes into a single word is not very different from making a phrase out of two words, though there are some important distinctions, as we shall see. The principle of compounding is that the meaning of the resulting word is not simply the sum of its parts, but has a further meaning that could not immediately be predicted by someone who knew the meaning of the free morphemes individually.

Thus *blackboard* is more than simply any board that happens to be black; it has a specific function in educational settings and incidentally is not always black. The *blackbird* is a specific type of garden bird, and there are many *black birds* in the world that are not *blackbirds*. Still more remote from the meanings of their parts are *paperback* and *shoehorn*. The former does have a cover made from paper, but the word itself does not indicate that it refers to a book. The shoehorn is a shaped piece of horn (or plastic) that aids the putting on of shoes, but the process aspect of its meaning is not evident in the word itself. It could, from the sum of its parts, mean a horn full of shoes, or a musical instrument shaped like a shoe.

What gives compounds their status as individual lexemes is precisely this obscurity in their meaning. Like other words, compounds can only be understood if the meaning is already known. This identity as an individual lexical item is emphasised by their phonological shape, which normally carries only a single main stress, unlike the equivalent phrase, which carries two word stresses:

'blackbird, 'black 'bird

The grammatical category of a compound word in English is always the same as the category of the second (or last) free morpheme. Thus a noun plus noun combination will be a noun overall (for example *sledgehammer*), as will an adjective plus noun combination (for example *high school*), whereas a noun plus verb combination will be a verb (for example *water-ski*) and a noun plus adjective combination will be an adjective (for example *fire-retardant*).

3.4 Lexical word classes

Each lexical item in English belongs to at least one word class, which determines its behaviour in larger structures and signals its similarity to the other words in that class. In the remainder of this chapter we shall explore the main word classes in English and illustrate their usage. A fuller investigation of the structures that these classes enter into can be found in Chapters 4 and 5.

First of all we need to introduce two rather different classes of word: **lexical words** and **grammatical words**. These were mentioned in Chapter 1 in relation to stress placement (Section 1.6.3), but the reason for distinguishing them was not examined at that point. Lexical words are those which contain the main semantic information in a text, and they fall into the four main lexical word classes: noun, verb, adjective and adverb. The qualitative difference between these classes of word and grammatical word classes (conjunctions, prepositions, pronouns, modals and so on) is that they are open-ended and can be added to readily. Thus, there are new nouns being invented all the time to cope with new inventions in technology and science, as well as new fashions and trends. In recent years, for example, the average British English speaker may have come across, if not used, the words *palmtop*, *flash drive*, *minging* and *chav*. The first two, being part of the international language of computing, will be familiar to other English speakers too. The second two, however, are part of youth culture and are more regional in use (*minging* meaning ugly or horrible and *chav* being a disparaging term for a certain style associated with working-class culture). Grammatical words, on the other hand, are very slow to change, and rarely do so. The only change that has taken place in relatively recent history is the gradual disappearance of the second-person familiar pronouns, *thou*, *thee*, *thy* and *thine*, except in very restricted and fossilised contexts such as religious services. In the following sections the main lexical word classes will be introduced and exemplified.

3.4.1 Noun

Nouns make up one of the largest word classes in English and were traditionally taught in primary school as 'naming' words. This description was discredited by early twentieth-century linguists because there are many nouns that do not name tangible things (for example *singing*, *laughter*, *perplexity*). Those linguists who took a structuralist approach considered that a word class needed to be defined not by a vague concept of general meaning, such as defining nouns as names, but by a rigorous assessment of the behaviour (function) and form of the members of the prospective class or category.

The basic forms of nouns in English are many and varied, and depend on their historical origins, their development and the extent to which they are derived from other word classes (see Section 3. 3. 2). Hence it is not feasible to summarise the forms of nouns themselves, though it is possible to use their inflectional morphology as one of the defining features of their class. However, since they have different inflectional possibilities we first need to consider an important distinction between two subclasses of noun: **mass** or 'non-countable' nouns and **'countable' nouns.**

Countable nouns can occur in combination with numbers, with the indefinite article, *a*, and can be pluralized by the addition of the {plural} morpheme. These include *cat(s)*, *table(s)*, *child(ren)*, *idea(s)* and *bicycle(s)*. The members of the other subclass, non-countable or mass nouns, do not occur with numbers or the indefinite article and cannot be pluralized. These include *air, sugar, water, horror, peace* and *future*. Note that there is no correlation between nouns referring to abstract concepts and being a mass noun (or *vice versa*). Note also that no linguistic categories are absolutely watertight, and there are examples that cut across any boundaries we try to set up. Thus many nouns are countable or non-countable in different contexts (compare *war* and *a war*). There are also many nouns that seem to belong fundamentally to one or other subclass but can also be used as though they belonged to the other class, though usually with a more specific meaning as a result. Examples include *How many sugars?*, referring to the number of spoonfuls or lumps, though the measurement is left implicit. Another example is the use of *coffees* to mean cups of coffee, and *papers* to refer to newspapers, as opposed to *coffee* and *paper* in general. All these nouns have a central mass or non-countable meaning, but are consistently associated with particular measurements or units (spoon, cup and so on) in our society. This allows for the mass noun to be used as though it were a countable noun, but without mention of the measurements themselves since they are taken for granted by members of the community.

The wordclass of nouns, then, can be defined morphologically for countable nouns, which can take the plural suffix, though this does not include all the proper nouns, except in odd contexts such as *Where are all the Johns and Marys?* A slightly more inclusive test of membership of the noun word class is the possibility of adding the possessive morpheme, *'s*, which is theoretically possible for all nouns:

Countable nouns:	*the dog's tail, an idea's origin*
Proper nouns:	*John's bike, Madrid's traffic problem*
Mass nouns:	*sugar's properties, anger's triggers*

Whilst word classes are not formally as well-defined as we may have thought, there is also the possibility of using syntactic function as a defining feature of the class. In the case of nouns, there are a number of potential functions that they can perform in English clauses, and these will be described briefly below. Fuller descriptions of these syntactic functions will be provided in later chapters. The syntactic system has mutually dependent aspects, and it is impossible to describe one of these aspects without referring to another aspect that has not yet been defined. This circularity is one of the strengths of the system as a means of communication, but makes it particularly difficult to unravel and describe in the linear fashion required by a book, and needed by students!

The basic function of a noun is to be the 'head' of a noun phrase, which means that it can occur after a definite or indefinite article or a determiner (*the cat, some air*), and may have a number of adjectives between the article and the noun (*the fat cat, the fresh air*). There is much more to the noun phrase structure than this summary, and it does not cover all the places where nouns are found in English. However it will work as a test of whether a candidate for inclusion in the noun class is indeed behaving like a noun if it *can* occur in these frames.

The other aspect of the function of nouns is how they operate, as part of noun phrases, in the larger context of clause structure. They have the most varied potential of any word class in being able to function (together with other parts of the noun phrase) as subject, object, complement and even adverbial, as follows (italic):

Subject:	*The crocodile* (ate my hat).
Object:	(The president announced) *his plans.*
Complement:	(This substance is) *refined sugar.*
Adverbial:	*Every night* (they sing karaoke).

There are some potentially confusing aspects of syntactic structure, if both form and function tests of word-class membership are not used. This is because words can change class in certain regular ways (zero derivation) and it is possible for a form to look like a verb (for example *playing*) but be used in a noun-like way: *Joshua Bell's playing was divine.*

The most important aspect of learning to make syntactic descriptions of data is practice in identifying repeated patterns. Try using the text below (or any other text) to practice identifying members of the noun class, and note the evidence you have used to make your decisions. This evidence should be similar to the tests described above, and refer to the form and/or function of the word.

Joe and Sophie had never been on a big ship before. Last summer they had to cross the sea to go on holiday. As it was going to take a whole day and a night they had a cabin with four bunk beds in it. It got tiring walking about on the decks because the ship moved all the time and made you walk in zig-zag lines. Joe and Sophie wanted to go and lie down on their bunk beds so Mum and Dad came too. Everyone went to sleep for a while and then Sophie heard a tapping sound near her head. She tapped on the wall and it went quiet Then the tapping sound came again. She tapped back and the wall replied to her. Joe was laughing and told her to tap a rhythm. She tapped five times. Twice slowly, twice fast and once slowly. 'Dum, dum, du-dum, dum.' The wall finished off with two loud taps: DUM DUM!'

The nouns in this passage include those which occur with the definite article or other definite determiners, such as *the ship* and *her head*; those which are clearly count nouns and plural, such as *beds* and *decks*; nouns which have been derived from verbs, such as *taps*, which is identified as a noun in this case by the enumerator, *two*, before it. There are nouns which are in Subject position, as in *the wall (replied)* and those which are Objects: *(to tap) a rhythm.*

3.4.2 Verb

Verbs are the other very large lexical word class in English, and were traditionally called 'doing' words when taught to young children. Like the noun class, the **lexical verb** class is more inclusive than the label implies as there are verbs (for example *have, be)* which do not describe doing, but being, or states, rather than processes and still others that describe events with no intentional action behind them (for example *die, fall*).

In order to group these words together, then, we need to identify their formal and functional features, as we did for the noun class. We have already seen that inflectional morphemes can be used to modify the verb in English (Section 3.3.1). These include the present-tense, third-person singular morpheme, which is written as *-s* in most cases; the past tense morpheme, written as *-ed* in all regular verbs in English; and the progressive form, which is written as *-ing* for all English verbs. Here we shall use the same information to define the word class of verbs, which form the pivotal point of an English clause. Many **minor sentences**, and many spoken ones, consist of a single word that is not necessarily a verb:

No! *Natalie!* *Me.* *Singing.* *Slowly.*

You may be able to work out likely contexts in which these words will occur as utterances in their own right. Note, however, that they must have a context in order to have a viable meaning.

With the exception of these and other minor utterance types, clauses in English need to have a verb in them. This verb may be the head of a verb phrase, but it may stand alone as a verb phrase too. The following clauses have a single verb functioning in the predicator role:

The students worked hard all year.

No one suspects me!

Although dancing as well as ever . . .

Dropped from the team . . .

To sit in the sun with a drink in your hand . . .

Later we shall look at more complex verb phrases that function as predicators. Here, we shall consider at the individual forms of lexical verbs in English and how they function. Note that the first of the two clauses above also form complete sentences, whereas the third, fourth and fifth are only part of an utterance. These incomplete utterances are examples of subordinate clauses, which we shall investigate in a later section. We are using them here simply to demonstrate the use of particular forms of verb: **non-finite forms**. These forms, often known as the *-ing* form, the *-en* form and the *i-* form, are also called the **progressive** form, the **perfective** form and the **infinitive form.** As we shall see later, these forms can be part of full verb phrases that function as the predicator in a complete clause. On their own, however, they do not link to the subject in a clear way (for example by an ending that indicates a person) and they do not establish the tense of the verb as either present or past. Note how they need auxiliaries to establish such aspects of the meaning of the predicator:

She was dancing as well as ever.

He was dropped from the team.

I shall sit in the sun with a drink in my hand.

Lexical verbs that do not need an auxiliary verb in order to function in main clauses are known as **finite forms**. They include the present tense form, which is normally indistinguishable from the infinitive form in terms of having no morphological suffix (for example *catch, sing*), the third-person present tense form, which normally adds an *-s* to base forms, and the past tense form, which adds *-ed* to regular verbs. Table 3.1 shows some examples of all the forms of English lexical verbs.

Table 3.1 The forms of English verbs

Citation form	Break	Play	Sing	Forget
Present tense	break	play	sing	forget
Present third person	breaks	plays	sings	forgets
Past tense	broke	played	sang	forgot
Progressive participle	breaking	playing	singing	forgetting
Perfective participle	broken	played	sung	forgotten
Infinitive	break	play	sing	forget

The most common pattern of forms in English verbs is the one represented in the table by *play*. You will see that there are effectively only four different forms (*play, plays, playing, played*), but because other common, but irregular, verbs distinguish, for example, the past tense (*-ed*) from the perfective form (*-en*), the regular verbs are also treated as though these forms were different. The irregular forms tend to belong to common verbs derived from Old English, rather than those with Romance language influences, such as French. Because they are very common they have not changed to match the sheer quantity of verbs with a pattern such as *play*, although there is some evidence that some such thing is happening. If you think about the way that people these days often muddle *sung* and *sang* and *rung* and *rang*, it seems that the distinction between past tense and perfective markers is less clear-cut than in the past. However, although the two forms might be merging in irregular verbs too, they are not moving towards matching the regular verbs, which would result in forms such as **singed* and **ringed*.

As with the noun word class, it is important to keep practising the identification of verbs in context. For this purpose you could try to identify all the main lexical verbs in the following passage, or another passage of your choice. Do not forget that some words may appear to be verbs but actually behave as nouns or adjectives, though there are none of these in the passage below. At this stage you may ignore all auxiliary verbs as they form a separate grammatical word class, though they share some of the same forms as the lexical verbs.

> *Joe knelt down and tried to see through one of the little panes of milky green glass. He couldn't see anything, but one of the panes of glass was missing. Maybe he could look through there? Just as he got his eyes close enough to see, Mum told him to get up off the dirty floor. Then she went on talking. Joe stood looking around for something to do. He wriggled his foot and found that if he pointed his toe he could get it through the gap in the glass.*

Note that many of the sentences, despite it being a children's story, are longer than a single clause. This means that there is more than one lexical verb in each one. The first sentence, for example, has *kneel, try* and *see* and the last sentence has *wriggle, find, point* and *get*.

The subclasses of lexical verb that can be identified tend to depend on the context in which they occur. Whilst the traditional grammars distinguished between transitive and intransitive verbs, we find it useful to distinguish further categories, depending on the clause structures in which they typically occur.

The **intransitive verb** will not be found with an object, and thus will occur in subject and predicator structures: *I'm* ***dying***. The **transitive verb** occurs with an object in subject-predicator-object structures: *She* ***hates*** *you*. **Ditransitive verbs** occur with both indirect and direct objects: *They* ***gave*** *me a beautiful present*. There are also subclasses of verb that tend to occur with compulsory adverbials: *John* ***went*** *home* and *I* ***put*** *the cigarette back in the packet*. Two further important subclasses of verb are **intensive verbs** (such as *be*) that occur with subject complements (*She* ***was*** *really tired*), and those which occur with objects and object complements: (*You* ***make*** *me happy*). The intensive verbs have a particular semantic effect in that they invoke existence (*there* ***is*** *a tree*) and equivalence (*she* ***is*** *my daughter*). These subcategories of verb are not watertight and some verbs can occur in a range of grammatical contexts. However it is useful to think in terms of verbs typically occurring in certain clause structures.

3.4.3 Adjective

The adjective word class is smaller than the noun and verb classes, and has both a more restricted set of forms than the verb and a more limited set of functions than the noun. Like the other lexical classes the adjective class can be divided into smaller subclasses, though only one of these can be formally identified. This is the class of **gradable adjectives**, which form comparative and superlative forms either by the addition of morphemes, or by the insertion of adverbs (Table 3.2).

Table 3.2 The forms of English adjectives

Adjective	Comparative	Superlative
big	bigger	biggest
smart	smarter	smartest
ferocious	more ferocious	most ferocious
scared	more scared	most scared

The remaining adjectives (non-gradable) can be considered to belong to groups, but these are largely semantic groupings, such as colour, material or nationality, and not strictly syntactic categories as they are not defined by their form or function. Interestingly non-gradable adjectives are sometimes treated as gradable, in a fairly creative way, by the addition of comparative and superlative adverbs. They tend to need a little context to make their meaning clear in a way that ordinary gradable adjectives do not:

He looked <u>more Chinese</u> than I expected.

That was the <u>most wooden</u> acting I have ever seen!

The basic function of the adjective is as the head of its own **adjective phrase**. The structure of such phrases is described in detail later; here we need only note that in English the adjective phrase is frequently restricted to the adjective itself, and only gradable adjectives regularly have preceding intensifying adverbs; for example *totally awful, particularly galling, very unhappy.* Adjectives are therefore perhaps easier to identify by their larger syntactic functions, rather than their function within their own phrases. The main two functions of an adjective are as the premodifier to the head noun in a noun phrase (*a <u>brilliant</u> artist*), and following an intensive verb as the complement of a clause (*the artist is <u>brilliant</u>*).

These functions are possible for most adjectives, and in most cases the meaning of the adjective remains constant, irrespective of the function of the adjective. However there are some cases where different meanings of the adjective arise in different positions:

A certain teacher of French . . .

The teacher of French is certain.

3.4.4 Adverb

The final lexical word class is the **adverb** class. In many ways this is the least class-like of all as it consists of a number of subclasses that have relatively little in common, except that they do not perform the most central roles in the clause and are often not essential to the grammatical completeness of the utterance in which they occur. The following words are all adverbs:

very, suddenly, now, quietly, then, really

There is one clear subclass of adverbs in that list. It is the class derived from adjectives by the addition of the *-ly* suffix. Most gradable (and some non-gradable) adjectives can be made into adverbs in this way. For example:

proudly, stupidly, weirdly, hungrily, beautifully, angrily

Another subclass of adverb is identifiable by its function as the premodifier in an adjective phrase. The members of this class are known as **intensifiers** because they in some way quantify the amount of the (gradable) adjective that is being invoked in the phrase. Note, however, that despite the name 'intensifier' the quantity is not always large:

dead proud; completely shattered; quite tired

It is probably worth making the point here that there are whole phrases in English that have a very similar function to adverbs, and we shall see later when looking at their syntactic function that they are classed with adverbs as having the function 'adverbial'. These are normally **prepositional phrases**, and like non-intensifying adverbs they add information about the circumstances of the process being described in the clause:

On Saturday, we went to the theatre.

When the match started it was raining in buckets.

In a flash they had disappeared.

These prepositional phrases can be replaced by adverbs, though they will not always be as specific as the phrases:

Then we went there.

When the match started it was raining hard.

Suddenly, they had disappeared.

When you are learning to describe the structure of English it can be frustrating to find that often there are two different ways of achieving the same effect, but the first of the rewritten clauses above demonstrates one of the strengths of this design feature of language. If English had a different adverb for every place a person could go to, as opposed to general ones (*there, here*), and for every point in time, rather than general references to relative time (*now, then, later*), the English vocabulary would be even bigger than it is and the resulting memory load on speakers would be impossible. Instead there are adverbs for the more general adverbial concepts, and the possibility of combining words into phrases for more specific circumstantial references.

The following passage from a letter of complaint has a range of adverbs of different types, as well as some prepositional phrases. Try to find these and work out to which subclass the adverbs belong.

In the meantime my neighbour had told me that the pavement outside had been mended, and when I saw the gap in my path, I went to investigate the repair work, only to discover that the 'new' slab was the identical size and shape as the one missing from my path. Of course this is not conclusive proof, but it does seem to be a strange coincidence. I phoned Brendan O'Malley, who gave me Johnson's number and a name to contact. This was perhaps unwise, though I didn't entirely realise that it was the subcontractor himself I would be speaking to. I had the impression from Brian (wrongly as it turned out) that Kennedy's had hired further subcontractors. I naively thought they would be as horrified as I was, and look into it. Instead, I had Mr Glazier assure me that 'his lads' wouldn't do any such thing, and they'd be round to see me within the hour when he told them. I said that I had no wish for anyone to come round.

The adverbs ending in -ly (*entirely, wrongly, naively*) are relatively easy to find, but there are also adverbs, such as *outside, instead, round* and *perhaps,* and the prepositional phrases include *by my house* and *within the hour.*

3.5 Grammatical word classes

The distinction between grammatical and lexical word classes was described earlier. To recap, the lexical word classes are open-ended and very large, whilst the grammatical word classes are small and very rarely change their membership. The grammatical word classes are sometimes described as closed systems, in contrast with the open class of the lexical words. This is because the members of grammatical classes are intertwined semantically, so that the addition of a new member or loss of an existing one would radically alter the meaning of some or all of the other members of the class. Take for example the loss of *thou, thee, thy* and *thine* in the relatively recent history of English. When they were in common usage, they were more or less equivalent to *tu* in contemporary Spanish and French, and were used to address family members and those of lower status than the speaker (for example younger). Once they had been lost in English the words *you* and *your* had to take over all the second person references they had previously not covered. Instead of *you, your* and *yours* being respectful, distancing and plural second person pronouns they became general purpose and referred to all second person **referents**.

We can envisage changes in the pronoun system because some have happened relatively recently, and there have also been discussions amongst feminists about whether a gender-neutral pronoun might be invented to cover *he and she* and avoid the use of odd combinations such like *s/he,* or to use the masculine pronoun for all individuals, as was common in the past.

It is not so easy to envisage changes in the other systems that form grammatical classes. The three coordinating conjunctions in English (*and, but, or*) seem to cover all the logical options, and this is precisely the point. Because they do cover the options, but cut up the possible options in a particular way, we find it hard to imagine another way of doing it. This is very interesting to linguists who study the interaction between language and thought, as it appears that, at least to some extent, the world's languages dictate the kinds of reality their speakers perceive, and make it hard for them to see things differently.

It is worth pointing out that although the grammatical classes tend to have less obvious semantic meaning when out of context (for example, what does the word *this* mean?), they are not devoid of meaning and some have more definable meanings than others. The most significant aspect of their meaning is perhaps the fact that they relate other (lexical) words to each other in particular ways. If you take the following sentence, for example, and take out all the underlined (grammatical) words, the result will be a list of lexical words with no clear links:

> *All the children will enjoy my party if they arrive on time*
> *children enjoy party arrive time*

We may be able to work out that *children* forms the subject of the predicator (verb) *enjoy*, that *party* is the object, that there is another clause with the verb *arrive* and probably some kind of adverbial containing *time*. However there is no evidence of how the two clauses relate to each other – that is, by the **conditional subordinator** *if* – and no information on how many children (all of them) or whose party it is.

Grammatical words, then, have a very important function in English: to make explicit the links between the lexical words and to create the context in which the lexical words can operate successfully.

3.5.1 Pronoun

Pronouns were mentioned a number of times in earlier sections, but in this section we shall look carefully at the class as a whole and how it works in English. Pronouns, although a grammatical class, function syntactically in similar ways to the noun class because they can be subjects, objects and complements. This makes sense because their role is to substitute for more complex nouns and noun phrases in order to make the language more efficient and avoid repetition. In the following passage the pronouns are underlined:

> *My sister and her family went to Malta for their holiday. She said they wanted to have a relaxing time with sun and sea, but they found that the hotel was miles inland, it didn't have a pool and the weather could be cloudy in August.*

Now see what happens to the passage when the pronouns are replaced by the full nouns and noun phrases they substitute for:

> *My sister and her family went to Malta for their holiday. My sister said my sister and her family wanted to have a relaxing time with sun and sea, but my sister and her family soon found that the hotel was miles inland, the hotel didn't have a pool and the weather could be cloudy in August.*

Some of these replacements sound forced, and some sound downright odd. This is because we don't generally repeat the full text referring to participants in our stories, unless there is a real danger of confusion. Instead, we use pronouns to refer back, 'anaphorically', and sometimes forward, 'cataphorically' to the people and things we are talking about.

Table 3.3 shows the pronouns of English and their relationships to each other.

There are also possessive determiners (*my, our, your, his, her, its, their*), but they do not replace the whole noun phrase. Instead they premodify the head noun, as other determiners do.

One of the striking things about English pronouns is that there is no variation in the form of the second person pronoun between subject and object functions:

Table 3.3 The subject, object and possessive pronouns in English

	First person	Second person	Third person
Subject pronouns:			
Singular	I	you	he, she, it
Plural	we	you	they
Object pronouns:			
Singular	me	you	him, her, it
Plural	us	you	them
Possessive pronouns:			
Singular	mine	yours	his, hers, its
Plural	ours	yours	theirs

<u>You</u> should come to my office at 10 a.m. (Subject)

The Head teacher will see <u>you</u> now. (Object)

The difference between the forms of the other pronouns is mostly quite straightforward:

<u>He/she</u> should come to my office at 10 a.m. (Subject)
The Head teacher will see <u>him/her</u> now. (Object)

<u>I</u> want to play tennis today. (Subject)
Will you play <u>me</u> later? (Object)

There are occasions, however, when people seem to worry about which to use, though there really should not be any difficulty:

<u>You and I</u> are best friends, aren't we? (Subject)

I don't think he likes <u>you and me</u>. (Object)

One reason for the confusion is that the effort to make certain that people use the subject pronouns (rather than saying, for example, *you and me are best friends*) has been taken up too enthusiastically in some quarters and applied to both subject and object functions:

You and I are best friends, aren't we? (Subject)

**I don't think he likes you and I.* (Object)

The possessive pronouns may occur in either subject or object functions:

<u>Mine</u> is a gin and tonic. (Subject)

They like <u>mine</u>. (Object)

It is true of all pronouns that we need context – either more text or something in the situational context – to work out the referent of the pronoun. This is most clear in the last case above, *They like <u>mine</u>*. We may be aware that the possessive pronoun *mine* refers to the speaker's possession, but we have no way of knowing from the clause just what it is that is owned by the speaker.

The other feature of the English pronoun in that is worth noting is the fact that the third person singular pronouns are divided into three groups, according to animateness and gender. Things that are clearly inanimate (*cups, houses*) are referred to as *it* (and any features they possess are indicated by *its*), whilst human beings are referred to according to gender as *she* or *he*, and their possessions are similarly gendered: *his* or *hers*. The animate beings (animals and so on) that share the planet with us are sometimes honoured with the human pronouns (*she, he*), but quite often, and probably largely because we cannot identify their gender, we use the inanimate *it* to refer to them. This, incidentally, is also true of babies, and for the same reason. Whilst it may seem rude to use *it* to refer to a baby in front of its parents, we then have the difficulty of remembering/identifying the gender in the absence of obvious signs, such as pink or blue clothing. Whilst we may struggle to find a way round this, when discussing the baby with people other than the parents we readily use *it*, as we do before the baby is born when we do not know the gender:

When did she have it?

When is she expecting it?

It will be interesting to see whether pronoun usage changes when referring to unborn babies, as increasingly parents seem to know the gender of their baby in advance.

3.5.2 Determiner

The **determiner** class is defined by its positioning within the noun phrase. Determiners are situated before the noun head of the phrase, and before any adjectives that may be in the noun phrase. The only words that may be placed before the determiner in a noun phrase are a small number of predeterminers, which we shall examine in a later section. The determiners form a single class in English because they cannot occur in combination with each other. There are three main subclasses of determiner and we shall investigate each in turn. These are the **articles**, the **demonstrative adjectives** and the **possessive adjectives**.

The article system in English is very simple in form, if less so in usage. There are two articles: the **definite article**, *the*, and the **indefinite article** *a(n)*. These are used roughly as follows. The definite article is used for referents that are either very clearly part of the context of the situation in which the utterance takes place, or that have been referred to earlier in the text. The indefinite article is used for (singular) countable nouns that have not been introduced earlier in the text and are not expected or evident from the context.

This statement of the uses/meanings of the two articles is hugely oversimplified and the real situation is much more complex, depending on style, context and so on. For example the definite article is often used to open literary works such as poems (see Semino, 1997, ch. 2) to make readers feel that they know the referent, although they have no way of doing so. Such stylistic and other discourse uses of articles are not the subject of this book and therefore will be set aside for now, though it is important to be aware that the whole story cannot be told in such a short space as this.

The demonstrative adjectives, *this, these, that* and *those,* function rather like the definite article when referring to things, people and so on that are identifiable in the context (textual or situational), but they differ from the definite article in being more specific about the proximity or distance between the speaker and the referents. Thus the **proximal** demonstratives, *this* and *these,* refer to things that are physically or emotionally close to the speaker and the **distal** demonstratives refer to things, people and so on that are physically or emotionally distant from the speaker:

This dress has always been my favourite.

That blouse looked awful on her!

Note that these examples demonstrate both physical and psychological proximity and distance, since the dress belongs to the speaker, and is liked, and the blouse does not necessarily belong to her, and is not liked.

The final subclass of determiners consists of possessive adjectives: *my, your, his, her, its, our,* and *their*. These words, which are mostly similar in form to the possessive pronouns, do not replace the noun head but combine with it in the way that other determiners do:

my garage, your friend,his tennis ball, her football, its hinges, our house, their bathroom

To summarise, the determiner class introduces noun phrases, and defines the head noun in certain ways in relation to the context (for example definiteness) and the speaker (for example possession and proximity/distance).

3.5.3 Preposition

The **prepositions** in English are legendary, mainly because there are so many of them. Foreign learners of English are known to find them difficult, and this is not only because of their huge number but also because their meanings are rather slippery. As we have already found, the meanings of grammatical classes normally create some kind of relationship between other words or referents in the text. The preposition always introduces a phrase that consists of itself and a noun phrase, and the meaning of the whole phrase usually indicates some circumstance in which the action of the clause is occurring, or the context of a previous noun phrase:

The tiger came <u>*into the room*</u>.

The cat <u>*in the garden*</u> *wasn't hers.*

These are two relatively straightforward examples (underlined) of prepositional phrases, and they respectively indicate the place into which the tiger came, and where the cat was. Note that the first one relates to the whole of the rest of the clause (where the action takes place) and the second one relates to the position of the noun phrase's referent: the cat. We shall revisit the different functions of prepositional phrases later; here we shall bring together some of the features of prepositions themselves.

The clearest examples of prepositions are those which relate actions or entities in time or space. The earlier examples dealt with space, so here are some examples of time prepositions:

<u>*In a day or so*</u>, *you will feel better.*

The concert <u>*on Saturday*</u> *is in aid of charity.*

As with the previous pair of examples, the prepositional phrases here relate to the action in the first sentence (when the process of feeling better will take place) and the noun phrase (*the concert*) in the second sentence.

In English prepositions make up a fairly large grammatical word class, with a large set of single-word prepositions supplemented by another large set of two or even three-word units that function very much like single-word prepositions (*as well as, over and above*). Common single-word ones include:

in, on, under, over, through, by, near, for, to, of

It is important to understand that some prepositions and adverbs have the same form but they are very easy to tell apart, as the preposition is always followed by a noun phrase and the adverb stands alone. Compare the following sentences:

I often go running <u>*through*</u> *the park.* (Preposition)

Will you take me <u>*through*</u>? (Adverb)

Note that the prepositional form is followed by the noun phrase *the park*, whereas the adverb form is intended to convey the whole of the situation in which the action will take place.

3.5.4 Conjunction

The coordinating **conjunctions** in English consist of a small, three-word set: *and, but, or,* which between them cover the logical possibilities of adding equal units together or contrasting them. There is more detail on this in Chapter 5; here we shall simply illustrate the fact that they allow more than one unit (word, phrase or clause) to operate in place of a single unit:

I like John. I like Andy. I like John and Andy
He was firm. He was nice. He was firm but nice.
Were you awake? Were you asleep? Were you awake or asleep?

Coordinating conjunctions, then, allow us to say things more succinctly and with less repetition, and they also allow us to create specific relationships, as in the sentences above. Thus the word *and* causes us to put the referents in the same category – people who are liked by the speaker in this case. The word *but* creates a co-occurrence of features that might be expected to contrast, in this case the question of whether you can indeed be *nice* if you are also *firm*. The final coordinating conjunction, *or*, shows that the speaker believes the two states (*asleep* and *awake*) to be mutually exclusive. A much larger class of **subordinating conjunctions** (including *if, so, that, although, then* and so on) is used in English not to give equal weight to parts of a structure, but to make clear that one unit or structure is less important grammatically (and thus also semantically) than another. We shall see the effect of subordination on structure in Section 5.4.3. The following are examples of subordinating conjunctions in context:

Although it was late, she rang the doorbell.

When you get to the hotel, give me a ring.

I know that you have taken it.

The subordinating conjunctions usually introduce a clause or other element (underlined in the above examples) that either sets the scene for the main clause, as in the first two examples, or acts as the object or complement of the main verb, as in the final example. Identifying a conjunction can be the key to understanding which part of a **complex sentence** is the subordinate and which is the main clause.

3.5.5 Auxiliary verb

Auxiliary verbs are so called because they support the lexical verbs by introducing some of the regular meanings that are needed by all verbs, such as tense. As we shall see when discussing the structure of the verb phrase, auxiliary verbs carry a great deal of meaning that in other languages are carried in inflectional verb endings. In English these functions are delegated to the auxiliaries.

The auxiliary verbs are made up of the **modals** (*may, must, might* and so on), *have* (perfective) and *be* (progressive and passive). Later we shall see how they work with each other and with lexical verbs. Here it is worth noting some of the uses of the auxiliary function: to construct questions, to provide emphasis and to carry negation.

Looking at questions first, the first auxiliary in a verb phrase can be put before the subject in order, to ask a question:

She will be coming. Will she be coming?

Jane has been hurt. Has Jane been hurt?

Dave might find it. Might Dave find it?

The emphatic use of the auxiliary is connected with stress and intonation patterns, but it is again the first auxiliary that carries the extra emphasis of an emphatic version:

She ***will*** *be coming*

Jane ***has*** *been hurt*

Dave ***might*** *find it*

The negation of English sentences is usually carried by the verb phrase in the form of a negative particle, which intervenes in the verb phrase after the first auxiliary and before the following auxiliary or lexical verb:

She won't be coming.

Jane hasn't been hurt.

Dave might not find it.

As these examples show, the negative particle is often attached to the auxiliary verb, though in the case of *might* the reduced form (*mightn't*) is less common now.

All three of these special uses of the auxiliary require some attention to the first auxiliary of a verb phrase. This may be a modal auxiliary or it may be *have* or *be*. Whichever it is, this verb is known as the **'operator'** because it has the special functions described above. In the absence of an auxiliary (that is, where there is only a lexical verb), the **dummy operator** – the verb *do* – is used instead:

Does Donald know the answer?

Donald ***does*** *know the answer!*

Donald doesn't know the answer.

The dummy operator, then, performs the three functions of the other auxiliaries, but it does not carry any meaning of its own to add to the verb phrase.

3.6 Further reading

Many general books on grammar, such as Brown and Miller (1991) and Huddleston (1988), cover morphology as well as syntax and are more detailed than the present volume. They also include discussions of lexical and grammatical word classes. For students who are specifically interested in morphology Matthews (1991) and Bauer (1990) are useful for theoretical issues and debates, whilst Bauer (1983) provides a very thorough description of word formation in English.

The larger English grammar reference books, such as Huddleston and Pullum (2002) and Greenbaum (1996), cover morphology, word classes and the topics of Chapters 4 and 5 of this book.

For useful reminders and alternative descriptions of many of the grammar topics in Chapters 3, 4 and 5, see the Internet Grammar of English at the following web address: www.ucl.ac.uk/internet-grammar/home.htm. There are also some very useful exercises for beginners on that site.

CHAPTER

4 Phrase

4.1 Introduction: structures larger than words

In the previous chapter we encountered the different word classes of English and looked at the internal structure of words. In this and the following chapter we shall consider structures that are usually made up of more than one word, and look at how they are put together out of the word classes we have already examined. Here, then, we shall be considering the ways in which words are combined to make **phrases**, and in the following chapter we shall investigate the structure of clauses, sentences and utterances. Mostly we shall look at well-made structures that appear not to be affected by the problems of on-line processing and other parole or performance issues (see 7.7.1) that characterise the spoken language. In this regard we shall investigate some of the issues of spoken grammar that mark it out as different from the grammar of written texts (for a full description of the grammar of spoken English see Carter and McCarthy, 2005).

There are a number of ways of approaching the description of syntax, and these depend to some extent on what your purpose is and which theory underlies your approach. In the case of this volume, the main purpose is to give students an accessible model of what is going on in English sentences that they can then use in their own work on different topics in English language studies.

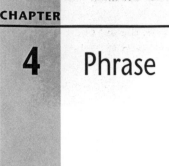

The approach taken here owes something to structuralist models and a little to functional and transformational-generative models of language. It will also be recognisable to people familiar with traditional grammatical training, though it differs in some significant ways from the old school grammars that based the description of English on the grammars of Ancient Greek and Latin. Where there are clear connections with any of the linguistic theories mentioned above, reference will be made to this, but the main task here is to give students tools that they can use.

As we saw in the Introduction to this volume, the use of an asterisk before an example in linguistics denotes an unacceptable form in the language being described. It is often used when demonstrating structures that simply do not occur, or hypothetical structures that would probably be rejected by speakers of the language. The use of a question mark before an example indicates that the example might or might not be acceptable to first-language speakers of English. It is less restrictive than the use of the asterisk.

4.2 Phrase structures

The circularity of the system of units and structures in English means that it is impossible to write about individual words and word classes without mentioning their functional roles in larger structures, including phrases. We have already met some of the structures that will appear in the sections below.

In English, phrase classes reflect the four major lexical word classes, so that there are noun phrases, verb phrases, adjective phrases and adverb phrases, each of which is centred on a head word of the relevant class, and each of which has certain potential additions to that head word to make a longer phrase. The only addition to this list is the prepositional phrase, which is really just a noun phrase with a preposition added at the beginning. We shall consider each of these classes in turn, and investigate their structure.

Before we do so, let us consider what makes a structure a phrase and not a clause. We saw earlier that single words can form complete utterances (for example Yes.) This is true of all word classes, and all phrase classes too, but without the full clause structure an utterance usually needs to include some information from the context for us to understand the significance of the word or phrase that is uttered.

Many traditional and more recent linguistic explorations of syntax have concentrated on the structure of more complete utterances that can stand alone and be understood. These structures are normally based on clauses, which have a conceptual completeness that is missing when a phrase is uttered alone. Phrases, then, like words, form part of larger structures and are not usually complete in themselves, without either the rest of the clause or some context that can fill in a clause-like conceptual structure. Take for example the following phrases:

On my chest of drawers near the window.

The longest walk I ever did.

Absolutely brilliantly!

These are a prepositional phrase, noun phrase and adverbial phrase respectively, and could occur as utterances on their own. However in that case they would be subject to some kind of contextual interpretation, such as a preceding question:

Where are the spare car keys?

What did you do on your birthday?

How did Jenny play?

The same phrases, when embedded in a full clause, would not require the same amount of contextual information to be interpreted at a basic semantic level, though context is always relevant to the full interpretation of all utterances.

The spare car keys are on my chest of drawers near the window.

On my birthday he took me on the longest walk I ever did.

Jenny played absolutely brilliantly!

These clauses are more interpretable than the phrases in the first set of examples, though for a full understanding the hearer would need to know the identity of the pronoun referents and who Jenny is.

Having established that phrases are, at least conceptually, part of a larger structure, we shall now consider the internal structure of the five phrase classes in English.

4.2.1 Noun phrase (NP)

The **noun phrase** is the most common and probably the most versatile phrase in English. It is based around a head noun, which is the irreducible core of the phrase and the shortest possible version of the noun phrase (underlined in the full clauses below):

Slippers are the new stilettos.

Power made him crazy.

Stephen found mould behind the bath.

In these examples, which are full clauses, the noun phrases we are concerned with are only one word long and consist of a single **head** noun.

Most noun phrases, though, have at least one **premodifier**, usually a determiner:

<u>These slippers</u> are the new stilettos.

<u>His power</u> made him crazy.

Stephen found <u>the mould</u> behind the bath.

Note that in English a noun phrase can have only one determiner, which is partly what puts the different determiners (articles, demonstratives and possessives) into a single class. Some languages allow a combination of article and possessive, but this is not permitted in English:

**The my carpet. *A his father.*

In addition to the determiner, the premodification of the head noun may include, in the following order, a predeterminer (determiner,) an enumerator, adjectives and a noun. We shall consider each of these in turn.

There is a small number of **predeterminers** in English, most of them concerned with quantification (Table 4.1). Predeterminers, as their name implies, tend to occur before determiners, though very similar quantifiers (usually without the particle, of) can occur without the intervening determiner (Table 4.2).

Table 4.1 Predeterminers in the noun phrase

Predeterminer	Determiner	Head
All (of)	my	sisters
None of	the	answers
Each of	those	books
Most of	our	water

Table 4.2 Quantifiers in the noun phrase

Quantifiers	Head
All	officers
No	answers
Each	book

To which subclass these quantifiers belong is open to question. They seem to be like predeterminers in meaning, but they could belong to the class that is mostly dominated by numbers, that is, the enumerators (Table 4.3).

Table 4.3 Enumerators in the noun phrase

Emumerators	Head
Ten	officers
Twelve	answers
Five	books

It is important to note that these candidates for membership of either the predeterminer or the enumerator class do not behave consistently with regard to combining with determiners. Some may occur with a determiner, and some may not (Table 4.4). The significant difference is that where a determiner does occur with enumerators proper it precedes the numeral (Table 4.5).

In summary, then, the predeterminer class has a varied expectation of co-occurrence with other deteminers, but where it occurs it is the first item in a noun phrase.

Table 4.4 Quantifier/Determiner combinations in the noun phrase

Quantifier	Determiner	Head
All	the	officers
*No	the	answers
*Each	the	book

Table 4.5 Determiner/Enumerator combinations in the noun phrase

Determiner	Enumerator	Head
The	ten	officers
Her	twelve	answers
Those	five	books

The **enumerator** class has already been introduced and is fairly straightforward, coming between the determiner and the adjective positions in the premodification of a noun phrase. As well as the **ordinal numbers** (one, two, three and so on), the **cardinal numbers** (first, second, third and so on) are also part of this class (Table 4.6).

Table 4.6 Ordinal and cardinal enumerators in the noun phrase

Determiner	Enumerator	Head
Her	three	dogs
Those	eleven	players
My	first	cappuccino

After the enumerator class, the premodification of a noun may include a number of adjectives. There is no theoretical restriction on the number of adjectives allowed in an English noun phrase, though more than three is unusual and a single adjective is most common, except in specific contexts, such as the description of products in catalogues:

Medium roast ground coffee.

These delicious shortbread Christmas tree shaped biscuits.

A deep, ribbed collar.

A few identifiable subclasses of adjective appear to have general restrictions on their co-occurrence as well as a tendency to occur in a certain order. For example the classes denoting colour, origin and material tend to occur after the subclass that might be labelled 'general adjectives'. These include size, shape and evaluation adjectives. They are not so much a structured class as a miscellaneous group of the most common adjectives that do not fit into the other, more-specific classes (Table 4.7).

Table 4.7 Adjective premodifiers in the noun phrase

Determiner	General	Colour	Origin	Material	Head
Those	gorgeous	red	Indian	linen	trousers
Her	long	green	Chinese	silk	skirt

The ordering of adjectives in noun phrases is not a strict rule of the grammar, and is probably a semantic restriction as much as anything, since it is unlikely that we would want to describe the noun head as being of two colours or from two different places (Table 4.8).

Table 4.8 Restrictions on adjective cooccurrence in the noun phrase

Determiner	General	Colour	Head
*My	gorgeous	red blue	trousers
*Her	long	Indian Chinese	skirt

The only way in which these phrases could be made to work would be to combine the meanings of the duplicated adjective class to mean 'somewhere between' red and blue, and 'a bit' Indian and 'a bit' Chinese.

As well as not having more than one of each adjectival subclass, changes in the order of these adjectives can sound rather odd. However this does not mean that they are ungrammatical, in the way that **the my house* or **pink those rabbit* would be:

?Those red gorgeous linen Indian trousers.

?Her Chinese long silk green skirt.

One of the effects of reordering the adjective classes is that the noun phrase sounds more as though it were being constructed on the spot, with the speaker thinking it through as she or he goes.

In addition to the subclasses already explored there is the verbal adjective class, which is made up of adjectives clearly derived from verbs, either using the *-ing* or the *-en* form of the verb but behaving in all other respects like an ordinary adjective:

The painted wooden boxes.

Those poor dancing bears.

It is less clear than with the earlier statement of ordering where these 'deverbal' adjectives are likely to occur in the premodification of the noun phrase. For one thing noun phrases with lots of premodifiers are relatively rare. Also, some changes in emphasis can be achieved with different orders, as we can see by changing the order of the premodifiers in the first of the above examples.

The wooden <u>painted</u> boxes

It is also unclear where an origin adjective would fit into the second of the above examples.

Those poor Russian <u>dancing</u> bears.

Those poor <u>dancing</u> Russian bears.

The first of these versions is probably most likely, but the second is also feasible. Once there are more than two adjectival premodifiers the order will depend on the tendencies in ordering discussed here, and also on the context, which could alter the emphasis for a number of reasons.

The final part of the premodification of nouns in English noun phrases is the noun premodifier. This is a noun that can precede the head noun, but functions in the same way as other premodifiers by limiting the possible range of referents of the noun phrase as a whole. Thus the noun phrase *a duck* may cover any referent that can be labelled 'duck', but the following noun phrases, with noun premodifiers, limit the possible referent to different subclasses of duck:

The Bombay duck.

My bath duck.

Dawn's garden duck.

An amusing way to try out noun premodification is to write random nouns on separate pieces of paper, then draw two out of a hat and put them together after a determiner (usually *the* is the safest choice). You will end up with some odd concepts, but it is usually possible to imagine a context in which you might hear the resulting noun phrase uttered. Some will be more ordinary than others, and some will be downright surreal. They will all be grammatically acceptable. Here are some phrases created in this way, ranging from normal to odd, and some suggested contexts (in brackets):

The book cupboard (the cupboard where we do/used to keep books).

His frog jumper (jumper with a pattern of frogs knitted in).

Those tree readers (people who can communicate with trees).

Note that these phrases could also contain the premodifiers discussed earlier (predeterminers, adjectives and enumerators), but if we included one from each category of premodifier the result would very odd indeed. The following are some noun phrases with a range of choices from the premodifiers possible in English noun phrases:

All my three dress patterns.

Those horrible yellow sneakers.

Before we look at the postmodification of head nouns, let us put the noun phrases we have just seen into a clause, to see them operating in different contexts:

All my three dress patterns are too small for me.

She keeps wearing those horrible yellow sneakers.

Although many noun phrases consist of only the head noun and a small number of premodifiers, there are two important types of **postmodifier** that you also need to recognise. The first is the prepositional phrase and the second is the relative clause.

The prepositional phrase will be explored in more detail in Section 4.2.5, but for now there is an easy way to remember the form of the phrase: it consists of a preposition and a noun phrase. If we add a preposition to the beginning of the slightly odd noun phrases we invented earlier the result is as follows:

In the book cupboard.

Up his frog jumper.

For those tree readers.

The resulting prepositional phrases can in turn be added to the end of other noun phrases to form the postmodification:

The dictionary in the book cupboard.

The chocolate up his frog jumper.

The cakes for those tree readers.

Note that these are still only noun phrases. They are not complete clauses and do not contain a verb. It is important to focus on this because there can be closely related clauses that might seem to be the same at first sight, but in this case the prepositional phrases are not postmodifying the noun as there is a verb between the noun phrase and the prepositional phrase:

The dictionary is in the book cupboard.

The chocolate is up his frog jumper.

The cakes are for those tree readers.

These complete clauses use the prepositional phrase in its only other function, as an adverbial clause element. We shall investigate these in Section 5.2.5, but for now let us place the noun phrases with prepositional phrase postmodification into clauses of their own:

The dictionary in the book cupboard is huge.

The chocolate up his frog jumper will be melting.

The cakes for those tree readers are nearly ready.

Here, the noun phrases (underlined) are functioning as the subject in a larger clause, though they could just as easily be objects:

You should consult the dictionary in the book cupboard.

Where did he get the chocolate up his frog jumper?

Don't eat the cakes for those tree readers.

Apart from the prepositional phrase, the other main form of postmodification in noun phrases is the relative clause. This is one of the areas of English grammar where it is difficult to know in which order to explain things. The relative clause, as its name implies, has a recognisable clause structure and this is discussed later in this volume. Rather than repeat the description of clause structure here, you are referred to Section 5.3. However a little of the structure of a clause will need to be introduced here in order for you to understand what is being described. The reason for this circularity in explanation is that there is a similar circularity in the structure of the English language. Whilst in general phonemes make up morphemes, which make up words, which make up phrases, which make up clauses, which make up sentences, which make up texts, there are some places in the structure where a 'higher' unit is embedded in a 'lower' unit. The noun phrase is one of these places.

We have seen that a noun phrase can include a prepositional phrase that itself contains a noun phrase. This is already quite complex (as we shall see below), but it can be explained quite clearly if the noun phrase is described first, as we have done here. We now find that noun phrases can contain clauses, though they are usually also contained within clauses.

Rather than drive ourselves mad trying to work out this conundrum, let us look at some examples of **relative clause** postmodification:

The trifle that Susan made for the party.

The thief who stole my car.

The ground where Australia lost the Ashes.

We shall see many more examples of relative clauses in Section 5.3.3; here it is important to note the context in which they occur. Unlike other subordinate clauses the relative clause is part of a phrase, not a clause element in its own right. It immediately follows the head noun of a noun phrase and is introduced by a relative pronoun (typically, but not only, *who*, *which* or *that*). The structure of the clause will vary according to whether a new subject is introduced (*Susan* in the second example and *Australia* in the third example above), and depending on what kind of relationship there is between the head noun and its role in the relative clause, since it may perform as subject, object, complement or adverbial in the subordinate clause.

For the purposes of this section, consider how we can recognise the relative clause as part of the noun phrase. If we put the whole of the noun phrase (including pre- and postmodification) into a clause it will be easier to recognise the relative clause as being subordinate:

The trifle that Susan made for the party was delicious.

The thief who stole my car has been caught by the police.

The ground where Australia lost the Ashes will be remembered.

Perhaps the most useful test to identify a noun phrase, however long it is, is the substitution test. If you are unsure whether a series of words is indeed a single noun phrase, try substituting the whole of it for a pronoun to see whether this is possible:

It was delicious.

He has been caught by police.

It will be remembered.

You cannot substitute only part of a noun phrase in this way as it makes nonsense of the rest:

**It that Susan made for the party was delicious.*

<u>He who stole my car</u> has been caught by police.

<u>It where Australia lost the Ashes</u> will be remembered.

To summarise, the noun phrase in English is made up of three functional elements, of which only the head is compulsory: Premodification, head, postmodification. These functions are normally filled by the word classes shown in Table 4.9.

Table 4.9 Form-function relationships in the noun phrase

Premodification	Head	Postmodification
Predeterminers Determiners Enumerators Adjectives Nouns	Noun	Prepositional phrase Relative clause

The aim here is to describe the most typical and regular patterns of English structures. Note that occasionally other word classes will form the head of a noun phrase, notably adjectives (as in *the poor* or *the rich*). These uses are dependent on the understanding that adjectives are fulfilling a noun-like role, as the head of a noun phrase. Hearers are thus likely to interpret adjective heads as implying that there is a missing noun, *people*.

The combinations of premodifiers are not restricted, except by the norms of length and the difficulty of understanding a very long noun phrase. The following is a long one that would be difficult to follow if it were delivered as part of a spoken utterance:

All of my three tall purple Chinese shining vases with gold leaf patterns . . .

Such noun phrases are relatively rare, except in catalogues, but another complicating factor in the noun phrase is the possibility of **recursion**. Because the noun phrase can contain a prepositional phrase that is mainly made up of a noun phrase, there is the possibility, in theory at least, of infinite repetition of this pattern. The following noun phrase is fairly long, but not terribly unwieldy:

. . . the pig in the sty on his farm in Wiltshire . . .

Note, though, that the levels of structure are quite complex, the first noun phrase being in three parts:

Pre-modification	Head	Postmodification
the	*pig*	*in the sty on his farm in Wiltshire . . .*

The second level of structure concerns the prepositional phrase that postmodifies the head, *pig*. It consists of the preposition, *in*, and a noun phrase with the following structure:

Pre-modification	Head	Postmodification
the	*sty*	*on his farm in Wiltshire . . .*

Here the embedded noun phrase, which is part of the prepositional phrase that postmodifies *pig*, has the head noun *sty* and another prepositional phrase that postmodifies *sty*. In other words, if the first prepositional phrase tells us where the pig is, then this one tells us where the sty is. The prepositional phrase at this level has a preposition, *in*, and a noun phrase with the following structure:

Pre-modification	Head	Postmodification
his	*farm*	*in Wiltshire . . .*

This noun phrase, if you read it as a stand-alone structure, seems very simple, but it does of course have one further level embedded within it. The postmodification of farm is a prepositional phrase with a preposition, *in*, and a noun phrase, *Wiltshire*. The structure of the latter consists solely of the head noun *Wiltshire*.

This demonstration of the potential complexity of the noun phrase structure in English shows how a simple rule, repeated a number of times, can include a great deal of information on one of the most basic structures of the language. It is also possible, of course, to do the same thing with relative clauses. Some writers of children's stories delight in playing with these kinds of recursive structure, perhaps most famously in the following form:

> *(This is) . . . the cat that chased the rat that ate the malt that lay in the house that Jack built.*

In order to make quite clear what is going on here, let us take it apart in the same way as the previous example. The 'top' level of structure is a noun phrase structured as follows:

Pre-modification	Head	Postmodification – relative clause
the	*cat*	*that chased the rat that ate the malt that lay in the house that Jack built*

The relative clause has a subject, *that*, a verb, *chased*, and the rest is an object, which is a noun phrase with the following structure:

Pre-modification	Head	Postmodification – relative clause
the	*rat*	*that ate the malt that lay in the house that Jack built*

Here we have a noun phrase with a postmodifying relative clause that tells us more about the rat. This relative clause has a subject, *that*, a verb, *ate*, and an object, which is a noun phrase whose structure is as follows:

Pre-modification	Head	Postmodification – relative clause
the	*malt*	*that lay in the house that Jack built*

In this case we have a noun phrase with a postmodifying relative clause that tells us more about the malt. This relative clause has a subject, *that*, a verb, *lay*, and an adverbial, which is a prepositional phrase containing the preposition, *in*, and a noun phrase with the following structure:

Pre-modification	Head	Postmodification – relative clause
the	*house*	*that Jack built*

In this example the noun phrase has a further relative clause that postmodifies house, which consists of an object, *that*, a subject, *Jack*, and a predicator (verb), *built*. It is only because we have now run out of noun phrases, with the object being represented here by the relative pronoun, *that*, that the process of extending the noun phrase has come to a halt. Let us look at the noun phrase in its original clause context:

> *This is the cat that chased the rat that ate the malt that lay in the house that Jack built.*

In the original, then, the noun phrase functions as the complement to the clause, which otherwise consists of only a subject, *this*, and a verb, *is*.

Having demonstrated the potential complexity of the noun phrase, let us look at some simpler examples in order to consider an important structure that occurs very often in English, particularly, but not only, in news reporting. In this structure two or more **noun phrases** are placed **in apposition** to each other, meaning that there can be more than one noun phrase in one of the normal clause functions (for example, subject), and if these have the same referent they are said to be in apposition. In the following the underlined phrases are all examples of apposition:

Mr Clark, the Home Secretary, said . . .

She saw Mr Bun, the Baker, going along the road.

My sister-in-law, Sandra, phoned me from Australia.

Blonde mother of three, Samantha, . . .

As you can see, these examples give information on either the occupation, the looks or the relationship with the speaker of the person referred to. Apposition can also be used for inanimate objects:

The Ford Fiesta, my new car, is a delight to drive.

4.2.2 Verb phrase (VP)

The **verb phrase** is the pivotal phrase in English clauses. It fulfils the role of predicator in the clause and effectively introduces a process (action, event and so on). Unlike in the noun phrase, recursion is not possible in the verb phrase, and with only a small number of exceptions all verb phrases fit into a fairly predictable and clear pattern, as described in this section.

It is important to note that some approaches, notably those deriving from **generative theory**, use the term verb phrase to refer to the whole of the predicate of the clause, that is, the verb and all that follows it. In the approach used here the term is used to describe only the verbal element of the clause, functioning as the predicator. To avoid confusion it is essential when reading other textbooks to establish which of these approaches is in use.

The first thing to note is that the simplest verb phrase will be a main lexical verb on its own. This is true of the vast majority of English verb phrases, and also of the clauses below, where the verb phrase is underlined:

The party started about 9 o'clock.

My brother always sings in the bath.

You bring us bad luck!

We have already examined the form of English verbs, so you should recognise the above as examples of the past tense, the present third person singular and the present second person singular respectively. As English has no future tense and things such as voice (active and **passive**), perfective and progressive are not built into its morphology (unlike, for example, French and Spanish), there is a range of auxiliary verbs instead. These precede the main lexical verb and introduce all of the variations of meaning that some other languages include in the form of the verb itself.

The full form of the verb phrase is as shown in Table 4.10, though as we shall see it is rare for all of these potential places to be filled at once.

Table 4.10 Verb phrase structure in English

Modal auxiliary	Perfective auxiliary	Continuous auxiliary	Passive	Main verb
might	have	been	being	followed

We shall consider each of the four auxiliary positions in turn. The modal auxiliaries in English are a subclass with at least the following members:

may, might, will, would, shall, should, can, could, ought (to)

There are other potential members of the modal class, including *need* and *dare*, but these are increasingly falling out of usage as modal verbs. **Modality** is an important semantic contribution to the interpretation of any text, and it is not found in modal verbs alone (see Simpson, 1993, ch. 3), but here we shall mainly consider the structure of the English verb phrase, rather than detailed variations in meaning and usage. In general, then, modal verbs are responsible for bringing in the speaker's own opinion about the substance of the clause being uttered, by indicating either how true or how desirable or acceptable he or she considers the circumstance being described. The likelihood or truth of an utterance is called **epistemic modality**, and its desirability is known as **deontic** or **boulomaic modality**. These two aspects of modal meaning can be represented by the same modal verb, with the semantics and context enabling the hearer to distinguish between them.

She <u>should</u> be here by now (I know that she left in plenty of time).

She <u>should</u> be here by now (It's not polite to be so late for a wedding).

The first example shows the use of *should* as an epistemic modal, with the speaker indicating some doubt about the truth of the statement. The second example demonstrates the deontic use of modals, whereby the speaker indicates what she or he thinks is the proper thing to happen. The modal verbs have no formal variation in morphology, and therefore they are always the same, irrespective of the person (first, second, third) or number (singular or plural) of the subject they follow:

I should go.

You should eat.

He/she/it should play.

We should sing.

They should leave.

More important, perhaps, is the fact that the modal verbs do not occur on their own, hence the inclusion of a range of lexical verbs in the examples given above. It is only when the lexical verb is completely predictable that the modal can stand in for the whole verb phrase. The following exchange provides an example:

A: *Might they bring a present with them?*

B: *They might.*

When a modal auxiliary is included in the verb phrase the subsequent verb form must be the infinitive form of the verb – one of the non-finite forms of the verb. In the above examples the lexical verbs follow the modal in infinitive forms – *go, eat, play, sing, leave* – but because the infinitive form is the same as other forms for many verbs, it is only clear that these are infinitives when the subsequent verb is one with a distinctive infinitive, such as the verb *be*: *You should be . . .*

Later we shall look at more complex cases, where some of the other auxiliary positions are also filled in. For now the significant points to remember are that modals do not change their own morphology but do influence the form of any subsequent verb, so that it is obliged to be an infinitive.

The second auxiliary position is the perfective auxiliary. This function is fulfilled by the auxiliary verb *have* which looks identical in all its forms to the lexical verb *have*, but must be kept separate for analytical purposes. The lexical verb *have* has a clear meaning or 'semantic content', approximating to the notion of ownership, though this is sometimes more metaphorical than literal (for example *I have a longing for a cool drink*). The perfective auxiliary, by contrast, brings the idea of completion to the meaning of the verb phrase:

She <u>has broken</u> the glass.

I <u>had cooked</u> the dinner.

Note that the perfective auxiliary, unlike the modal verbs, will agree with its subject as long as it is the first verb in the verb phrase. It can also take the present (*has*) or past (*had*) tense form, and this choice will differentiate between actions or processes completed in the immediate past and those completed at an earlier moment.

The other important feature of the perfective is its effect on the subsequent verb, whether that is another auxiliary or a main (lexical) verb. Those verbs which follow the perfective auxiliary have to take the *-en* form, which is another of the non-finite forms of the verb.

She <u>has taken</u> the dog.

They <u>had sold</u> their house.

I <u>have asked</u> lots of questions.

You may recall that the *-en* form of many verbs is either irregular (for example *sold*) or similar in form to the past tense *-ed* form (*asked*). Nevertheless, whenever the perfective auxiliary is followed by a verb for which a distinctive *-en* form is possible, this is the form that is used (for instance *taken*).

The next auxiliary position in the English verb phrase is the progressive auxiliary verb, *be*. Like the perfective it has the same range of forms as a very common lexical verb, but they should be considered as different verbs. The lexical meaning of *be* is hard to capture, but it can be summed up as to do with existence and equivalence:

This book <u>is</u> the best I have ever read.

There <u>is</u> a beach on the other side.

The auxiliary verb, *be*, however, conveys the idea that the process being described by the utterance is in some sense continuous – either in the past or in the present:

She <u>is</u> making a cake.

The priest <u>was</u> saying a prayer.

In the first of these examples the verb phrase, *is making*, tells the hearer that the process is ongoing since the auxiliary is in the present tense. In the second example the process is in the past because the auxiliary is in the past, but there is a focus on the duration of the process that is lacking in a past tense or perfective version:

The priest said/has said/had said a prayer.

These three versions all place the action in the past, and none of them evokes the length of time during which the prayer was being said, unlike the progressive version.

The final auxiliary to discuss is the passive auxiliary, which also takes the form of the verb *be*. Again this needs to be distinguished from the lexical verb *be*, and from the progressive auxiliary, which is formally identical to it. In fact the only way that we can tell the difference is by what follows it. In the case of the passive auxiliary, the subsequent verb has to be in the *-en* form rather than the *-ing* form, which follows the progressive.

Jessica was throwing her javelin (progressive).

Jessica was thrown from her horse (passive).

The significant contribution of the passive voice to meaning is that it changes the relationship between the subject and the predicator. In all active (non-passive) verb phrases, in some sense the subject is the doer of the process (even if the verb is a fairly inactive one, such as *notice* or *fall*). With passive verb phrases the subject is the goal of the process, and suffers the consequence of the process described, rather than being the initiator. This can be seen in the examples above, where Jessica is doing the throwing in the first sentence but is affected by it in the second.

The passive auxiliary, like the perfective and the continuous, carries person/number agreement and tense if it is the first auxiliary in the verb phrase:

The old man <u>was affected</u> by the collapse of his pension scheme.

I <u>am surprised</u> by your words.

When the passive auxiliary is no longer the first auxiliary in the verb phrase the usual restrictions apply. Thus after a modal auxiliary its form will be an infinitive, after a perfective it will be *-en* and after a continuous it will have the *-ing* form.

We are now in a position to summarise the English verb phrase structure and the formal restrictions that the auxiliaries place on the subsequent verb (Table 4.11).

Table 4.11 Summary of English verb phrase structures

Modal	Perfective	Progressive	Passive	Main (lexical)
might	have			seen
	has	been		trying
		is	being	burned
should		be		buying
can			be	bought
	have	been	being	considered
will	have	been	being	thought

4.2.3 Adjective phrase (AjP)

The majority of adjective phrases in English are very simple; usually an adjective on its own, or premodified by an intensifying adverb:

She is pretty.

Your house is incredibly untidy.

We saw in Section 3.4.3 that the main functions of adjectives are to premodify the head noun in a noun phrase or to serve as a complement, usually after the lexical verb *be* or another intensive verb. In the two examples above they are both complements, while below they have a premodifying function:

The pretty girl.

Your incredibly untidy house.

The only further complexity that is possible in adjective phrases is a kind of postmodification that is sometimes known as an **adjectival complement**. This takes a variety of forms but is commonly either prepositional or clausal:

(She is) sad about her friend's illness (prepositional).

(They are) likely to come to the party (clausal).

In these examples the adjective phrase is the part of the section that is not in brackets and forms the complement of the clause. The analysis of the prepositional phrase or clause complement of adjectives is the same as elsewhere.

4.2.4 Adverb phrase (AvP)

The **adverb phrase** is the simplest of all English phrases, being made up of only an adverb and any premodifying intensifiers that are also part of the adverb class:

. . . *very closely.*

. . . *right slowly.*

. . . *amazingly subtly.*

In general only adverbs that are gradable – normally those deriving from gradable adjectives – are able to be premodified by intensifiers. Other adverbs occur alone.

The two major functions that adverb phrases fulfil are as an adverbial in a clause structure or as a premodifier to adjectives in adjective phrases:

. . . *very obviously drunk.*

. . . *They nearly always arrive late.*

The first of these examples is an adjective phrase, with an adverb phrase as premodifier. The second has the adverb phrase (underlined) as a clause element, telling the hearer how often the action occurs.

4.2.5 Prepositional phrase (PP)

The inevitable circularity in defining the terms and units in syntax means that if you are reading this book in the order it is printed you will now know almost all you need to know about prepositional phrases. The form of prepositional phrases has been described in a number of places and is very simple to summarise, as it is made up of a preposition and a noun phrase.

The function of prepositional phrases has also been touched upon. The use of prepositional phrases as postmodifiers in noun phrases was explored in some detail (in Section 4.2.1), but they also have a clause function, as adverbials, and this has only been mentioned briefly. In addition, although it is quite easy to identify prepositional phrases there is considerable potential for confusion between the two functions of these phrases. We shall now explore some of the ways of distinguishing the functions, as well as some of the possible ambiguities.

To take the adverbial function first, we have seen that adverbs and adverb phrases are the typical forms that function in adverbial roles in clauses. The adverbial role can be summed up as detailing the circumstances in which the action of the clause takes place. This might include the time, the place and the emotional setting (for example if it is a surprising or depressing process), and in many cases these circumstances are outside the compulsory structure of the clause.

> *In a moment or two the cortege will emerge from the Abbey . . .*

Note that the adverbial prepositional phrase (underlined) in this example is not vital to the grammar of the sentence, though it clearly adds information.

The other function of prepositional phrases, as we have already seen, is to postmodify the head noun in a noun phrase:

> *Those children with the expensive trainers . . .*

This prepositional phrase elaborates what we know about the head noun, *children*, and would be part of the section replaced if a pronoun (for example *they*) were substituted.

4.3 Further reading

Brown and Miller (1991) cover the topics in this chapter, including recursion and the general principles of phrase structure, though in a slightly different way, drawing upon both generative and functional models of language. This will be of interest to students who are coping well with the present book and are interested in seeing the same structures described differently. Huddleston (1988) is a more straightforward match for this book, but at a greater level of detail. For a more comprehensive investigation of phrase structure see Huddleston and Pullum (2002) and Greenbaum (1996), as well as the many useful encyclopedias and linguistic dictionaries.

The verb phrase has received many dedicated treatments, including in the books by Palmer (1974, 1986), Leech (1971) and Allerton (1981).

The Internet Grammar of English (www.ucl.ac.uk/internet-grammar/home.htm) has an explanation of phrase structure that students may find useful, as well as exercises for practising analysis.

CHAPTER

5 Clause and Sentence

5.1 Introduction: idealised structures

This chapter continues the useful myth that there is an ideal language that can be described in books and that represents the core of what speakers draw upon in their everyday language use. This idealised form of English reflects the most stable form of the language, and one that has been described most consistently over the years: the written language.

As linguists we are interested in both written and spoken language, and phonetics and phonology were developed in response to the increased interest in the spoken language that developed in the twentieth century. The study of grammar, however, has tended to develop out of the traditional concern that scholars of the nineteenth century and earlier had with 'correctness' and 'better' forms of the language. This evaluative approach disappeared when linguists became aware that all human languages, including those with no writing system, were equally complex and equally suited to their purpose and functions. However the structuralist approach of de Saussure and others retained the view that there was a notional ideal language that speakers and writers had as a foundation to their flawed and imperfect use of the system. This conviction remained part of the approach taken by Chomsky and other generative linguists, who thought that the idealised version of the language was what we stored cognitively and used imperfectly. These notions have been regularly challenged by those working in contextual studies of language, including discourse analysis, pragmatics and conversation analysis. These studies have shown that the spoken language is as patterned as the written, though in different ways. Carter and McCarthy's *Grammar of Spoken English* (2005) is a recent attempt to capture not just the contextual but also the structural features of this form of language.

Despite all these developments, those studying language need some tools to begin their work, and the grammars that have been constructed in response to the 'ideal' form of the language remain the clearest and easiest to assimilate because they concentrate on the text alone, leaving the contextual aspects of meaning to be studied separately. This chapter concludes the introduction of these tools of analysis by considering the structure of **clauses**, which are the building block of English sentences and utterances.

Although we shall not be investigating detailed differences between the spoken and written language, it should be kept in mind that there are many potential differences between complete grammatical sentences in English and the utterances that English speakers produce. However all the sentences we shall investigate in this chapter can be uttered or written, and so we are concerned with the fundamental structure of the language.

Clauses can be combined in various ways to make complex and **compound sentences**, and we shall consider these in Sections 5.3.2 and 5.3.3. For now we shall treat the clause as equivalent to the sentence, and expect to see only one verb phrase in each example. The defining feature of a complete clause is that it must contain a predicator (the verbal element) and usually other clause elements (subject, object, complement, adverbial), as introduced below.

5.2 Clause functions

It is useful for students who are learning how to analyse the grammar of English to understand the difference between form and function at all the different levels of analysis. You have already seen this distinction at work in the noun phrase, where there are members of the noun (form) class perform different functions, such as premodifier and head. We have also seen how the adjective can function as a premodifier or as a complement. This section will introduce an important set of **clause** elements that make up the major structure of English texts, and explain the relationships between the various phrase classes (noun phrase, verb phrase, adjective phrase and so on) and their clause functions.

During the process of learning to analyse syntax it may seem that in some ways it would be simpler if languages did not make a distinction between forms and their functions. This could only occur if there were a one-to-one relationship between form and function, so that, for example, noun phrases could only be subjects and there were different forms for the object and complement functions. The loss of economy inherent in such a scheme would make the language very unwieldy. The fact that a smallish number of forms can each play a number of different parts in clause structure allows for a huge range of different utterances. By such means, human languages make a relatively small demand on the memory whilst reaping a huge advantage in terms of the complexity and range of things that can be said.

There are only five clause elements in English: subject (S), predicator (P), object (O), complement (C) and adverbial (A). The following sections will examine the clause functions in more detail, but for now there are a few general observations that can be made about the model of syntax explored here. First of all, as we shall see shortly, clause functions relate to the role that a unit (word, phrase or clause) plays in the larger structure. Although there are some straightforward connections between the functions and forms that fulfil them, it is helpful to view the two as separate. Thus although noun phrases often function as subjects, and though subjects are very often fulfilled by noun phrases, there is no intrinsic connection, and it is important to know that a noun phrase may have a number of functions that are not as a subject clause element.

Another general point that needs to be made is that clause elements can be the level and point at which recursion occurs. This means that units that are normally at a higher level may occur within a lower level of structure, leading to the potentially infinite length of structures that we saw earlier in relation to noun phrase postmodification. In the case of the clause, although clause elements are parts of a clause, at times they may be made up of subordinate clauses, meaning that the clause structure contains another clause structure, and this may in turn have a clause element that is a subordinate clause, and so on.

5.2.1 Subject (S)

The **subject** clause element is a syntactic function that is mainly fulfilled by noun phrases, but may also be fulfilled by a subordinate clause. The first of the sentences below is an example of a noun phrase (underlined) and the second of a clause as subject (underlined):

> <u>*My son*</u> *went to university in Wales.*
>
> <u>*To perform at Madison Square Gardens*</u> *was her highest ambition.*

There are a few places where a predicator will not be preceded by a subject. These include **imperative** structures, such as *Go to bed immediately*, where the implied subject of a command is clearly the second person, that is, *you*. They also include subordinate clauses where the subject is entirely predictable or 'elliptical':

> <u>*After closing the curtains*</u> *she turned on the television.*

Here the subordinate adverbial clause (underlined) has no subject for the predicator *closing*, but the structure makes clear that *she* is the subject of both clauses.

On all occasions when the subject is not so clearly predictable it will be made explicit, although the precise semantic relationship the referent will have with the verb will vary according to the semantics of the verb chosen. Thus although we think of subjects as stereotypically doing something, if the verb chosen is *suffer* or the verb phrase is in the passive form, the subject may be far from an actor and more like a recipient or patient. Such observations have been made since the early days in syntactic analysis, and the problems of identifying the relationship between clause elements and semantic functions remain under discussion. This is one of the fundamental problems of linguistic description; how to reconcile the formal regularities of language with the semantic irregularities and variations. Some grammatical descriptions, such as the functional approach taken by Halliday (1985), attempt to place such matters in the centre of the description, but the exact relationship between the forms and their patterns of meaning remains fraught even there.

5.2.2 Predicator (P)

The **predicator** is the only place in the clause where form and function map onto each other one-to-one. We are calling the function (that is, the verbal 'slot') the predicator here to differentiate it from the verb phrase form. However, although only verb phrases usually function as predicators it is worth noting that some parts of the verb take on noun or adjective-like functions at times:

The singing detective (lives down my street).

My broken heart (will never mend).

Her playing (was sublime).

It is not always clear whether we should treat such examples as the word class they function like, or the one that their own form suggests. This is a matter for more advanced work; here they are pointed out to avoid confusion in anaylsis.

As already mentioned, all full clauses contain predicators, and in main clauses and finite subordinate clauses the predicator (underlined) normally follows the subject:

The lorry braked hard.

None of the supporters had seen the goal.

All my three remaining grandparents are deaf.

As we saw earlier, the verb in English has relatively few forms of its own, but occurs with auxiliary verbs in making the full range of meanings connected to the process being described. Where there is a subject and a predicator, the verb form of the predicator will take account of the subject. Thus, the final example above has a plural form of the verb, are, to match the plurality of the subject noun phrase.

When the predicator occurs in non-finite subordinate clauses with no subject, it will be the first element in the clause or follow a subordinating conjunction:

Having identified the body (Miss Sharpe grew quite tearful).

After being questioned so aggressively (the man collapsed).

In these examples the subordinate clause is the setting for the main clause (in brackets) and the predicator (underlined) in each case has no preceding subject because it is assumed that the subject is the same as that in the main clause (that is, *Miss Sharpe* and *the man*).

5.2.3 Object (O)

Like the subject, the **object** function is mainly fulfilled by noun phrases, though a clause also take its place.

Seven baby frogs crossed the path in front of me.

I always hope that he will remember me.

In these two examples, the underlined sections represent the object in each case, with *the path* being a noun phrase functioning as an object, whilst *that he will remember me* is a subordinate clause with the same function.

Whilst in many cases the object corresponds to the element affected by the verb, it also has many other potential semantic relationships with the process described, depending on the verb chosen and other factors. For example the sentence below shows an object that is not affected but created by the action of the verb.

My mother knitted a tea cosy.

In addition to these **direct objects** there is a minor clause element known as the **indirect object**. This function is normally fulfilled by either a noun phrase or a pronoun, and precedes the direct object, as we can see from the following:

My mother knitted me a tea cosy.

Jennifer sent her boss a postcard.

The indirect object can alternatively be placed into an adverbial, usually a prepositional phrase, with little change in meaning.

My mother knitted a tea cosy for me.

Jennifer sent a postcard to her boss.

5.2.4 Complement (C)

A **complement**, as opposed to a compl*i*ment (for instance *Don't you look lovely today!*), is a syntactic function that can be fulfilled by a nominal element (a noun, noun phrase or noun clause) or an adjectival element: (an adjective or adjective phrase).

Complements occur after particular verbs. These include intensive verbs such as *be, seem, become, appear*:

Sofia is a teacher (noun phrase).

Carrie is tall (adjective).

Sam became a doctor (noun phrase).

Carlos became very angry (adjective phrase).

Jennifer seems clever (adjective).

Other verbs that are followed by complements are verbs of change, such as *make, paint, colour, rub* and verbs of perception such as *think* and *consider*: These verbs have objects (bold) as well as complements (underlined).

Mary made ***me*** *successful* (adjective).

Carrie painted ***the door*** *red* (adjective).

Sam's training made ***him*** *a doctor* (noun phrase).

Carlos coloured ***his*** *sky blue* (adjective phrase).

Jennifer rubbed ***her feet*** *raw* (adjective).

Nasser thought ***Saskia*** *immature* (adjective).

The word complement literally means 'completing', so this function is used not to introduce something entirely new into the sentence but to complete what we know about something or somebody already mentioned.

In the first of the two sets of examples above we are told something extra about *Sofia, Carrie, Sam, Carlos,* and *Jennifer,* the subjects of the sentences. The complements follow the verb directly and are known as **subject complements**. In the second set of examples we are told something about *me, the door, him, his sky, her feet* and *Saskia* that is, the objects of the sentences. These complements follow the direct object and are known as **object complements**.

It is sometimes difficult to distinguish between objects and complements, especially when the complement is a nominal of some kind. If we only consider their form, the following sentences seem to have the same structure (noun phrase plus verb phrase plus noun phrase):

Sofia is the teacher.

Sofia hates the teacher.

Speakers of English will know, however, that the complement in the first sentence refers to the same thing as the subject (*Sofia = the teacher*) (Figure 5.1) but in the second sentence *Sofia* and *the teacher* are different people (Figure 5.2).

Sofia is the teacher

Figure 5.1 Example of SPC structure

Sofia hates the teacher

Figure 5.2 Example of SPO structure

The results of this method of distinguishing objects from subject complements by appeal to meaning can be confirmed by using a syntactic test. Objects can usually be moved to the subject position without changing the basic meaning if the verb is changed to a passive form:

The teacher is hated by Sofia.

Verbs that can be followed by subject complements cannot be made passive:

**The teacher is been by Sofia.*

A similar problem can arise when a verb is followed by two nominals. The sentences look alike on the surface (NP + VP + NP + NP), but the two noun phrases after the verb can function as either indirect object plus direct object or direct object plus object complement. The semantic key to the answer is to consider whether the two nominals refer to the same or different things:

My mother made me a tennis player.

My mother made me a cup of coffee.

In the first sentence the two nominals after the verb are the same person (Figure 5.3). This means that there is a direct object and an object complement in this sentence. In the second sentence the two nominals after the verb refer to different things (Figure 5.4). The child (*me*) and the *cup of coffee* are clearly not referring to the same item, so these are indirect and direct objects respectively.

A syntactic test similar to the one used for subject complements can be employed here. The direct objects in both sentences can be made into the subject of passive sentences:

My mother made me a tennis player

Figure 5.3 Example of SPOC structure

My mother made me a cup of coffee

Figure 5.4 Example of a SPOO structure

I was made a tennis player by my mother.

I was made a cup of coffee by my mother.

However the complement cannot be made the subject of a passive sentence, though the indirect object can:

**A tennis player was made me by my mother.*

A cup of coffee was made for me by my mother.

The examples of complements discussed so far are simple and invented but examples in real texts are usually more complicated. The following is an extract from a travel brochure about Madagascar, and it contains three examples of subject complements:

Isalo National Park in the southwest is a landscape of sandstone rocks cut by canyons and eroded into extraordinary shapes. The rock-clinging elephant's foot plant and the Aloe isaloensis are icons of this reserve. Isalo is sacred to the Bara people, who bury their dead in caves in the canyon walls.

One of the things that we notice in real texts is that the large majority of subject complements follow the verb *be* rather than one of the other intensive verbs. In this extract there are two singular present tense forms of the verb *be* (*is*) and one plural present tense form (*are*). After these verbs there are three phrases, two of them rather long, each complementing the subject of their respective clauses.

. . . a landscape of sandstone rocks cut by canyons and eroded into extraordinary shapes.

. . . icons of this reserve.

. . . sacred to the Bara people, who bury their dead in caves in the canyon walls.

The first two are nominal, with head nouns *landscape* and *icons* respectively. The last one is adjectival, with *sacred* as its head. Although there are many more words in these examples they have the same structure as the invented examples (Table 5.1).

Table 5.1 Complements in clauses

Subject	Verb Predicator	Complement
Mary	is	the teacher
Isalo National . . . southwest	is	a landscape ... shapes
The rock-clinging . . . isaloensis	are	icons of this reserve
Isalo	is	sacred to the Bara people . . . walls

One of the reasons why such structures are common in travel brochures is that they enable the writer to make quite bold statements without being at risk of contradiction. The intensive verb acts like an equals sign, making the sentence appear to be stating a given truth whereby the subject and the complement are clearly identical.

This can have interesting consequences in terms of manipulating the reader, particularly when politicians use such structures as categorical statements, as in the following quote from the British prime minister, Tony Blair, in a national newspaper: *'It is a false illusion that the answer to the problems of the north is somehow to punish the south'* (*Guardian*, 15 February 2000, p. 10).

Here the 'equation' is between the complement noun phrase *false illusion* and the delayed subject, which is a noun clause: *that the answer to the problems of the north is somehow to punish the south*. Both of these ideas are presented as 'packages' by being put into nominal forms. By using an intensive verb and a subject-verb-complement structure the reader is being asked to accept that they are identical or equivalent.

Subject	Verb Predicator	Complement
. . . that the answer to the problems of the north is somehow to punish the south	is	a false illusion

Note that the effect of making the complement nominal, rather than adjectival, is to strengthen the force of the statement. Tony Blair could have said the following instead, choosing the adjective *false* instead of the noun phrase *a false illusion*:

> *It is false to claim that the answer to the problems of the north is somehow to punish the south.*

If he had chosen this form there would have been more chance of his hearers being inclined to argue with the equivalence he was trying to assume between the complement and the subject.

5.2.5 Adverbial (A)

The final clause element in English is the **adverbial**. It is both useful and potentially confusing that the name of this clause element is so similar to the name of the word class of adverb and phrase class of adverb phrase. In some grammar books the term adjunct is used for a similar range of functions, but we shall stick with adverbial here. The important difference between the adverbial function and adverb forms, as with all clause elements, is that a number of different forms fulfil the function of an adverbial clause element, and not all of them are based on adverbs. Although the most regular forms that play this role are adverbs and adverb phrases, another very frequent form that has an adverbial function is the prepositional phrase. In addition noun phrases, particularly when they refer to moments or periods in time, can function in this way.

> *The train pulled away from the station very slowly* (adverb phrase).
>
> *Unfortunately, I won't be able to come to your wedding* (adverb).
>
> *In a moment, I shall pour you a cup of tea* (prepositional phrase).
>
> *Every day of my life I practise for four hours* (noun phrase).

As noted, these examples respectively demonstrate an adverb phrase, an adverb, a prepositional phrase and a noun phrase (underlined) functioning as an adverbial in the clause. The common factor is that they all describe the circumstances in which the action or process of the clause takes place. The traditional description of this clause function included the definition of adverbs as time, place or manner adverbs, and although we are now applying these concepts to a function rather than a form, they are still useful as a conceptual reminder of the kinds of adverbial we can expect to see. Perhaps even more useful as a memory aid is to consider them to be answering the implicit questions introduced by words such as *when, where, how* and *why*. These questions do not quite cover evaluative adverbials such as *unfortunately* or *sadly*, but they do cover most other cases of adverbial meaning.

Though syntax is intended to be the study of form and structure, rather than meaning, as we have seen it can be difficult, and even undesirable, to divorce the two. We have already seen that adverbials have a range of forms, but their distribution is a little more unified and they are mostly optional in terms of the grammaticality of the clause in which they occur. As a result they have a potential for mobility in terms of position that the other clause elements lack. If we look again at the examples given above we can see that the adverbial elements can be omitted without any damage to the acceptability of the clause, although some meaning is inevitably lost.

The train pulled away from the station.

I won't be able to come to your wedding.

I shall pour you a cup of tea.

I practise for four hours.

There is also some flexibility in the possible positioning of the adverbial, as we can see from the following:

<u>Very slowly</u> the train pulled away from the station.

The train <u>very slowly</u> pulled away from the station.

The train pulled <u>very slowly</u> away from the station.

The train pulled away <u>very slowly</u> from the station.

I won't, <u>unfortunately</u>, be able to come to your wedding.

I won't be able, <u>unfortunately</u>, to come to your wedding.

I won't be able to come to your wedding, <u>unfortunately</u>.

I shall pour you a cup of tea <u>in a moment</u>.

I shall, <u>in a moment</u>, pour you a cup of tea.

I practise for four hours <u>every day of my life</u>.

I practise <u>every day of my life</u> for four hours.

Not all permutations are equally likely and some sound odder than others, but in principle at least the optional adverbial can move into positions between other clause elements, and sometimes also interrupt clause elements; for example by occurring between the auxiliary verb and the lexical verb in a predicator (underlined, including an adverbial):

She might, sadly, find things rather different.

What is missing from the account of adverbials so far is the fact that there are some clauses where the adverbial element is compulsory. There will be more examples of this phenomenon below, and obligatory adverbials have already been touched upon when discussing the verb word class. However it is important to note here that the flexibility and mobility of the optional adverbial does not apply equally to the obligatory kind. The reason why obligatory adverbials occur at all is that there are some lexical verbs whose meaning relates the subject of the predicator not to other individuals (such as objects) or to some quality or identification (such as complements), but to some kind of circumstance, such as time or space. The form of these obligatory adverbials is most commonly the prepositional phrase, usually relating to place, though it may sometimes refer to the timescale of a process, and on occasion it can be an adverb or a noun phrase:

The teacher put the books away/in the cupboard

The festival lasts for a week/all week.

The first of these examples shows the obligatory adverbial of place that follows the object of verbs such as *put*. This can be either in adverb form (*away*) or in the form of a prepositional phrase (*in the cupboard*). In the second example the adverbial tells us when the process took place, and takes the form of a prepositional phrase (*for a week*) or a noun phrase (*all week*). These adverbials are central to the meaning of the clause in a way that the optional ones are not, as can be seen when we omit them:

**The teacher put the books . . .*

**The festival lasts . . .*

These examples are clearly not grammatically complete, and yet there are some verbs, such as *come* and *go*, that can operate without their adverbial element of place, though it is usually implicit from the context in a way that is not true of optional adverbials:

The parcel came.

John went.

The hearer of these utterances is called upon to work out what place has been arrived at or left. It may be evident from the context:

I waited in all morning and finally the parcel came (to my house).

I started hoovering the house, and John went (left the house).

In the absence of textual clues we make assumptions about the regular meaning of such common verbs, but the important thing is that a place is clearly implied by the verbs *come* and *go*, in a way that the earlier (optional) adverbials were not implied by their verbs. To remind you of these examples, here they are again:

The train pulled away from the station <u>very slowly</u>.

<u>Unfortunately</u> I won't be able to come to your wedding.

<u>In a moment</u> I shall pour you a cup of tea.

<u>Every day of my life</u> I practise for four hours.

There is no hint in the obligatory part of these clauses of the manner of the train's leaving, the emotion felt at missing the wedding, the imminent pouring of the cup of tea or the regularity of the practice. Note, however, that there are also obligatory adverbials in some of these, and they cannot be deleted without the speaker making some assumptions about the knowledge she shares with the hearer.

**The train pulled <u>very slowly</u>.*

<u>Unfortunately</u> I won't be able to come.

The result of deleting the obligatory adverbial in the first example is to make the clause ungrammatical, unless the train is understood to be pulling something along. In the second case the loss of the obligatory adverbial means that the hearer needs to be already aware of the location implied by the verb *come*.

5.3 Form and function relationships

At this stage it will be useful to summarise some of the form–function relationships that have been introduced so far, as a checklist. Here the clause elements (functions) are listed with their possible forms (word, phrase and clause class):

- S: noun phrase; noun clause (more on this later); verb (see above).
- P: verb phrase.
- O: noun phrase; noun clause; verb.
- C: noun phrase; adjective phrase.
- A: adverbial phrase; noun phrase; prepositional phrase.

5.3.1 Simple clause structures

Having introduced all the lower-level units and structures we are now in a position to investigate the structure of clauses in English, drawing on the knowledge that has been built up in the earlier part of this chapter and the previous two chapters. In this section we shall consider only simple clauses, identified by having only one main verb phrase, though more complex clause and sentence structures will be introduced in later sections.

The simple clause in English is made up of the five clause elements discussed in the previous section. To recap on their names and principal forms:

- Subject (S): usually a noun phrase and near the beginning of the clause.The verb must agree (in person and number) with this element.
- Predicator (P): always a verb phrase and agreeing with the subject in person and number. Normally follows the subject fairly closely.
- Object (O): usually a noun phrase and following the predicator. Only follows transitive verbs.
- Complement (C): either a noun phrase or an adjective phrase. Only follows a limited group of intensive verbs, most notably *be*. Has the same referent as the subject (or the object if there is one).
- Adverbial (A): usually a prepositional phrase or an adverb phrase. Optional element that may occur in any position in the clause, and that, if omitted would not destroy the grammaticality of the clause. Some obligatory adverbials are more restricted in position (after the predicator).

All clauses in English are based on just seven basic clause structures (excluding optional adverbials):

• SP:	*Jane*	*lied.*		
• SPO:	*The three kings*	*forgot*	*their lines.*	
• SPC:	*The journey*	*was*	*a nightmare/horrendous.*	
• SPA:	*Mr Stevens*	*went*	*to London.*	
• SPOO:	*Philip*	*sent*	*me*	*a present.*
• SPOC:	*My mum*	*made*	*me*	*an artist/artistic.*
• SPOA:	*The conductor*	*placed*	*his baton*	*on the music stand.*

These basic structures underlie most of the utterances and sentences in English, though there is always the possibility of adding optional adverbials. Here are the above examples in the same order with additional adverbials (underlined) added in a number of positions:

Yesterday Jane lied to my father.

Unfortunately the three kings completely forgot their lines in the school play.

On the whole the journey was a nightmare/horrendous from start to finish.

In the end Mr Stevens obligingly went to London on my behalf.

Every birthday Philip sent me a present from Paris.

Happily my mum made me an artist/artistic.

At the end of the concert the conductor quietly placed his baton on the music stand.

Note how the adverbials have a range of forms, including adverb, noun phrase and prepositional phrase. In all cases, however, they add the same kind of information, giving some background and circumstances of the process being described.

It is important to practise recognising the structures of simple clauses. Below there are some more, with no additional adverbials, for you to consider. There is only one of each basic structure here, so you can use some elimination to help you. Note that some of the clause elements are deliberately long in order to try to catch you out. Once you have worked out the basic structures you may like to try adding some optional adverbials.

Various different friends gave me the same advice.

The three teachers in the staff room were smoking.

All of the people in the photo had come from the East.

The small dirty dog licked my hand.

Sadie Brown is very beautiful.

The wet weather made my car really muddy.

We sent the old clothes to the Oxfam shop.

The following clauses have additional adverbials, though the basic structure of each one is still one of the seven listed above.

As a rule we hide all our valuables in the washing machine.

Carefully the shop assistant unpacked the crystal vase from its box.

Eventually, with a terrible groan, the train started.

In an hour or two I shall be Mrs Barraclough.

Happily nobody was hurt in the crash.

Another good way to practice identifying clause structures is to synthesise your own clauses. In other words, instead of taking an existing clause and trying to work out its structure, you make up your own clauses to a particular pattern, using all you have learnt in this chapter so far. Here is one set of instructions that you might follow:

1 Choose one of the seven basic clause stuctures, for example SPO;
2 Choose a verb to be the predicator. If you are going to make an SPO structure your verb will have to be able to take an object. In other words it needs to be a transitive verb, such as *kiss*.
3 Decide on the form that the verb phrase will take (for example perfective in the past plus a main verb, such as *had kissed*).
4 Build yourself a couple of noun phrases using the structure described in Section 4.2.1. For example premodifier (determiner plus adjective), head (noun) and postmodifier (prepositional phrase or relative clause).
5 Now choose which will be the subject of your verb and which the object.
6 Finally, put them all together; for example *My elderly aunt from Dorset had kissed her illicit lover who turned up unexpectedly.*

You can have some fun with these synthesised sentences, particularly if you have someone else to play with. Make up noun phrases and swap them with your partner, and see whether they work with the verbs you have chosen, whether they result in something semantically odd but grammatical, such as *the hot potato ate my arm*, or whether they are completely ungrammatical, such as **Three purple snails died those woolly cardigans*, where the verb *die* (unlike *dye*) cannot be followed by an object.

The structures of the sentences introduced earlier in this section are as follows:

Various different friends (S) *gave* (P) *me* (O) *the same advice* (O).

The three teachers in the staff room (S) *were smoking* (P).

All of the people in the photo (S) *had come* (P) *from the East* (A).

The small dirty dog (S) *licked* (P) *my hand* (O).

Sadie Brown (S) *is* (P) *very beautiful* (C).

The wet weather (S) *made* (P) *my car* (O) *really muddy* (C).

We (S) *sent* (P) *the old clothes* (O) *to the Oxfam shop* (A).

As a rule, (A) *we* (S) *hide* (P) *all our valuables* (O) *in the washing machine* (A).

Carefully, (A) *the shop assistant* (S) *unpacked* (P) *the crystal vase* (O) *from its box* (A).

Eventually (A) *with a terrible groan,* (A) *the train* (S) *started* (P).

In an hour or two (A) *I* (S) *will be* (P) *Mrs Barraclough* (C).

Happily (A) *nobody* (S) *was hurt* (P) *in the crash* (A).

The basic clause structures each have characteristics that may be useful to students when they use syntactic analysis in their studies of English texts, whether literary or non-literary in origin.

5.3.2 Coordinated structures

Many sentences in English, of course, are more complicated than these simple clauses, and there are two processes that can produce further structural patterning. The simpler of the two is **coordination** and the more complex is subordination or embedding. Both these processes can operate at any level of structure, so it is important not to confuse the coordination of, for example, premodifying nouns in a noun phrase with the coordination of two whole clauses:

For dinner I had <u>*veal and ham*</u> *pie with peas.*

<u>*I had veal pie and Jane had the vegetarian lasagne.*</u>

The conjunction, *and*, in the first example is simply joining the two nouns, *veal* and *ham*, to make a single premodifier of the head noun, *pie*. In the second example the whole of the SPO clause, *I had veal pie* is added to the whole of the SPO clause, *Jane had the vegetarian lasagne*.

What is happening in the conjoining of any structures is very simple. Instead of a single member of a class taking on a function such as the head of a phrase or subject, or a premodifier, two such units are given equal status in having the same function and, depending on the conjunction, are added together (using *and*) or seen as opposites in terms of their desirability (using *but*) or mutually exclusive options (using *or*). The following are examples of the three conjunctions operating at the level of the word, and in the function of adjective phrase heads:

> *The woods are* *lovely and dark*.
>
> *The woods are* *lovely but dark*.
>
> *The woods are* *lovely or dark*.

This sentence is adapted from the poem by Robert Frost, 'Stopping by Woods on a Snowy Evening'. In it the narrator says *'the woods are lovely, dark and deep'*, which conjoins not two but three adjectives. I have simplified it for our purposes here, but it is worth noting that anything that can be done with two units can generally also be done with three or more.

Note the subtle differences in meaning in the examples. In the first case the two adjectives seem to complement each other; it is almost as though it is because the woods are *dark* that they are also *lovely* (see Simpson, 1993, ch. 5). In the second version there seems to be a difference of evaluation: although the woods are seen as both *lovely* and *dark*, these are good and bad qualities respectively. The final version presents us with alternatives. The woods cannot, in this particular version, be both *lovely* and *dark*.

Let us now consider some examples of phrasal coordination. All phrases can be joined by conjunctions, but here we shall look at the verb phrase as predicator, to see how it operates:

> *My children* *were running and jumping* *for sheer joy.*
>
> *The audience* *were crying but laughing* *at the same time.*
>
> *Athletes* *were* *training or resting* *according to their schedule.*

Although these are examples of phrasal coordination, in each case the second phrase has the auxiliary verb (*were*) missing through ellipsis, which is the deletion of entirely predictable elements of structure. As with the coordination of words, these examples provide mutually supportive notions (*running and jumping*), apparently contradictory but concurrent processes (*crying but laughing*), and mutually exclusive processes (*training or resting*) respectively. It is important to note that the role of a coordinated structure is exactly the same as it would be for a single item performing the same function (Table 5.2).

Thus coordination does not change the structure in any significant way, but simply adds some content to it. The coordination of clauses, however, is a slightly special case, as the clauses concerned do not enter into any higher structure, except as a main clause that is being coordinated with another main clause.

Table 5.2 Coordination within phrases

Subject	Predicator	Complement
The woods	are	lovely and dark
The woods	are	lovely
The woods	are	dark

The clauses that are being coordinated may have the same structure, as in the first two examples below.

> *Jenny painted the gate and I rubbed down the window frames.*
>
> *My father was a car salesman but my mother was a bus driver.*
>
> *Julia will make a cake or you can go to the baker's.*

Table 5.3 Coordinated clauses with matching structures

Subject	Predicator	Object
Jenny	painted	the gate
I	rubbed down	the window frames
Subject	**Predicator**	**Complement**
My father	was	a car salesman
My mother	was	a bus driver

There is, however, no requirement for the clauses to be identical in structure, and the third of the above examples has two clauses with different basic structures.

Table 5.4 Coordinated clauses with different structures

Subject	Predicator	Object
Julia	will make	a cake
Subject	**Predicator**	**Adverbial**
you	can go	to the baker's

5.3.3 Subordinate structures

The use of **subordination** in syntactic structure is another of the recursive features of human language, and one that allows us to make an infinitely large number of utterances out of a large, but finite, stock of units. Subordination is also known as **embedding** and is similar to **rank-shifting** in Firthian and Hallidayan linguistics (see Halliday, 1985).

What is meant by subordination is essentially that a higher-level unit is included in one of the lower-level units, meaning that there is a circularity to the description of the structure. As we have seen, this is the case with the repeated use of postmodifiers in the noun phrase, where the prepositional phrase, for example, may occur within a noun phrase but also contains a noun phrase (which may in turn contain a prepositional phrase containing a noun phrase, and so on).

The main forms of subordination are where phrases contain other phrases in this way, producing a continuous cycle of embedding, and where clauses are embedded either within phrases or as substitutes for phrases in clause elements. We shall consider each of these types of embedding in turn.

The most common type of phrasal embedding within phrases is the one already mentioned, where a noun phrase occurs within a prepositional phrase that is postmodifying a head noun:

The chair in the corner of the room in my house in Tuscany.

Here, *in Tuscany* is embedded in the noun phrase, *my house in Tuscany*, which is embedded in the phrase *the room in my house in Tuscany*, which in turn is embedded in the phrase beginning with *the corner*, and this whole phrase is embedded in the main noun phrase beginning with *the chair*.

This process can also occur when the prepositional phrase as a whole is functioning as an adverbial but contains a number of layers of embedding within it:

She took her dog <u>to the vet on Stainbeck Lane in Meanwood</u>.

Here the prepositional phrase beginning with the preposition *to* contains the noun phrase *the vet on Stainbeck Lane in Meanwood*, in which the head noun, *vet*, is postmodified by another prepositional phrase with another noun phrase within it: *on Stainbeck Lane in Meanwood*. This prepositional phrase in turn also has a prepositional phrase that postmodifies the head noun *Lane*: *in Meanwood*, in which the word *Meanwood* functions as a noun phrase at the lowest level.

The other significant way in which noun phrases can be embedded in other noun phrases is as a premodifier. The section on the structure of the noun phrase (4.2.1) introduced the notion of nouns functioning as modifiers to other nouns.

The garden furniture.

My patio lamps.

A new orange juicer.

Whilst such examples are very common, particularly in the world of consumer products, it is also possible for the premodifying noun position to be filled not just by a noun but by a noun phrase.

the sunken garden furniture.

my paved patio lamps.

a new blood orange juicer.

What is striking about these structures is that they are syntactically ambiguous, and it was only with great difficulty that I found adjectives that were clearly semantically related to the first of the two nouns and not the second. If you use fairly common general adjectives you will find that the resulting structures are equally likely to be interpreted in either fashion, with the adjective premodifying either the first or the head noun:

The white garden furniture (a white garden, or white furniture?)

My new patio lamps (a new patio or new lamps?)

A new cheap orange juicer (cheap oranges or cheap juicer?)

It is often world knowledge and experience that allows us to see these ambiguities and reject the sunken furniture, paved lamps and blood juicer that are syntactically possible interpretations of the earlier examples!

The other type of embedding is less complex than noun phrase embedding. Adjective phrases can be found within other phrases, replacing the single-word premodifiers in noun phrases but usually consisting only of an intensifying adverb and the head adjective. Because there is no possibility of phrases being embedded within adjective phrases, the embedded adjective phrases do not give rise to any possibility of recursion.

That very old dog.

An incredibly beautiful sculpture.

These examples are typical of the use of adjective phrases within noun phrases, and they do not cause any particular analytical problems.

Moving on to the subordination of clauses, there are two levels where subordinate clauses can be found. The first is at the level of the clause element, where the embedded clause takes the place of a complete clause element. The second is the embedding of clauses in the noun phrase as relative clauses. Because they have already been touched upon we shall deal with relative clauses first.

As we have seen elsewhere, the relative clause is one of the options for postmodifying of a noun phrase:

> *The bag <u>that I took to the festival</u>.*

Here we have a noun phrase with a determiner (*the*) premodifying the head noun, *bag*, and a relative clause (*that I took to the festival*) postmodifying it. Note that although it contains a clause, this noun phrase would not normally stand alone as a complete utterance as it does not form a main clause. However any structure can stand alone as an utterance if the missing information is clear or implicit from the context. In this case the noun phrase uttered alone might answer the question *Which bag are you taking*? It can be confusing to try to identify relative clauses and be sure that this is what they are. Two tricks of analysis are to look out for a relative pronoun (*that, which, who, where, when*) and to see whether the whole of the phrase, including the relative clause, can be replaced by a single pronoun, in this case *it*.

The relationship between the relative clause and the nouns they postmodify can vary according to the clause function played within the relative clause by the referent of the head noun. You can see from the example above that the referent of the noun, *bag*, is invoked again by the relative pronoun, *that*, as the object of the subordinate predicator. The resulting structure of the relative clause is therefore as follows:

> *that* (object) *I* (subject) *took* (predicator) *to the festival* (adverbial).

Relative clauses can focus on the referent of the preceding noun in different ways, as following examples show:

> *The resort <u>where the family spent their holidays</u>.*
>
> *The waiter <u>who served us</u>.*
>
> *The year <u>when I finally finished the book</u>.*
>
> *The present <u>which my cousin sent me</u>.*

In these examples the relative pronoun functions as adverbial (of place) subject, adverbial (of time) and direct object respectively. It is only the predicator and the complement functions that cannot be performed by a relative pronoun. The last two of the above examples demonstrate that the speaker has the option to omit the relative pronoun when it is followed by a subject of the subordinate predicator.

The year I finally finished the book.

The present my cousin sent me.

This omission is an entirely recoverable ellipsis; both speaker and hearer are able to fill it in if asked to do so. Thus, an analyst who wonders whether something is indeed a relative clause, even though no relative pronoun is included, may simply try putting the relative pronoun back in to test its status as a relative clause:

The year that I finally finished the book.

The present that my cousin sent me.

In semantic terms the relative clause can be either **restrictive** or **non-restrictive**. This can be illustrated by returning to a phrase we examined earlier, but punctuated in two different ways to illustrate first restrictive and then non-restrictive relative clauses.

The bag that I took to the festival has gone missing.

The bag, that I took to the festival, has gone missing.

The first version restricts the number of bags that could be referred to by the relative clause – it is the one that was taken to the festival that is being referred to. The second version uses the relative clause as background information, and somehow assumes that the hearer is already aware of the bag. It is not using the relative clause in quite the same way to identify the referent.

We shall now turn to the types of subordinate clause that, unlike the relative clause, function as a whole clause element in the higher-level structure. There are two important classes of subordinate clause and we shall investigate each in turn. These are the clauses that function in the place of noun phrases and are therefore known as noun clauses, and those which function as adverbials and are, predictably, known as adverb clauses.

The **noun clause** can function as a subject, an object or a complement in a higher-level clause structure:

Singing with the band was Mary's greatest pleasure.

They stopped walking the dog along the canal.

Her highest ambition was to perform at the Edinburgh festival.

These examples have subordinate clauses with non-finite verb phrases (*singing, walking, to perform*) in predicator position, and no specified subject because the notional subject of the non-finite verb phrase is usually presumed to be the same as the subject of the higher-level clause. The structure of the higher clause in each case is shown in Table 5.5.

Table 5.5 Structure of sentences containing subordinate clauses

Subject (noun clause)	Predicator	Complement
Singing with the band	was	Mary's greatest pleasure
Subject	**Predicator**	**Object (noun clause)**
They	stopped	walking the dog along the canal
Subject	**Predicator**	**Complement**
Stuart's highest ambition	was	to perform at the Edinburgh festival

The structure of the lower, embedded, clauses is drawn from the same range of options as main clauses, so we can expect to find the same variations on the seven basic clause structures – possibly with additional adverbials – that are found in main clauses. The difference with subordinate clauses is that the subject can be omitted if it is entirely predictable, as in these cases, and the predicator can be a verb phrase in non-finite form. Table 5.6 shows the structures of the subordinate clauses from the set of examples above.

Table 5.6 Structure of subordinate clauses

Subject (ellipted)	Predicator	Object	Adverbial
(Mary)	singing		with the band
(they)	Walking	the dog	along the canal
(Stuart)	to perform		at the Edinburgh festival

Two of these examples have verb phrases with progressive (*-ing*) forms, and the last one is in the infinitive form. It is also possible for noun clauses to contain a fuller structure that is similar to that of main clauses, with the subject included and a finite verb phrase agreeing with the subject in number and person where relevant. These noun clauses are usually introduced by a subordinator, often the all-purpose subordinator *that*:

That the poodle had won first prize at Cruft's amazed everyone.

The audience said that the band played an encore.

The decision was that we should go in one car.

These noun clauses are functioning as subject, object and complement respectively. Note that the subordinator, *that*, can be omitted in objects and complements:

The audience said the band played an encore.

The decision was we should go in one car.

Like the relative pronoun, this ellipsis is entirely recoverable and can be filled in by a hearer or analyst. The structure of the main clauses is shown in Table 5.7. The internal structure of the subordinate clauses is just as straightforward (Table 5.8).

Table 5.7 Structure of sentences containing noun clauses

Subject (noun clause)	**Predicator**	**Object**
That the poodle had won first prize at Cruft's	amazed	everyone.
Subject	**Predicator**	**Object (noun clause)**
The audience	said	that the band played an encore
Subject	**Predicator**	**Complement (noun clause)**
The decision	was	that we should go in one car.

The other type of subordinate clause is the **adverb clause**. As its name suggests it has an adverbial function, and like other adverbials it is often quite mobile as well as being optional. Here are two examples:

Table 5.8 Structure of noun clauses

Subject	Predicator	Object	Adverbial
the poodle	had won	first prize	at Cruft's
the band	played	an encore	
we	should go		in one car

After receiving the Nobel prize for literature, he never wrote another book.

Although the weather is hot now, you should take plenty of warm clothes.

Adverb clauses are usually quite easy to spot as they are often separated from the rest of the higher-level clause by a comma and are always introduced by a subordinator; in the above cases these are *after* and *although*. Note that you can omit the clause entirely or move it to the end of the higher clause without making the utterance ungrammatical:

He never wrote another book.

He never wrote another book after receiving the Nobel prize for literature.

You should take plenty of warm clothes.

You should take plenty of warm clothes, although the weather is hot now.

Like noun clauses, adverb clauses may either have a non-finite verb phrase as their predicator (for example *After receiving the Nobel prize for literature*) or it may be a finite verb phrase (for example *Although the weather is hot now*). They also have the usual range of possible clause structures. The ones featured here have the structures shown in Table 5.9.

Like Noun clauses, Adverb clauses with finite verb phrases may also have an elided subject, where the referent is the same as that of the subject in the main clause. This is the case in the first of the above examples.

Table 5.9 Structure of adverb clauses

Subject	Predicator	Object	
(He)	receiving	the Nobel prize for literature	
Subject	**Predicator**	**Complement**	**Adverbial**
the weather	is	hot	now

5.4 Information structure

The normal clause in English is structured in such a way that the new information tends to occur towards the end of the clause. This tendency can vary, as we shall see, but before we look at unusual examples we shall first examine the neutral information structure of English clauses.

If you study the way in which sentences build up into longer texts, you will realise that many sentences start with a subject that has already been encountered earlier in the text:

> *By this time we were getting close to the man and we saw him wave and signal to someone else that we couldn't see in the next field. We all dared Amy to ask him what he was doing and as usual she took up the challenge. 'But you've got to walk on. Don't stand around staring or I'll go red', she said. 'Hannah can stay with me though.'*

As we can see in this paragraph, the subject of the first sentence is *we* and the identity of the referents has presumably already been explained. *The man* also seems to be already known about as he is introduced with the definite article. In texts the subject often links backward to the introduction of the referent in an earlier sentence. This happens here in the second sentence, where *he* refers back to *the man*, and *she* refers to *Amy*. The subject clause element is therefore often quite low in information content whilst the information content of the element following the predicator, whether it is an object, a complement or an adverbial, is usually much greater.

This neutral structure of information in English clauses is reflected in the normal utterance stress that is allocated when speaking. As we saw in Section 2.4.1 the main utterance stress in a clause, assuming there is only one, will normally be on the final clause element, unless contrastive stress is used.

5.4.1 Cleft sentences/fronting

As well as contrastive stress there are other, more structurally based, ways of altering the information focus of clauses. Some of them are particularly typical of the written language and others are more common in speech, although these categories are not watertight.

Because the order of clauses in English is fairly fixed it is hard to focus on subject referents since they normally come early in the clause, and it is also difficult to pinpoint other clause elements when they are not the final element in the clause. There are at least two methods of picking out one clause element and placing it in a focal position, thereby downgrading the importance, in information terms, of the remainder of the clause.

One of these methods is known as **fronting**, and as its name implies it simply requires the focal clause element to be put at the beginning of the clause. In English there are two common kinds of fronting, which is also known as **inversion**: the first is when the subject and predicator elements are put in reverse order, and in the second the subject and first auxiliary elements are reversed. The following sentences illustrate these two inversions:

Here's the hotel. (APS).

Very cautious is his nature. (CPS).

Hardly had I arrived (before . . .) (A auxiliary, S lex).

Many times did I consider (. . .) (A auxiliary, S lex).

Note that the inversion of subject and predicator occurs mainly in SPA and SPC clauses and tends to be in fixed phrases, or literary style. It is also limited by some speakers to simple present or past verb forms with no auxiliaries, as the second of the sentences below illustrates:

There she stood.

?There she was standing.

The inversion of first auxiliary and subject leads to the situation in the third and fourth of the earlier sentences, where the verb phrase predicator is effectively 'interrupted' by the subject.

The other method of focusing on the information in a clause element is to create what is known as a **cleft sentence**. This involves using a fairly information-light frame, such as *It was . . . that . . .*, and then slotting the required clause element into the focal point after the verb. The remainder of the basic clause ends up in a relative clause (beginning with *that*) and its importance is accordingly lessened.

If we take a clause with every possible clause element in it we can try putting each of the elements into the focal position in turn:

The British electorate voted Tony Blair prime minister in 1997.

This sentence has all five clause elements, as follows:

The British electorate (subject) *voted* (predicator) *Tony Blair* (object) *prime minister* (complement) *in 1997* (adverbial).

If we take each element in turn, we find that with the exception of the predicator we can put any of them into the focal position in the cleft sentence frame:

It was the British electorate that elected Tony Blair prime minister in 1997.

It was Tony Blair that the British electorate voted prime minister in 1997.

It was prime minister that the British electorate voted Tony Blair in 1997.

It was in 1997 that the British electorate voted Tony Blair prime minister.

In texts you encounter in daily life you will find that cleft sentences are surprisingly common, particularly in news reports and political texts.

5.4.2 Transformations

Although the model of grammar presented here is not extensively based on transformational-generative grammar, some insights of this branch of linguistics are so useful that it is hard to imagine describing English without them. The most useful for this level of study is the idea of the **transformation**, which is a patterned relationship between sets of sentences that can be explained by a simple rule.

The example we shall explore here is **passive transformation**, though a similar explanation could also be applied to the cleft sentences and fronting described in the previous section.

The theory of transformation, simply expressed, suggests that since there is a regular pattern of changes between, for example, active and passive pairs of sentences we might hypothesise that the active sentence is more basic, and by the use of a single rule, rather than a rule for each verb, we could capture this regularity. Without using the sometimes complex notation of transformational grammar, the rule can be summarised as follows:

NP1 + VP + NP2 → NP2 + VP by NP1

Here notation NP denotes noun phrase and VP denotes verb phrase, and the numbers identify the noun phrases, which change order from active to passive, as we can see from the following:

The dog ate my dinner. → My dinner was eaten by the dog.

The painter decorated my bedroom. → My bedroom was decorated by the painter.

The film scared my sister. → My sister was scared by the film.

The arrow in this notation denotes 'becomes' or 'transforms into'. These pairs of sentences, then, illustrate a much more general rule of English: almost all active sentences that have transitive verbs as their predicator and therefore also have objects can undergo passive transformation. The meaning change inherent in this structural alteration is also regular, with the emphasis in the passive sentences being on the suffering of the action, to the extent that the actor or the initiator of the action (the subject of the active sentence) can be dropped altogether:

My dinner was eaten.

My bedroom was decorated.

My sister was scared.

Transformations are one way of explaining a particular feature of human language: the ability to construct an infinite number of sentences or utterances. If all active–passive pairs of sentences, as well as other sets of structures, can be reduced by half by the introduction of a single rule, this makes the grammar of the language more manageable.

5.5 Further reading

There are many books on syntax in general and English syntax in particular. Some of these are specifically for learners and are aimed at improving the English of students whose first language is not English. The books recommended here are aimed instead at students of English language as an academic subject, who can of course be both native and non-native speakers.

For students who wish to reinforce their knowledge without necessarily going into more detail it is worth reading general language textbooks such as Kuiper and Scott Allan (2004) and Ballard (2001), or simple grammars such as Collins (1998). The volume by Jeffries (1998) is complementary to these works as it is concerned with the meaning of structures, rather than introducing the structures themselves. A step further in terms of detail and complexity is provided by Brown and Miller (1991) and Burton-Roberts (1997). Huddleston (1988) offers a clear introduction to a similar syntactic treatment to the one found here, and the volume by Quirk *et al.* (1985) is a comprehensive grammar of English that has a great deal of detail but little discussion of theory.

General linguistics handbooks such as that by O'Grady *et al.* (1996) will take the reader into grammatical theory a little more, particularly generative theory, and are not limited to the description of English. For students who wish to follow the development of transformational-generative grammar, Chomsky's seminal works (1957, 1965) are the place to start. There are a great many commentaries on these and later works as well as introductions to transformational grammar, such as Radford (1988) and Horrocks (1987). Recent developments from Chomsky's work include government and binding theory, which is introduced in Cowper (1992). Bloor and Bloor (1995) is the most accessible book available on the detail of functional grammar, though Halliday (1985) is the source of much of this work.

As with the previous two chapters, the Internet Grammar website is worth using for practice and to obtain alternative explanations of much of the material in this chapter. It can be found at www.ucl.ac.uk/internet-grammar/home.htm.

CHAPTER

6 Semantics

6.1 Introduction: lexical meaning

As we saw in the Introduction to this volume, the model used here to describe language has different layers of structure and its semantic component operates at a number of these levels. We have touched upon the way that phonology contributes to meaning, both by allowing individual sounds (phonemes) to change meaning (tested by minimal pairs) and in the use of stress and intonation at a suprasegmental level. Meaning is also contributed by morphemes, as we saw in Chapter 4, as these not only have lexical meaning themselves but may also contribute grammatical modifications to the main lexical items, through inflection and derivation. Meaning is also contributed by the particular combinations of words and morphemes that make up the syntax of the language, but because of the complexity of structural descriptions there was little chance in the syntax chapter to go beyond some of the more basic ways in which syntax delivers meaning. The study of **semantics** in linguistics has historically been targeted at the two components of language: the **lexis** (vocabulary) and the grammar. In this chapter we shall limit our discussion to the **lexical semantics** of English, leaving aside the much more complex problems of what happens to meaning when words are combined, and still further when they occur in context to other volumes.

It is an overly simplistic, but nevertheless useful, approach to take the view that words have meaning, particularly referential meaning, and that they are combined by syntax into structures that relate their meanings in certain ways. Thus, a noun that is chosen to be the head of the subject in a clause is often likely to perform the action of the predicator, and to affect the referent of the object in some way, as we can see in a sentence such as *Joe opened the letter.* Readers will immediately see that this decoding of meaning from units and their combinations is not always straightforward. Firstly, there are features of meaning that derive not from the words and structures but from their placing in a given context. This **pragmatic meaning** is beyond the scope of this volume, though it will be mentioned again in the final chapter. Secondly, within a text there may be many variations in the meanings that result from the simple combining of words in structures. To take the same SPO structure of *Joe opened the letter*, we can see that the actual relationship of meaning between the subject and object in the following sentences differs widely:

Joe opened the letter.

The baker made a cake.

Mr Simpson wanted a new car.

I believe the earth is flat.

Those dinosaurs are chasing my car.

Here the object can be specific and directly affected by the action of the predicator, as in *Joe opened the letter*, or brought into existence by the predicator, as in *The baker made a cake*. The next sentence, *Mr Simpson wanted a new car*, has a non-specific object that is not affected by the predicator; no particular car is the referent and there is no change in the pool of possible referents (that is, all available cars) as a result of Mr Simpson wanting one of them. The subsequent sentence, *I believe* <u>*the earth is flat*</u>, has a clause (underlined) as its object. In this case there are some issues of meaning that relate to the truth values (or otherwise) of utterances. This sentence may or may not be true, according to the belief of the speaker, but the subordinate clause would be considered to be false by most contemporary speakers. Interestingly, language is not constrained to being true, but can be used to propose both falsehoods of this kind and also fantastic and unlikely scenarios, such as the final utterance in our list: *Those dinosaurs are chasing my car*. This sentence is similar to the first one in terms of the relationship between subject and object (the object is clearly affected by the predicator), though the scenario conjured up is obviously not a real one.

Unfortunately we do not have room to explore all the different aspects of meaning that have been raised by the examples above, though some of them will be revisited later. For now we have to limit ourselves to the lexical semantic element of the language; that is that part of the language that is relatively stable and where the most common meanings of words can be described in a systematic and insightful manner.

Up to this point we have used the term 'word' as though it were transparent in its meaning. Although speakers of the language may think that this is so, it takes only a few moments' thought to realise that there are a number of ways in which we use the word 'word'. You might consider how many words the following passage has:

> *Saffron wanted to be a dancer. She had danced since she was little, and everyone said she should dance on the stage. One day she was dancing in a little room at the back of the church hall, where she waited for her dancing class with her mum. Her mum was talking to the other mums while they waited.*

Deciding whether to count each occurrence of a single word (*she, the, was*) separately is one decision; another is whether to count *dance, dancing* and *danced* as separate words, let alone *dancer* and *dancing* when used as an adjective (*her dancing class*). Of course there may be occasions when linguists want to count each and every occurrence of a word, or when they wish to discuss a word in general, such as the verb *dance*, without necessarily worrying about which inflectional form it should take. The latter is particularly useful in semantics, where the meaning (denotation) of a word will not change radically when its ending is changed in a regular (inflectional) way. The term **'lexeme'** is normally used to refer to such a collection of forms that are grouped together under the same denotation. This term is used frequently in the remainder of this chapter.

6.2 Multiple meaning

We shall begin the exploration of lexical meaning by looking at two rather different kinds of multiple meaning. What is meant by multiple meaning is that a single lexical form may have such different uses that we are compelled to recognise them as being separate in some significant way. This may be such a significant difference in meaning that we conclude that they are in fact different lexemes. This relationship, whereby two completely different words happen to have the same form, is known as **homonymy**. The other, more common, differences in meaning are less extreme than homonymy and normally concern differences where the user can still see that the words are related. This relationship between what are known as **senses** of the same lexeme is called **polysemy**.

As we shall see below, polysemy is both more common and more complex than homonymy, which is mostly an accident of historical development. Polysemy, on the other hand, is the basis of much of the rest of lexical semantics, since it is the polysemous sense that is the unit of lexical semantics and enters into relationships with other **word senses**.

6.2.1 Homonymy

There is a limited number of full homonyms in English. The one most often quoted in text books and definitions is *bank*, which has two distinct sets of meanings: those relating to riversides, and those relating to the storage and retrieval of money. I say 'sets of meanings' because for each homonym there is a range of polysemous senses. You will usually find that dictionaries list what they consider to be homonyms as separate entries, and polysemous senses as subentries. After reading this section it might be interesting for you to look up some dictionary entries and see whether you agree with their classification of homonyms and polysemous items.

Other homonyms in English include *sole* – a fish versus 'the only' – and *cleave*, which is a fascinating pair of homonyms as the two meanings are diametrically opposed to each other. One of them means 'to stick fast to something', as in *I cleave to God* (the uses of this sense are all quite dated now, and often Biblical in style). The other means 'to divide in two, usually violently', and is very rarely used in the verb form nowadays though a number of derived forms remain in use, such as *cleft* (*cleft stick, cleft palate*) and *cleaver* (butcher's knife).

Homonyms that are frequently quoted, then, tend to be few in number and sometimes rather obscure. It may be that this is not really representative of how the users of language make the classifications, and we shall see shortly that there are other, more everyday, candidates for homonym status. It is tempting to suggest that homonyms should be defined diachronically (that is, historically) by whether they share a common **etymology** (the history of their derivation). This is of course interesting, but in a sense is irrelevant to ordinary users of language, who will simply use two apparently identical words in different ways without being conscious of whether or not they are distantly related. This more synchronic approach, which is concerned with the state of language at any one moment in history, will be taken here.

The main test of whether two meanings of the same form are homonyms is whether they share any semantic features, and how central these shared features are to the meaning. I have considered the meanings of regular lexical forms such as *ring*, *wave* and *tip* with many groups of students, and after some reflection and experimentation with these words in various contexts the students have almost always concluded that *ring* and *tip* are homonyms, each with their own set of polysemous senses, but that *wave* is a single lexeme, albeit with a range of fairly diverse uses. The following are the kinds of analysis that have typically resulted from asking a group of English speakers to consider these words:

- *Tip*, 1a: the end of something long and thin, or tapering, such as a pen, a baton or an iceberg.
- *Tip*, 1b: a small piece of advice.
- *Tip*, 1c: a recommendation about placing a bet.
- *Tip*, 1d: a small monetary reward for a service rendered.

- *Tip*, 2a: to upend or turn over.
- *Tip*, 2b: a place where rubbish is deposited in a disorderly fashion.
- *Tip*, 2c: a place that looks like a rubbish tip (metaphorical).

- *Ring*, 1a: to make a resonant sound, as when striking metal or glass.
- *Ring*, 1b: the resonant sound as of metal or glass being struck.
- *Ring*, 1c: an electronically produced sound similar to 1b.
- *Ring*, 1d: to phone.

- *Ring*, 2a: a circular mark or item.
- *Ring*, 2b: a circular piece of jewellery.
- *Ring*, 2c: to encircle or surround.
- *Ring*, 2d: to draw a circle around.
- *Ring*, 2e: to place a metal circle around a wild bird's leg for the purposes of monitoring behavioural patterns.

- *Wave*, a: to move backwards and forwards.
- *Wave*, b: to move the hand backwards and forwards in greeting or farewell.
- *Wave*, c: a surge or swell in a body of liquid, usually the sea.
- *Wave*, d: having an undulating shape (hair, wheat fields, patterns).
- *Wave*, e: a passing phase of the body or the emotions (a wave of nausea/horror).

The students concerned did not carry out a major research project to come to these conclusions, but the compilers of most recent dictionaries, such as the *Collins Cobuild Learners' Dictionary* (1996), have used enormous computerised databases of language to find out the range of uses of word forms and inform their decisions on homonym classifications and polysemous sense identities. The above definitions also vary a little from what one might find in a dictionary that is usually concerned with the word class of the different meanings as well. What is quite interesting is that there is some clarity in the minds of these native speakers about whether or not the various uses of these words are related to each other. The result is two separate meaning groups for *tip* and *ring*, but only one for *wave*, where the metaphorical connections between the uses is clearer perhaps. Of course one can always find some way to link even the more diverse meanings; such is the capacity of the human mind for pattern-finding. Thus one might argue that the meaning of *Tip* 2a is extended from *Tip* 1a because when you tip over a rubbish bin, for example, you are focusing on the end of something, though obviously it is not a narrow or tapering kind of tip. Some students also made the case quite forcefully for the sound of ringing to be circular, perhaps because of the shape of the traditional bell. However the consensus was always as given above.

If you look homonyms up on the internet you will find a number of fascinating websites where people have collected numerous examples of what they call homonyms. However most of them are actually **homophones**, and some of the web sites acknowledge this misnaming, though they persist with it. Homophones are much easier to identify than homonyms as they are spelt differently, despite sounding the same. Their great attraction is their potential for punning, especially as they do not seem to be stored in our memories as a pair, and we can therefore be quite surprised that some words apparently sound the same (though it does sometimes depend on your accent). Here are some examples:

- *Bear*: a large wild mammal.
- *Bare*: wearing no clothes or without adornment.

- *Elicit*: to find out information from someone.
- *Illicit*: illegal or against a moral code.

- *Allowed*: permitted.
- *Aloud*: in an audible voice.

- *Paste*: a thick liquid or soft solid.
- *Paced*: walked up and down.

- *Hostel*: a place for people to stay.
- *Hostile*: aggressive.

All of the above work for both British and American accents of English (and probably others too), with the exception of *hostel* and *hostile*, which in British English are normally pronounced /hɒstəl/ and /hɒstaɪl/ respectively, while in many American accents they are both pronounced as /hɒstəl/. There is little further to say about homophones, but they do give us an insight into the nature of homonyms, which are similarly accidental in nature and should therefore be equally treated as incidental to the regular patterning of the language, in just the same way as we feel inclined to with homophones.

There is one further logical category that we have not yet dealt with:

homographs. These are words that have a single spelling but very different uses or meanings. Just like homonyms and homophones, in a sense these are not central to the structure of the language, and are accidental in many cases, but they nevertheless form part of our consciousness about language, and can be used in jokes and visual punning. The following examples:

- *Invalid* /ɪnvəlɪd/: someone who has a disability.
- *Invalid* /ɪnvælɪd/: not valid or acceptable.

- *Moped* /məʊpɛd/: a small motorbike.
- *Moped* /məʊpd/: sulked.

- *Row* /rəʊ/: a line of similar items.
- *Row* /raʊ/: an argument.

- *sewer* /suːwə/: underground pipes to carry away waste water and effluent.
- *sewer* /səʊwə/: someone who sews.

If these examples have any value in our description of the English language, apart from being oddities, it is to use our own sense of them as a basis for comparison with our sense of the related meanings we shall encounter in the next section, which examines polysemy. The very fact that we are sometimes surprised by the similarity of these items, and perhaps somewhat amused by them too, demonstrates that their similarity is somehow incidental to the language, rather than being an essential part of it.

6.2.2 Polysemy

As noted in the previous section, polysemy is a set of related senses of a single lexeme, in contrast with the unrelated meanings of homonyms, homophones and homographs. In the present section we shall explore what these related senses are, and how they underpin many of the semantic relationships considered in the remainder of this chapter.

Let us return to some of the examples examined in the previous section. First, it is important to note that the senses that are listed for the two homonyms of *tip* are related to the other senses of the same lexeme in a variety of ways. In the case of *tip* 1, there appears to be a general meaning (1a) and then a number of meanings that are metaphorically related to this general meaning, in that they all take the semantic feature of size (small, end of something) and use it to refer to small things that people give one another, in specific settings such as racecourses (1c), restaurants (1d) or more general advice (1b).

- *Tip,* 1a: the end of something long and thin, or tapering, such as a pen, a baton or an iceberg.
- *Tip,* 1b: a small piece of advice.
- *Tip,* 1c: a recommendation about placing a bet.
- *Tip,* 1d: a small monetary reward for a service rendered.

Though all the examples relating to *Tip* 1 are nouns, there are, of course, also verbal forms of *Tip* 1 b–d. Polysemous senses of a lexeme may vary in word class without altering the semantic relationship between the senses, though the grammatical features of a word sense will have some impact on their usage. If we look at *Tip* 2, there appears to be a general verbal meaning (2a) that is extended to a specific place where the activity of tipping is likely to happen (2b) and then, by metaphorical extension, it is also extended to places that remind the speaker of rubbish tips, such as teenage children's bedrooms and so on:

- *Tip,* 2a: to upend or turn over.
- *Tip,* 2b: a place where rubbish is deposited in a disorderly fashion.
- *Tip,* 2c: a place that looks like a rubbish tip (metaphorical).

As well as having a range of possible grammatical forms, and different kinds of relationship (derived, metaphorical etc.), word senses often have a different set of sense relations. It is relatively simple to demonstrate the different sets of words that some of the senses of the two *ring* homonyms relate to.

- *Ring,* 1a: ding, dong, bang and so on.
- *Ring,* 1d: phone, call and so on.

- *Ring,* 2a: square, rectangle, box and so on.
- *Ring,* 2b: necklace, bangle, choker and so on.

These sets of words are not **synonyms**, but words with related meanings and similar semantic features, known collectively as 'semantic fields'. They demonstrate quite clearly that the senses of a polysemous word, while related in some way, nevertheless operate in a different semantic context from each other.

6.3 Lexical description

Lexical semantics as a subdiscipline arose from the structuralist theory of language, which considers that the vital aspects of human language are its arbitrariness and its systematicness. The argument is that if words only mean something by convention, rather than having any intrinsic reason for their shape or sound, then by extension the whole vocabulary of a language is a system of meaning relations, and an important part of the meaning of an individual word sense is its relationship with other word senses.

This argument extends the idea of mutual definition, which has been put forward in relation to grammatical word classes and applies it to the whole category. According to this idea, the addition or subtraction of a member of any lexical word class potentially affects other members of that class. A term describing a new kind of computer (for example *laptop, palmtop, desktop*) will inevitably, it is argued, have an effect on the existing words in that field. Back in the days when computers were the size of rooms the word *computer* meant just that – a huge set of processors and other accessories. In the age of the personal computer the term has been narrowed in most usage to refer to the desktop computer that many of us have in our homes and offices. The arrival of *laptops* and *palmtops* produced the need for the new term *desktop*, because their portability marked them out as different from the standard personal computer. What is striking is that the word *desktop* meant nothing before the advent of smaller computers, and because it was not needed it did not exist.

The meanings of words, then, are seen in this view as being made up of lots of contrasts; that is, distinctions of meaning between the word under consideration and those like it. These contrasts and any similarities can be captured by the use of semantic feature analysis, and sets of words with overlapping and similar meaning are often known as **semantic fields**. We shall investigate these two approaches to lexical description in the following sections.

6.3.1 Semantic features

The proposal that word meanings can be seen as made up of **semantic features** is one of the outcomes of thinking that language is systematic. If that is the case, then one might expect lexical meaning to be made up of repeated features, that appear in different combinations in different words but can still be recognised as recurrent building blocks of meaning. This view of lexical semantics also corresponds to two other impulses in the development of linguistic theory: the search for universals, and the creativity of human language.

The search for universals of human language in the twentieth century took linguists from all subdisciplines into more and more abstract searches for some kind of underlying pattern in the phonology, grammar and semantics of human language as a whole. This was not hugely successful, because there are some culturally specific meanings that a language conveys that would be unlikely to occur more widely. However, the use that anthropologists made of principles such as semantic features demonstrated that there was indeed some mileage in trying to break down lexical meaning into its component parts, so that they could work out how different words related to each other in languages of tribal groups such as native Americans which had not so far been described in grammars and dictionaries.

The classic example, drawn from the experience of these twentieth-century anthropologists, is the kinship vocabulary of languages, which can be described on the basis of a very small number of semantic features, such as +/– MALE, +/– GENERATION, +/– BLOOD RELATIVE and so on. With a restricted area of the vocabulary such as kinship terms, the semantic features required were relatively few and could demonstrate unusual terms (to English ears), such as those meaning 'aunt on my father's side' or 'male relative of the same generation as the speaker'.

The early promise of universal semantic features was inevitably left unfulfilled. Though some of the more general levels of vocabulary can be compared and contrasted in this way, the more subtle and detailed vocabulary of any human language requires similarly subtle semantic features to distinguish between the lexemes. To take just one example, it may only be English that distinguishes between the different ways of talking that are captured by the words *burble* and *mumble*. Nevertheless we need a semantic feature or two to define the similarities and differences between them. They both involve verbal behaviour, and both result in some kind of difficulty of understanding for the hearer. In the case of *burble* it can be suggested that, the difficulty arises from the confused syntax and lack of clarity in the text structure. In the case of *mumble* it is a phonological difficulty, caused by careless pronunciation or low volume.

Whilst we may find similarities in vocabulary in different langages at the level of *walk* and *run* or *talk* and *listen*, the real detail of any individual lexical structure requires a lot of language-specific features of meaning. This does not invalidate the usefulness of semantic features as an economic and organised way of describing word meanings, but it does call into question their universality.

Let us consider one area of English vocabulary in order to see the kinds of semantic feature that are needed to describe a set of lexical items that share some of their features. The verb *laugh* can be characterised using the following semantic features:

- [HUMAN COMMUNICATION]
- [VOCAL/AUDIBLE]
- [NON-LINGUISTIC]
- [SHOWING PLEASURE OR AMUSEMENT]

There are a number of other verbs that share these features but are more specific in describing the kind of laughter. For example *giggle* and *titter* both seem to indicate laughter that is [HIGH-PITCHED] and possibly also [REPETITIVE], whilst *guffaw* and *howl* indicate a [SINGLE] and [LOW-PITCHED] laugh and a [LOUD] laugh respectively.

6.3.2 Semantic fields

We have already touched upon the concept of semantic fields as areas of lexis describing aspects of the world by the means of word senses with related meanings. These fields of vocabulary can be defined very broadly, as in fields such as 'animals' or 'movement', or they can be defined very narrowly, as in fields such as 'inadequate ways of walking' (*limp, hobble* and so on) or 'loud verbal communication' (*shout, yell* and so on).

Semantic fields are sometimes described as though they were a mosaic of words mapping out the whole of the semantic picture of a language, with different languages inevitably mapping out slightly different pictures. This analogy works quite well in some ways. It highlights the fact that semantic space is continuous, whereas words are discrete and a language must therefore make arbitrary decisions as to where the boundaries are between meanings. It also gives a visual analogy for the idea that languages tend to 'cut up' the perceived world into different sizes and shapes, according to the social reality of the community in which the language is spoken.

The point at which the mosaic metaphor begins to break down is when we realise that language would have some strange features if it really were a mosaic. Firstly there would be some gaps, so it could be like a Roman mosaic, with bits that used to be there but are now missing (that is, words that have fallen out of use), or it could be like an unfinished mosaic (that is, concepts that are possible in a particular language but are not named). The latter idea is quite strange in a way. It may only be because of contact between different human societies, and the march of progress in our own, that new ideas take root and thus need to be named. But until these ideas exist there may be no semantic space for them in our mosaic. In other words a new piece of floor to be covered with tesserae will suddenly appear and push the rest of the mosaic into a new pattern!

Perhaps we have been using the mosaic analogy for long enough now, although the final point that needs to be made about semantic fields will push it still further. It seems that one of the problems with a very 'neat' conception of the coverage of semantic space by words is that there is much more redundancy or overlap than this analogy would imply. English in particular has many layers of words, some more specific than others, and some almost synonymous but with subtly different connotations, and among these layers of vocabulary the same semantic space is covered again and again.

In fact, if we think of word meaning as made up of semantic features it becomes clear that there is repeated coverage of the same semantic feature in many words. The concept of human movement by use of the legs might be best captured in general by the verb *walk*, but in a few moments most English speakers could think of many more words that indicate walking. They may be more specific about the manner of walking, as the examples below demonstrate, but they all have a number of semantic features in common, which can be summarised as [MOVE], [ANIMATE], [HUMAN], [USING LEGS].

[WITH DIFFICULTY]: *trudge, tramp, limp, hobble, stagger*
[WITH EVEN STEPS]: *march, pace, stride, goosestep*

There are many other groups of words that share their core semantic features with these words but have different specificities, and each area of the semantic map has similar layers of vocabulary, ranging from the very general to the very specific. The most specific of all are words that occur in particular contexts (for example *goosestep*), or 'registers' associated with an occupation or social context.

Semantic fields, then, are groupings of words that share some of their semantic features, usually the core ones. They may operate at a general level of the vocabulary, so that the field of movement includes *walk, run, swim* and *fly*, or they may be seen to operate at increasingly specific levels, such as the walking verbs listed above, or swimming words such as *crawl, butterfly, breaststroke* and *backstroke*. For the purposes of semantics, the word class to which members of semantic fields belong is less important than their semantic features, though we often find ourselves describing a group of nouns or a group of verbs together.

To date there has been no systematic and comprehensive attempt to describe the words of English in their respective semantic fields, though there are many publications that use the idea of the semantic field as their organising principle. The most famous of these, of course, is *Roget's Thesaurus*, but this merely lists words with similar meanings and predates the theory of semantic fields. Others (for example McArthur, 1981, and Summers, 1993) try to combine the ordering principle of a thesaurus with the definitions of a dictionary, particularly for the benefit of learners of English. A quick comparison of some of these publications will demonstrate the difficulty of coming to a single description of this kind.

The reason why such a task is difficult can be found in the distinction between langue and parole, which has been the foundation of much of the linguistic description of the last century (see 7.7.1). In theory there is a fixed and stable system, the **langue**, and a more messy reality of usage, the **parole**.

In practice there is an evolving and only partially stable system, which may differ slightly from speaker to speaker, and usage that pushes the instabilities of that system ever further whilst relying on the system itself for interpretation of the parole.

Thus, whilst speakers may each have a vocabulary that is stored in a hierarchical (that is, more or less inclusive) set of semantic fields, the texts we encounter every day usually invoke a slightly creative set of semantic fields that do not quite map onto the ones we have as our personal thesaurus. We quite happily interpret these fields as though they were part of the langue, because we know in principle how semantic fields work and we can easily cope with a new or partly new one.

In order to use semantic fields as an analytical tool we probably need to incorporate semantic feature analysis, and be able to argue, in any one case, that the words we claim belong in a single field are related in some important ways.

6.4 Sense relations

As we have already seen the individual polysemous senses of a lexeme can have different sets of relations with other word senses. The interrelations of word senses are collectively known as **sense relations**, and in a structuralist model of language they are seen as one of the systematic aspects of the linguistic code, defining word meaning in terms of the word's relations with other words, rather than seeing language as a simple naming of the world.

There is a range of possible sense relations into which a word sense can enter, based on the similarities and differences between them. There is a tradition of naming these relationships, as *synonymy*, *hyponymy* and so on, and we shall continue to use these names, though as we shall see the different sense relationships have more in common than this naming convention implies.

All the sense relations of a word sense are based on the extent to which semantic features are shared with other word senses. 'Synonymy' is a relationship of identity, where the semantic features are largely the same; 'hyponymy' is a relationship of hierarchy, where the semantic features of a more general word form part of the description of a more specific word; 'meronymy' is a part-whole relationship, where the semantic features of the whole form part of the description of the part; and 'oppositeness' is a relationship where many semantic features are shared by two word senses but they have diametrically opposed values for one prominent semantic feature. We shall now examine these relationships in more detail.

6.4.1 Synonymy

English is known for the size and richness of its vocabulary, arising, it is often claimed, from the many languages that have influenced it over the ages following the invasion and settlement of many different groups. This extensive vocabulary might lead us to conclude that there must be many synonyms in the language, but in fact there are very few, or at least very few exact synonyms.

For word senses to be truly synonymous they would have to be identical in their semantic features, connotations and grammatical identity and behaviour. Such synonyms would cause a problem of redundancy, as speakers would be storing two words for a single meaning and use. What has happened instead of the extreme redundancy of multiple synonyms is that words have developed specialist meanings, or particular connotations, or sometimes even particular syntactic contexts in which they occur. This can be seen in the examples of semantic fields in Section 6.3.2, where there are many words for different types of walking, all of them subtly different, and conjuring up a different picture of the manner of walking.

English, then, has a very large number of what we might call partial synonyms, which overlap in some core parts of their meaning but differ in detail. This relationship is difficult to quantify as there are different levels of overlap. We might argue that *talk* and *speak* are quite close synonyms, though their range of use is different and their grammatical features vary. Even if we narrow down the senses to those meaning [VERBAL ACTIVITY] (to exclude *'Can you speak French?'*), *speak* can be used in frames where *talk* would never occur: *'Did you speak?'*, though they seem to be equivalent in some contexts: *'I was talking/speaking to my neighbour'*.

There are many words that share no semantic features, or only the most general ones. The words *carrot* and *car*, for example, are both [TANGIBLE] but share no further semantic features. There are many words between these two extremes that could be described as partial synonyms. Nouns that describe human emotions are one example: *anger*, *fury*, *rage* and *resentment* are quite close in meaning, as are *fear*, *terror*, *trepidation*, *anxiety* and so on. These two groups also share some of their core features, so a text that contains members of both fields will certainly be full of members of the semantic field of human emotion. For example:

> *She didn't know where the anxiety stemmed from. She had been angry at first; resentful of how she'd been treated. But the terror had come from nowhere, causing her to feel trepidation at the most ordinary of human interactions.*

The lesson we can learn from this is that membership of semantic fields is a more useful analytical tool than synonymy, except when we wish to draw attention to the partial synonymy of pairs of members of a semantic field.

6.4.2 Hyponymy

The other semantic relationships we shall examine are simply more specific versions of partial synonymy, which underlies them. **Hyponymy** reflects the hierarchical nature of some areas of the vocabulary, though it should be stressed that it is not possible to define the entire English lexis in hierarchical terms.

Where there is a hierarchy, the word senses that occur 'higher up the tree' are semantically simpler than the members of the field that are lower down and their meanings are included within the meanings of the lower items. The higher the word the fewer semantic features it will have. These higher-level word senses are known as **superordinates**, and the more specific word is its hyponym. The relationship between two or more hyponyms of the same superordinate is **'cohyponymy'**. Thus the superordinate *mammal* is described by fewer semantic features than its hyponyms *cow* and *horse*, though these cohyponyms include all the features of *mammal* and some specific ones of their own. Table 6.1 provides a description of these words.

Table 6.1 Sharing of semantic features in hyponymous sense relations

	Animate	Livebirth	Suckling young	Quadruped	Bred by humans	Bred for milk production	Bred for riding and pulling vehicles
Mammal:	✓	✓	✓				
Cow:	✓	✓	✓	✓	✓	✓	
Horse:	✓	✓	✓	✓	✓		✓

Note that these definitions are not ones that scientists would necessarily use. The word senses of a language are used by everyday speakers in ways that will not always concur with the scientific definition. Thus a scientist might not include the production of milk as part of the vital definition of *cow*, whereas it is an important part of what ordinary users of the language understand by the word.

Hyponymous sense relations should not be confused with part–whole relationships. The former can be tested by the frame 'An *x* is a kind of *y*', where *x* is the hyponym and *y* is the superordinate term. Thus *A cow is a kind of mammal* and *Limping is a kind of walking* both demonstrate hyponymous relationships, though the same frame does not work for part–whole relationships, as can be seen from **A foot is a kind of leg.*

Hyponymy can work at more than one level of hierarchy. Therefore the hyponym of one superordinate can also be the superordinate of a lower-level hyponym. This works particularly well in the natural world, where hierarchical structures have long been recognised and therefore named, even in non-scientific language:

Plant – tree – oak.

Animal – mammal – cow.

The multilayer hierarchy is less comprehensive in semantic fields that deal with human affairs and social realities, though there are some patches where we can sketch in a few hyponymous levels:

Emotion – anger – fury.
Relative – Parent – Mother.

Hence, we could to argue that *anger* is a type of *emotion* and *fury* is a kind of *anger*, since *fury* has more semantic features than *anger* to define its strength. Similarly *parent* is a kind of *relative* and *mother* is a kind of *parent.* Note that these hyponymous relations, like all sense relations, are language-specific rather than universal truths. Not all languages would treat these meaning relations in quite the same way.

Hyponymy is a patchy relationship that shows the capacity of human languages' to organise some aspects of human experience into hierarchical structures in a quite detailed way, whilst other areas of experience remain more vaguely connected in loose semantic fields with just a few connecting semantic features. Many of these hierarchies have unexplained gaps where there could, theoretically, be a superordinate word but it happens not to exist. For example in English there is no ungendered word equivalent to *parent,* to cover both aunts and uncles, and no gendered words equivalent to *sister* and *brother* to cover female and male cousins respectively (Figure 6.1).

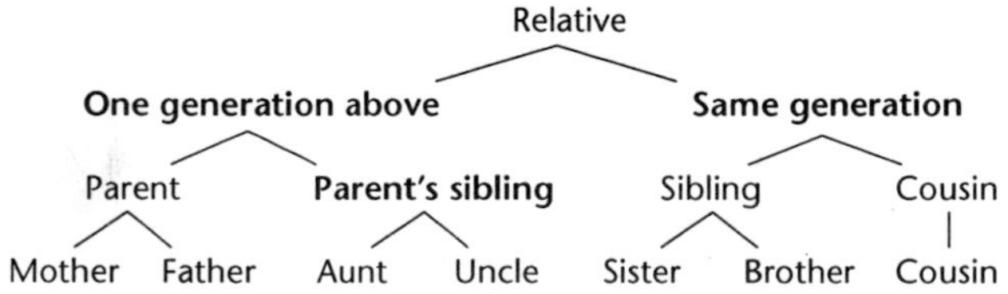

Figure 6.1 Lexical gaps in English kinship terms

It is noticeable here that in order to describe the semantic features of kinship words in English, we find ourselves proposing the existence of a hierarchical level that has no English labels attached; this is the level at which kinship terms can be divided into generations (older, younger and same generation).

6.4.3 Meronymy

The part–whole relationship between some word senses has already been touched upon to distinguish it from hyponymy. Meronymy, like all sense relations, partly reflects the world being described by the language. For example an arm is indeed part of the body, though the extent to which body parts are viewed as separate entities is partly a perspective, as opposed to an unchallengeable reality. In some cultures, such as Chinese, the hand and arm are treated as a unit and there is only one name for the combination. It is also true that we tend to use words variably, with the result that meronymy is not entirely stable. Whilst it might be acceptable to say that the hand is part of the arm in some contexts, we also use the word *arm* to refer to the limb from shoulder to wrist, excluding the hand, and the word *body* may be used to refer to the torso, excluding the limbs, despite the fact that the leg is part of the body.

However the way in which relationships of this kind are set up and broken down is of great interest. It can be instructive to look carefully at the lexis of a passage you are analysing to see the extent to which sense relations, including meronymy, are being exploited. The bizarre perception of body parts that can result from various extreme conditions has often been portrayed in literature by the use of a body part vocabulary, in a way that denies the essential part–whole nature of the relationship between the body and its constituent parts.

Carol Ann Duffy (1993), for example, begins her poem 'Small Female Skull' with the following line: 'With some surprise, I balance my small female skull in my hands.' It turns out that she is describing being in pain, possibly from a hangover (this is not clear) and she portrays her head as though it did not belong to her. A similar effect is achieved by William Golding (1956) in his novel *Pincher Martin*, which is about a man drowning and increasingly seeing his body parts as separate from himself.

6.4.4 Oppositeness (antonymy)

Perhaps one of the most important sense relations in language is that of **oppositeness**. It is not really a single sense relation because there are a number of different types of oppositeness, as we shall see later in this section. Nevertheless the popular concept of an 'opposite' is important enough in the psychology of language users for us to put them into a single section.

As with the other sense relations, oppositeness exists between polysemous senses of a lexeme, and this can be demonstrated when there are different established opposites for different senses of a word. The opposite of *lose*, for example, is *win* when referring to a game but *find* when referring to misplacing something. Despite these differences the two senses are related enough to be polysemous, though they are substantially different in usage. This pattern is repeated for many lexemes in English.

Oppositeness is also like other sense relations in that the words concerned share the majority of their semantic features. They are only significantly different in relation to *one* semantic feature, usually one that has strong social significance. Thus the opposite adjectives *long* and *short* have the following semantic features in common:

[PHYSICAL PROPERTY], [SIZE], [RELATING TO LONGEST DIMENSION]

Then, because in human life it can be important whether that dimension is large or small, they are distinguished for the semantic feature:

Long: [RELATIVELY LARGE IN THIS DIMENSION]

Short: [RELATIVELY SMALL IN THIS DIMENSION]

Notice that opposites are not, as we might imagine them to be, word senses that are utterly unlike each other. Such relationships, for example between *butter* and *philosophy*, are of little use in human affairs. The relationship of oppositeness, then, is really a special case of partial synonymy, with the particular dimension of contrast being socially important. Many of the common opposites are taught to children at an early age. Many books for toddlers are one-word-per-page picture books with opposites such as *hot* and *cold, tall* and *short* and so on. We can draw a conclusion from this need to teach children opposites: they are not innate. In other words, although there are some physical opposites (such as *hot* and *cold*) that exist independently of human life, these are essentially constructs of social perception, and only seem to be essential because we know them from a very early age.

It is also worth noting that not all words have opposites. We have already established that *butter* and *philosophy* are not each other's opposites, but neither do they appear to have their own opposites. Whilst some might argue that *margarine* is the opposite of *butter,* this is only the kind of opposite that children are arguing for when they insist that *dog* and *cat* are opposites. In other words, having found out that opposites exist children are keen to see the pattern replicated in all of their vocabulary. Adults are also capable of this, and can be heard 'playing' with language in this and similar ways. But in the case of established and conventionalised opposites, entrenched in the langue, there are a limited number.

The conventional opposites of the langue also tend to be found at a fairly basic level of generality. In other words the word senses that have opposites usually occur in the kind of vocabulary acquired quite early by both children and second-language learners. We learn of *push* and *pull*, then, but not that *shove* is the opposite of *tug*. These words are hyponyms of the more general *push* and *pull* respectively, and though we can see how they might be related in the same kind of way as *push* and *pull*, theirs is not an established relationship.

So far we have treated opposites as though they were a single category of sense relation. In some ways this is true; opposite relations all require the same overlap of semantic features, with a single prominent feature being the one on which the word senses are opposed. However, there are a number of different types of opposite, distinguished by their logical properties in relation to each other, which it is helpful to use when analysing opposition usage in texts. We shall consider the main four types of opposition: 'complementaries', 'gradable antonyms', 'converses' and 'directional opposites'.

Complementaries are what one might view as the stereotypical kind of opposite, though they are not necessarily the most common. They involve word senses that are mutually exclusive, so that if one applies, by definition the other does not apply. Thus if a person is *male*, by definition he is not *female*, and vice versa. If an animate being is *alive*, it is automatically construed as not having characteristics of being *dead*. If a statement is *true* it cannot also be *false*. These are adjectival examples, but complementaries can also be nouns and verbs. One cannot be a *man* and a *woman*, *live* and *die* at the same time, or tell both the *truth* and a *lie* at the same time.

Note that we are not talking about how the world really is. It is of course true that some people do feel themselves to be both male and female, and some are physically so (hermaphrodites). There are some statements that do indeed fall somewhere between the truth and lying, or manage to achieve both things at the same time. The issue for us here is to see how the language system – the langue – treats our experiences and categorises them as though they were mutually exclusive, rather than being one of the other types of opposition. This categorisation can, however, be manipulated in context. After all, we do say things such as *I'm half dead* when we are tired, or *He's such an old woman* when we want to insult a man. But in a sense these are the parole, getting around the langue and using our knowledge of the system to create new meanings by deliberately flouting the known relationships of sense.

Gradable antonyms are the (usually adjectival) opposites that we teach most readily to children, and they represent the two ends of a spectrum with intermediate points along its length. Thus although *hot–cold, big–small, good–bad, dirty–clean* and so on are opposites, they do not mutually exclude the other in the same way as complementaries. Something that is *not big* is not necessarily *small*, a person who is *not bad* is not necessarily *good*, and so on. Because these antonyms are gradable they can be, and often are, intensified by premodifying adverbs: *very hot, quite big, rather good, extremely bad.* In a few very common cases some of the intermediate points are also named by an inner set of opposites:

hot . . . warm . . . cool . . . cold.

Converses are logically interesting because both words apply to a particular situation but represent two different perspectives of that situation. The transactions involved in buying and selling or borrowing and lending are good examples of converses. Whilst the same transaction is implied by the words *buy–sell* and *borrow–lend* they look at it from the point of view of the buyer/borrower or seller/lender respectively. Whilst complementaries explicitly negate their opposite (to be a man is not to be a woman), converses invoke their opposite; to be a *husband* necessarily means that there is a *wife*, and *vice versa*. The moment one or other disappears (through death, divorce and so on), the identity of the other is also cancelled. Another converse relationship is *teacher–student.* The converse is sometimes not a true opposite because the opposing words are not contradictory. However they are popularly treated as opposites and make an interesting contrast with complementaries, being mutually dependent rather than mutually exclusive.

The final category of opposite is **directional and reversive opposition**. This is a smaller category than the others, and introduces a different perspective on opposition, as it describes processes that reverse the effect of each other. Thus *button–unbutton, enter–leave* and *marry–divorce* are all directional in this sense. Prepositions fall into similar patterns, so that *up–down, towards–away* and so on indicate reverse directions. Whilst there is a case for distinguishing between directional and reversive opposites, it is beyond the scope of this book and they will treated as one class for our purposes.

6.5 Semantic contexts

This chapter has focused on the semantics of individual lexical items and this section does not diverge from this pattern. There is a great deal more that can be analysed about the semantics of larger structures than the word, up to and including whole texts, and the situational context in which they are produced and/or received. Unfortunately, this too is beyond the scope of this book, though we will touch upon some textual features in Chapter 7.

Nevertheless it can be argued that the kinds of context in which a word sense regularly appears form part of the identity of that word sense, and that such regular patterning should therefore be part of the linguistic description of the semantics of that word sense.

There are two basic aspects to the context of any linguistic item or structure: the linguistic context and the non-linguistic or situational context. If we consider ways in which this could affect what speakers generally know about a word sense, it is likely that they would have some idea of words that often occur together or within a few words of each other (collocates), and in which social contexts word senses are likely to occur or be appropriate (connotation). These two aspects of a word sense's meaning are different from the semantic features discussed earlier, although connotation at least fits into a view of lexical semantics that sees word meaning as primarily relational. Whilst relationships between word senses that share semantic features are principally paradigmatic, the relationship between collocates is syntagmatic. Connotation is perhaps less relational than the other aspects of a word sense's meaning, linking as it does to the world outside the language itself.

6.5.1 Collocation

There are a number of ways of looking at the likely linguistic context of a word. We could consider the syntactic frames in which it occurs, and this is largely a regular feature of the word class (and subclass) to which it belongs. We can also look at the semantic frames in which it regularly occurs, to see whether there is any pattern of occurrence that we can identify as a generalisation for that word sense or a group of similar word senses.

There are two useful ways of approaching the question of semantic co-occurrence. These have arisen from different theoretical models of language, but both have a contribution to make when analysing texts. On the one hand, transformational-generative grammar proposes the idea of **selectional restrictions**, which limit the possible co-occurrence of a lexical item by determining the semantic features of likely subjects, objects and so on. On the other hand the concept of **collocation** was proposed by linguists working in the tradition of lexicography, who recognised that there were statistical co-occurrences of lexical forms that could not always be explained in general terms, and in some cases were apparently completely arbitrary.

As we shall see, these approaches are not entirely distinct, though like many models of language neither of them tells the whole story. Let us begin by investigating some examples of each approach.

Selectional restrictions were originally envisaged as a necessary limitation on possible combinations of words produced by a grammar. The idea was that in order to stop a grammar producing anomalous sentences, such as *The carpet ate my dog* or *John painted the theory*, individual words should have restrictions on their occurrence in certain contexts. The most efficient way to achieve this was to define the characteristics of words that could occur with verbs and adjectives, so that the verb *eat,* for example, would have a selectional restriction on its subject, which would have to be animate, and on its object, which would have to be edible. Similarly the verb *paint* would be required to have a human subject and a concrete but normally inanimate object, to prevent constructs such as *tables painting babies* and *elephants painting perceptions*.

You may have noticed that although the examples given in the last paragraph were odd, they were not as unacceptable as grammatically disordered or incomplete sentences such as *The was my singing but.* The difference is of importance, because it points out one of the ways in which speakers of English can deal with new and sometimes anomalous sentences. As long as the grammar is reasonably intact, hearers and readers can decode semantically unusual sentences with some degree of success. The examples in the last paragraph, for instance, could probably all be interpreted successfully, given the right context. Thus *The carpet ate my dog,* whilst unusual, might be an amusing metaphorical interpretation of what happened when a small dog running into a room slides on a polished floor and ends up underneath a large rug. Interestingly, after I had written this paragraph I saw an episode of a surreal situation comedy called *Black Books,* in which a child disappeared into a large sofa and the protagonist began to complain about *sofas that eat children*.

The fact that selectional restrictions can be broken quite readily is a good illustration of how langue and parole work together in actual texts and utterances, drawing on the hearer's knowledge of the normal restrictions of co-occurrence on a word, and having to interpret any breaking of these restrictions as a metaphorical use of the word.

Collocation is different from selectional restriction in two ways: collocation is not a strict restriction so much as a tendency to co-occur; and co-occurrence is not based on semantic features but on individual items. Thus the collocation of the adverb *stark* with *naked* but not with *nude* appears to be completely arbitrary and to have no general semantic feature at its core. These accidents of usage are perhaps the most interesting collocations, since they characterise a great deal of colloquial English, and for second language learners the use of appropriate collocations can make the difference between sounding foreign and sounding like a native speaker.

We tend to use the term collocation, then, to characterise the likely co-occurrences of words that cannot be captured by generalisation. The words *resounding* and *monumental*, for example, might conjure up a particular collocate or set of collocates for most readers. The collocational tendencies of these words may make us think of *success* or *win* for *resounding* and *mistake* or *error* for *monumental*. These examples demonstrate that in practice there is not a great difference between selectional restrictions and collocation, because we could make a generalisation about *resounding* occurring with a positive noun and *monumental* with a negative one. The difference however, is, that this collocational tendency can be broken without the need for reinterpretation, assuming metaphorical meaning or producing an unacceptable sentence.

A *resounding defeat.*

Your monumental achievement.

Collocations are statistical tendencies and can be measured by computer to confirm or contradict our impressions. Many of the more subtle collocational tendencies are below the level of our consciousness and can only be clearly demonstrated by statistical measures of this kind (see Louw, 1993). However we use and respond to collocations all the time, and as analysts we can invoke the idea of strong or unique collocation to explain phenomena that we come across in textual data.

6.5.2 Connotation

Connotation is used as a technical term in lexical semantics, but there are many other uses of this word, both in everyday life and by other academic disciplines, that only partly overlap with the use intended here. A distinction between **denotation** and connotation is made by structuralists, particularly when it is applied to cultural and literary texts. This distinction is similar to but less technically distinct than the one we are using here.

All that was discussed under the heading of semantic features, semantic fields and sense relations can be described as the word's denotation. It is the basic referential meaning of the word sense and its relationships with other word senses. However this may not be the whole meaning of a word sense in a language, since words also have the capacity to conjure up the circumstances in which they are typically used (for example place and time) and the participants involved.

Take for example the verb *lie*, which we can define as *to make untrue statements*. The near-synonym, *fib*, might be defined slightly differently, with an emphasis on the less serious nature of the crime, but it is significant, that the word is likely to be used in the context of children, both to them and by them. The less serious nature of the lie may arise, therefore, from what is essentially a connotation; that this is word connected with the world of children.

Connotations come in a number of forms that are associated with the participants in the interaction, the place of interaction, the time of the interaction and the speaker's evaluation of the process being described. We shall consider these in turn, although there is some overlap between them.

To begin with the participants, we have already seen that the age of participants can be relevant, since some words are normally associated with talking to children, or with their own speech. These words include obvious 'babytalk' words such as *gee gee, horsey, doggy, toothy pegs* and *tummy* as well as words such as *fib* and *naughty*, which might be used to and by slightly older children. The connotation of words that are likely to be used by other age groups, ethnic groups, and people with social or professional roles, such as teachers, lawyers and so on, are also part of the word sense's identity. For example an utterance such as *Steve needs more space for his decks* has the connotation of youth in British society in the early twenty-first century because of the specific use of the word *decks*, and this may be true more generally as the disc-jockey phenomenon has affected music across the world. By contrast the utterance *I have to caution the suspect* includes two words that are rarely used in this sense outside the criminal justice system. They therefore have the connotation of police officers or other officials in this system as their regular users.

Word senses also have connotations arising from their association with a place. These can be regional associations, such as the Scottish connotation of words such as *haggis*, and the Yorkshire connotation of the dialect word *ginnel* (meaning *alleyway*). They can also have associations with places of work, hobbies and leisure activities, such as are found in the registers associated with particular acitivities. Examples are *mid-off* and *leg-side*, which not only have *de*notations in the cricket world but also have *con*notations of the world of cricket to those outside the game, even when they do not understand the denotation of the terms themselves. A slightly more general connotation associated with place is concerned with the formality or informality of the situation. English has a great many near-synonyms that are distinguished largely by their level of formality, so that their denotation may be identical but whilst some could suitably be used in front of the queen, a prospective employer or a teacher, others are fit only for friends, family and the pub:

Purloin, steal, nick, knock off.
Smallest room, lavatory, toilet, loo, bog.

At the extremes of informality, of course, there are taboo words that we use in inappropriate settings to shock or explicitly reject the social constraints of decorum. I shall not list any of the taboo words for *loo*, but readers might know some of them! Note also that at the extremes of formality the words begin to sound comically overdone or dated (*purloin*), or they are euphemisms, some of which are rarely used in serious contexts now (*smallest room*).

Since word usage changes over time and with different generations, speakers also have connotations of how new or old a word is, as part of their understanding of that word and its usage. This type of connotation is of course tied to the type of person who uses the word (for example a teenager or old person), but it is essentially about the time connotation of the word itself. Words such as *cool* (in the sense of *okay* or *good*) and *minging* (*ugly* or *disgusting*) are, at the time of writing, relatively new words used by teenagers in Britain. There are also greetings that mark out a person as elderly, such as *Good day*, and words for common items in the home that tend to sound dated once they have been superseded by the latest technological advance, for example *wireless* and *radiogram*. These have the effect of making the person sound dated. In some ways all of these connotations have in common the fact that they are additional to their denotation and can, by their very use, evoke the particular atmosphere or context with which they are associated.

The final type of connotation we shall discuss here is slightly different from the others. It concerns the speaker's evaluation of the item or process being described by the utterance. Thus whilst we might describe someone's voice in neutral words such as *speak*, we might also portray the act of speaking in either a positive or a negative light by choosing words with evaluative connotations:

Sybil spoke the words of the poet.

Sybil squawked the words of the poet.

In both cases the denotation is that Sybil recited some words written by a poet. In the first version we are not told what the speaker thought of the delivery. In the second we are clear about this because the word *squawked*, connotes that the speaker was not impressed.

6.6 Further reading

Jeffries (1998) introduces a range of ways in which linguistic units and structures make meaning, and the discussion is not restricted to lexical semantics. The most thorough and readable description of lexical semantics can be found in Cruse (1986), and Cruse (2000) goes beyond word meaning to take in the theory and description of semantics at all levels and introduces pragmatic meaning too. For more theoretically dense and comprehensive treatments, particularly of logical and formal semantics, see Lobner (2002) and Kearns (2000). Though these books go way beyond the scope of the present volume, some of their introductory material ought to be accessible to new students of linguistics and English language. Much older, but still very readable, treatments of semantics are Palmer (1976) and Lyons (1977), the latter being more detailed than the former. Nida (1975) provides the original description of the componential analysis of meaning in English, and this has not been superseded.

CHAPTER

7 Theory, Text and Context

7.1 Introduction: Beyond the sentence

This book is mainly about teaching readers to analyse the sounds, meanings and structures of English texts so that they can go on to use these skills when studying specific uses of language, whether these be literary, political or everyday uses of English. Nevertheless there are some general theoretical issues that are appropriate to introduce at this stage, because understanding what we are doing when we analyse language is the key to analysing real texts. Similarly it is important to know what is round the corner, so that our clause analysis can be set into a broader conceptual and textual scene. To this end, this chapter contexualises the levels model both theoretically and practically. We shall look at the structures of English that are larger than the sentences and clauses of the previous chapter, and on our way we shall take in both formal (mostly written) texts, and the nature of conversation. As for the theoretical context, we shall consider some of the questions that linguists have been asking during the last hundred years, and introduce some very important global distinctions that underlie the analytical tools introduced so far in this book.

This chapter, then, takes the reader into the world of structures that are larger than the sentence, and considers the extent to which patterns are discernible in these larger structures. Because we are starting to consider whole texts here, we are inevitably drawing closer to the situational context in which texts are produced and/or received, such as who the producer is, who the text is for, and so on. This is the point at which *Studying Language* (Clark, 2006) takes over, so we shall only touch upon some of these issues in this chapter. Similarly, when introducing the theoretical concepts we shall stop short of the ground covered in *Thinking about Language* (Chapman, 2006), which deals exclusively and more thoroughly with general questions of linguistic analysis.

7.2 Cohesion

Once the description of language up to the level of the sentence is achieved, the next question to address is whether there are any structuring devices above this level. Of course we would expect there to be some constraints on the flow of sentences or utterances in a text, but are these only social constraints, or might there also be some linguistic patterning that holds sentences or utterances together? One of the answers to this question is known as **cohesion**, which is the linking mechanism between sentences and serves to make sure that a text is not simply a random series of unconnected sentences, but has enough information for the reader/hearer to interpret the text as a whole.

The idea of cohesion arose from the work of Halliday and Hasan (1976), within the field of functional linguistics. They suggested that there were specific types of linking mechanisms that pointed out to the reader/hearer the proper way to interpret sentences in the context of adjacent sentences. If you take the word *him*, for example, there is no obvious way for a reader to understand who it refers to, unless there has been mention of someone in an earlier sentence that will make it clear:

Tony Blair arrived in Egypt this morning. He said he was delighted to be there.

Even if the referent is not a famous British Prime Minister like Tony Blair, a pronoun in such a position has a specific link to the last-mentioned male in the previous sentence, which gives the hearer a clue as to his identity. Notice that the norm is for referents to be introduced with a fuller description or name, and then to be referred to by a pronoun afterwards. This effectively means that the pronoun is pointing backwards in the text, to the point where the referent was first introduced. This is known as **'anaphoric' reference**. The forward-pointing or **'cataphoric' reference** is used less frequently in straightforward texts, though it can cause suspense and is therefore used fairly often in literary texts:

Tony saw <u>him</u> at once, at the end of the corridor. <u>His father</u> had been missing for thirty years, but Tony still knew the shape of him.

Cohesive links are textual rather than contextual, and they make an explicit connection between the sentences in a text. They fall into six different groups that work in slightly different ways, though the same effect is achieved by all of them. The six groups, which will be explored in more detail below, are: repetition, reference, substitution, ellipsis, conjunction and lexical cohesion.

7.2.1 Repetition

The most straightforward type of cohesive link between sentences is that of repetition. The exact repetition of words, or the repetition of identical syntactic frames, but with different words, both make clear that the sentences are linked to form a text:

> *The child in the mirror is me. The child in my arms cries. I look down at my child and feel afraid.*

Although this passage does not make clear whether the child in each case has exactly the same referent, there is nevertheless a semantic link between the sentences because of the repeated word, *child*, and this causes the reader to try to make sense of the passage, rather than rejecting it as a random series of sentences, because the repetition is evidence enough of its status as a text.

The following passage uses a repeated syntactic frame, rather than a repeated word to give the same effect:

> *We shall root out vandalism. We shall cut out waste. We shall single out failing hospitals and schools.*

This kind of repetition is normally known as parallelism and is common in literary texts, particularly poetry. Both passages rely on their repetitive elements for their cohesion and to indicate to readers that the sentences are related. Thus although the cohesion of a passage may be fairly limited, the least connection of this kind can trigger a reader's inclination to look for further links.

7.2.2 Reference

The term **reference** is used rather more narrowly here than it is in philosophical approaches to language, where it means the direct connection between a word and the world. Here it is a more linguistic matter and refers to the ability of some words to refer to others in earlier (or later) parts of the text. This linking with items in other sentences has the required cohesive effect and is a particular property of demonstrative adjectives, the definite article and a small number of other words, for example *such*, as we can see from their use in the following passage:

There was a small café in the square, with mullioned windows and Ye Olde Tea Shoppe in large letters over the door. The café was full of walkers in wet clothes, quietly steaming over their tea and cakes. Such cafés were ten a penny in this tourist area, but this café was the place where they'd met, she was sure of it.

The first time the café is mentioned, the indefinite article is used because it is new to the text. Whilst the reader will still not actually know the café, it has a definite article in the next sentence and both *such* and a demonstrative (this) in the following one, because the café as a site of interest to this story has now been established and there needs to be a clear indication that the café in each successive sentence is the same one that was mentioned in the first one.

7.2.3 Substitution

Closely related to reference is the cohesive device of **substitution**, which is often carried by pronouns and the dummy auxiliary verb *do*, to avoid the need to repeat the same words too many times. We saw an example in Section 7.2. where with *Tony Blair* was referred to as *he* in the sentence following the one in which he was first mentioned. Here we shall illustrate the substitution of a main verb and its object by the dummy auxiliary *do*:

I should have bought an iPod. Janie did.

The substitution of *did* here replaces the whole of *bought an iPod,* though it is noticeable that the auxiliary part of the verb phrase is contrasted, since the speaker uses the modal perfective *should have* to describe her or his own actions and the emphatic use of *did* to describe Janie's actions.

Other regular substitutions are *the same* or one of the demonstrative pronouns *(this, these, that, those*) for a noun phrase or noun clause, and *so* for a clause:

I wanted a pizza. John wanted the same.
Sarah thought he had behaved appallingly. We all thought the same.
Dave said he'd mend the computer. Kiran did so.

The underlined sections in the first sentence in each case are substituted by those in the second. Note that the subordinate noun clause is replaced by *the same* rather than by *do,* which emphasises its similarity with noun phrases.

7.2.4 Ellipsis

A similar cohesive mechanism is **ellipsis**, which takes substitution one step further by completely omitting very obvious sections of an utterance. This grammatical process also has other functions, for example it avoids unnecessary repetition and is more economical. However the very fact that a word or phrase is so predictable that it can be left out and speakers will still know what it is, means that there is a cohesive link to the sentence in which the full form occurs:

> *Haworth is best in winter. Hawes in summer.*

The second sentence here is linked to the first by the fact that we know that the verb and complement *is best* is missing. As we have seen in various parts of this book, such ellipsis is common within sentences, but as a cohesive mechanism across sentence boundaries it is most frequent in informal and spoken language styles.

7.2.5 Conjunction

The use of conjunctions to link sentences is well known and is a skill that is taught to children when they learn to write more sophisticated texts at school. The signposting that conjunctions provide fall into four semantic sets:

- Additive, for example *and, furthermore, besides, similarly.*
- Adversative, for example *but, yet, however, nevertheless.*
- Causal, for example *so, for, because.*
- Continuative, for example *well, anyway, after all.*

Conjunctions have the semantic role of indicating in which way the new information links to the previous sentence. It may be additional (additive), conflicting (adversative), explanatory (causal) or simply the next thing that is to be said on the subject (continuative). As far as cohesion is concerned, though, the function of conjunctions is the same: to indicate that the sentences are linked in some way. If we look at an example of a continuative conjunction we can see that it can be used to link otherwise quite disparate sentences:

> *Judith was really late for her French class. Anyway, Joel said that he'd been on a bus that had broken down.*

This pair of sentences is typical of informal chat between friends who share a great deal of the background information in question, including the context and the identity of the people mentioned. The sentences might work as a text even without the conjunction (*anyway*), but it works as a marker for the hearer to link the two statements. We might presume that the larger story is about being in trouble for being late, but it could equally be that Judith and Joel are a couple who had played truant to be together. The only thing that the continuative establishes is that they are related in some way. The context has to do the rest.

7.2.6 Lexical cohesion

The final type of cohesion to consider is **lexical cohesion**, where the choice of lexical items will cause the reader to make connections between sentences in a text. The forms that lexical cohesion takes are as varied as the sense relations discussed in Chapter 6. As long as there is some kind of semantic link between the items in adjacent or nearby sentences, then there will be lexical cohesion. These links can be membership of a semantic field, which would involve a similar set of semantic features, hyponymy, cohyponymy, oppositeness or even similarities of connotation. Most texts have some element of lexical cohesion; there are normally a few semantic fields in play in a text, and the vocabulary will reflect these interlocking fields.

In a narrative the last-named person of the right gender will normally be the referent of a personal pronoun, as we saw in the example with Tony Blair. When there is more than one person in the story, however, there may be a need to repeat a name, or some version it, before resuming the use of a pronoun. What emerges is a 'chain' of substitution and reference, linking all the different ways of referring to the same person

If you link up all the cohesive elements the extract below you will find that the result is a very visible demonstration of the fact that language is very far from being the linear string of words we sometimes believe. The 'knitted' effect of the lines that link the cohesive ties can be more or less dense, depending on the nature of the text and how cohesive it is (Figure 7.1).

In the front room ***our*** dining ***table*** looks to have come off ***a wrecked ship*** and there is ***an*** immense rolltop ***desk*** (possibly from ***the same ship***) used by ***Our Father*** for writing ***his*** sermons. ***The desk*** has ***wooden*** legs and ***cast-iron*** chicken's ***feet***, ***each*** clutching a huge ***glass marble***, though three of the ***marbles*** are cracked and ***one*** is gone, replaced by a chink of ***coconut husk*** in the interest of a level ***writing surface***. In ***our*** parents' room, more ***furniture***: ***a wooden bureau*** and ***an old phonograph cabinet*** with no workings inside. ***All brought*** by other brave Baptists before ***us*** though it is hard to see quite ***how***, unless one envisions a time when other means of travel were allowed, and more than forty-four pounds. ***We*** also have a ***dining table*** and a rough handmade ***cupboard*** containg a jumble-sale assortment of ***glass*** and ***plastic*** ***dishes and cups***, one too few of ***everything***, so ***we*** sisters have to bargain: ***knives for forks*** while ***we eat***.

Source: Kingsolver, 1998, p. 70.

Figure 7.1 Cohesion in an English text

7.3 Conversation

Whilst all of the analytical tools that have been discussed in this book can be used to investigate the spoken language, there are particular features that make up the structure of interactive conversation. Conversation is a different kind of text that is jointly created by more than one speaker in real time, and it therefore has a number of significant features that are not shared by texts (either written or spoken) produced by one person, and in which there is time to consider and revise textual features.

The field of **conversation analysis** is concerned with many of the features of parole, which is the practical use of the idealised language system that has been the subject of much of this book. These features include mistakes, rewordings, unfinished utterances and other performance features, but nevertheless there is regularity, even in the apparent mistakes and corrections that speakers make. The topic of conversation analysis takes us into an area between the description of a language and the description of its use. We shall therefore, restrict ourselves to illustrating just two aspects of conversational practice.

7.3.1 Turn-taking

One of the regulating principles of conversation is the mechanism for **turn-taking** and how speakers negotiate the smooth transition from one speaker to the next. Of course not all conversations are equally successful in this way, but it is surprising how many of them proceed with most of the transitions happening quite neatly.

For conversation analysts the **transition relevance place (TRP)** is the potential point in the structure of the turn where another speaker may enter the conversation. This is often at a boundary between clauses, though it can also occur between phrases. The intonation of the current speaker will give clues as to her or his view of whether the turn is nearly over, for example by using a low falling tone towards the end of a sequence of tone units, and the new speaker will use structural and suprasegmental information to ascertain when to enter the conversation. The following is a successful example of a speaker transition at a clause boundary:

A: *Then I was on my way home when I got a call from George.*

B: *Where had he been all evening?*

It is possible, of course, for speakers to make transitions when a TRP has not been reached, and where it is clear that they are not waiting for a suitable TRP, this will be interpreted as interruption:

A: *Then I was on my way home when [I got a call from George.*

B: *[Where were you?*

If the new speaker appears to have anticipated a turn by only a little, this will be interpreted as an overlap:

A: *Then I was on my way home when I got a call from [George.*

B: *[Where had he been all evening?*

Three kinds of activity are involved in turn-taking in a conversation: taking the turn, holding the turn and yielding the turn. Speakers may or may not cooperate with each other in turn-taking, and the results can be incomprehensible to a listener if the turn-taking gets out of hand, as it sometimes does during political interviews on the radio. Mostly, however, turn-taking – even with interruptions – is smooth enough to allow the conversation to take place successfully.

7.3.2 The cooperative principle

In the previous section the concept of cooperation was introduced as a vital part of the joint negotiation of conversational turn-taking by participants. Cooperation is important semantically as well as structurally, and is the foundation of much of how we communicate in context, which is studied in pragmatics and conversation analysis.

Grice's (1975) **cooperative principle** states that interacting speakers will, on the whole, cooperate with each other in a number of ways, and that this cooperation is expected by the participants in a conversation. It is this expectation of cooperation that allows normal life to function, since talking to people with no idea of whether they are using the same rules as you would make communication impossible. Conversely it is this expectation of cooperation that also makes certain types of non-cooperative communication possible, including lying, exaggeration and other, more entertaining, types of communication, such as monologues, stand-up comedy, fantasy literature and so on.

The four **Gricean maxims** proposed as examples of this cooperation are quantity, quality, relevance and manner. These require participants to say only the appropriate amount (quantity), to speak the truth (quality), to stay relevant to the content and purpose of the conversation (relevance) and to be clear and use an appropriate style (manner).

7.4 Context

The importance of **context** to understanding and analysing language use cannot be exaggerated. The language we use is affected by the people we interact with, our status in particular situations, our recent experiences, our place of origin, our political, religious or social outlook and many other factors. Some of these are described by sociolinguistics, dialectology, pragmatics, conversation analysis and stylistics and are beyond the scope of this book. Here, we will investigate just two aspects of meaning that are both textual and contextual in nature. They both link to the analytical aims of the book, but also lead towards other, more contextual, approaches, such as will be found in the rest of this series.

7.4.1 Deixis

There is one feature of reference that is so pervasive and significant in terms of textual meaning, that it deserves mention here, although it belongs to wider discussions of language use and theory. This feature, **deixis**, is textually based in English, and yet it has the capacity to make direct links with the situational context of the speaker or writer.

Deixis refers to the capacity of some words to shift their reference, depending on who says (or writes) them and/or the speaker's position in space and time. The simplest example is from the pronoun system in English, where the words *I* and *you* differ in their reference according to who is saying them. One of the reasons why we talk to small children in the third person (*Mummy is going downstairs now*) is that they do not understand until a certain stage in their development that *I* will sometimes mean *Mummy*, and sometimes *Daddy*, and it might mean *the milkman* if he is the one talking!

Another example comes from the adverbs of place, *here* and *there*, which mean 'near to the speaker' and 'far from the speaker' (or near the hearer), thus changing their exact referent depending on who is speaking. The utterance *shall I come over there*, said on the phone, has the referent of *there* as the place where the hearer is. When the hearer replies *No, don't worry, I'll come over there*, the referent of *there* changes to where the first speaker is.

What is confusing to explain in fact works quite simply in everyday life, once we have learnt the system of deixis relating to the language we speak. Note that deixis can work differently in different languages, for example the Spanish use the verbs *come* and *go* differently. If you meet someone in the street and ask them to your house in Spanish, you use the verb *go* (*ir*), not the verb *come* (*venir*), as we would in English. This is because the Spanish are more literal about the deixis of these verbs, and since neither the speaker (host) nor the hearer (invitee) is actually at the house referred to, *come* is not seen as appropriate. By contrast the English usage depends on a psychological deixis whereby the host is metaphorically 'at' his or her house when an invitation is spoken, and the verb *come* therefore seems perfectly appropriate.

7.4.2 Metafunctions

The approach taken in this book is not dependent on the functional approach to language description of the Firthian school, and its main proponent, Halliday. This is not because functional linguistics is unpopular or ineffective. In fact it has been very widely used in some areas of linguistic activity, including stylistics, critical discourse analysis and teaching English as a foreign language.

We shall limit ourselves here to looking at one of the general claims of functional linguistics, which is the idea that language use can be characterised in some or all of three ways: **interpersonal**, **ideational** and **textual**. These three broad functions of our use of language are known as **metafunctions** and they preside over all the other lower-level functions and forms of language, and direct some of their effects. Utterances do not necessarily have only one of these functions at any one time and the precise combination of functions can only be determined when the full context is known.

To take a simple example, the utterance *Sheila has eaten her cabbage* can have an ideational function if it is a case of simple transfer of information, for example a babysitter speaking to an absent parent on the phone to allay fear about the child's nutritional intake. The same utterance can function interpersonally if it is said to another child over the dinner table as a rebuke to that child for not being as good as Sheila. Finally, it can could have a textual function as the answer to a question, perhaps, where the link between the question (e.g. *What is the code sentence I will recognise him by?*) and its answer is part of the process of text creation.

The above example has been given only one function at a time by the constructed contexts. An example of a text that has all three functions at once is *When I've finished reading this article*. This utterance clearly has a textual function as the answer to a question, which is shown by the subordinator *when*. Depending on the question it can also have an ideational function that genuinely gives some information (for example *When will you drive me to the gym?*) Depending on the previous context (for example the nagging of a repeated question) and the relationship between the participants (e.g. demanding child and mother), it is possible that the sentence also has an interpersonal function, meaning, *please do not keep nagging me – I will finish what I want to do first.*

This book is largely concerned with the textual and ideational metafunctions; the others in the series will deal with aspects of the interpersonal.

7.5 Design features of human language

Many introductory books on language begin by asking *What is language?* This is indeed an important question, but it is sometimes difficult for students to answer it until they have looked at specific aspects of language and learnt a little about how it works in practice. This is the reason why the question of what characterises human language has been left until the last chapter of this book.

Claims are often made about human language and how it differentiates us from the other higher mammals. The design features of human language are the fundamental features of linguistic systems that have not yet been shown to exist in other animal societies, and at the moment are mostly considered to be unique to human languages. Sometimes it is implicitly claimed that the importance of the design features is that they mark the superiority of the human race. This dubious argument will not be agreed with here, given the negative impact that human activity is currently having on the planet. However it is important to recognise that the design features demonstrate the complexity of human language and show how it works at a very general level.

Charles Hockett (1958, 1960, 1965) began a debate that rages to this day, about what are the essential and/or unique characteristics of human language. His own list of design features ranged from 10 to 16, and discussions of the list by others have prioritised different features. Those which are almost never omitted are the four we shall discuss below.

7.5.1 Arbitrariness

As we saw in the Introduction to this book, the structuralist theory of language points out that the basis of human language is arbitrary, and this has become a recognised feature of linguistic design. What is meant by arbitrary in this context is that human language is a conventional system of units and structures that have no intrinsic connection to the world that it claims to describe and manipulate.

Evidence of **arbitrariness** comes from the differences between human languages, which name and identify the world differently, but equally effectively, for the purposes of human society. Thus the fact that the French call butter *beurre*, the English have a similar word, *butter*, and the Italians have another similar word, *burro*, might make us believe that there is something about butter that requires this kind of phonological form to name it. But when we consider that the Spanish word for butter is *mantequilla*, and that the Spanish word *burro*, means donkey, it becomes clear that the naming of things in our world is merely an accident of history and convention. There is nothing more that we need to say about arbitrariness, though it feeds into other aspects of our description, as we shall see.

7.5.2 Duality of patterning

Another design feature of human language is **duality of patterning**, which refers to the fact that language is organised on at least two levels. The material of language is made up of individual sounds, and these are combined in various ways to make words. These words are also combined in various ways to make higher-level structures. These two levels of unit and combination are independent of each other, and mean that an infinite number of different utterances can be made out of a rather small number of speech sounds.

In our levels model, presented in Table I.1 in the Introduction the levels of patterning go beyond two, but the basic design feature is normally considered to be the way that meaningless sounds combine to make meaningful words and structures. The levels model is an elaboration of this concept, but does not alter the mathematical fact that the number of units (sounds and words) that people have to learn is really quite small and that it is the process of combining of these units that allows us the expressive range we enjoy.

7.5.3 Open-endedness

Sometimes also called **creativity**, **open-endedness** refers to the capacity of human beings to use their language to say new and different things every day for a lifetime and to be able to understand unique sentences as well.

The infinite capacity of languages to allow new utterances is due partly to the duality of patterning, but also to some recursive features of syntax that allow elements to recur or repeatedly be embedded in other elements. This recursion can be thought of as a bit like the effect of two mirrors facing each other, with infinitely repeated images getting smaller and smaller. There comes a point when the recursion makes comprehension very difficult, but it is not ungrammatical as a result:

> *The man that I met who went to my school which was burnt down last year . . . has just died.*

Statistically, then, human beings have an infinite number of utterances available to them. But perhaps equally importantly they can refer to things and events that do not exist or cannot happen; in other words they can create fantastic worlds as well as lying. It is no accident that the imaginative freedom that underlies fiction writing and poetry is the same freedom that allows us to mislead our fellow human beings. The open-endedness of language is the basis of both.

If we take a simple sentence such as *George told me about the smugglers*, this could be a true sentence, spoken (or written) about a real person and a real situation. It could also be an untrue sentence, spoken about a real person and a real situation. It could be a sentence spoken (or written) as though it were about a real person and a real situation, though either (or both) may be false. Of course it could also be a sentence spoken (or written) as part of a fictional story, where truth does not matter. Finally, if we change the vocabulary a little it could be a sentence that clearly describes an unreal world, and therefore exists entirely in the textual world (of sci-fi literature in the following case): *The Martian told me about the smugglers.*

7.5.4 Displacement/stimulus-freedom

Related to the creativity of language is the ability that human beings have to talk about times and places that are not part of their current reality which is called **displacement** or **stimulus-freedom**. This ability to get away from having to talk about the stimuli that are in front of us is a great asset for human development and a function of our ability to empathise with others in different times and places.

Children learn to displace gradually and there are times when they become distressed because their parents leave the room, or when it is hard to teach them to wait for a treat. This is because they have not yet learnt of the existence of any time or place apart from the one in which they are living. The importance of being able to talk of places and times other than the here and now can be made clearer by imagining a world in which adults behaved like two-year-olds. It would be impossible to make an appointment with the doctor, remember how to get to a place that we had visited before, or book a holiday in a place where we had never been!

Whilst this may be unimaginable it is worth considering that many wild animals live lives that are mainly dictated by the presence of stimuli. Thus hunger will cause them to eat or look for food, and danger will cause them to run or hide, but despite the likelihood that animals will have some memories (for example of good places to find food), it is unlikely that a pride of lions will sit down at the end of the day and talk over the various hunting achievements of the afternoon.

7.6 Dimensions of language

There are two important sets of dimensions of language that all linguists find the need to refer to at times. The first of these, the paradigmatic and syntagmatic dimensions, refers to relationships between linguistic items themselves. The second, diachronic and synchronic perspectives, considers two ways of approaching language study.

7.6.1 Paradigmatic and syntagmatic relationships

The distinction between the **paradigmatic** and **syntagmatic** dimensions of language is related to the difference between units and structures as discussed in the Introduction to this book. The units of language, from a structuralist viewpoint at least, are defined by the relationships they hold with other units of the language. Some of these relationships are to do with the fact that two or more units can fulfil similar functions in a structure, and some of them are concerned with the combination of units in a structure.

Paradigmatic relationship refers to relationships between similar items that could replace each other in the same slot in a structure. Thus the nouns *cake, biscuit* and *sandwich* have a paradigmatic relationship with regard to the gap in the utterance *Who's going to eat the last . . . ?* In other words the functions we have explored when examining phrase structure and clause structure have a large number of potential forms that could fulfil them. The head of a noun phrase, for example, could be any noun in English, and a few adjectives too. These are all said to be in a paradigmatic relationship with each other with regard to this function.

By contrast the items occurring alongside each other in a structure are said to be in a **syntagmatic relationship**. Thus the verb *eat* in the above utterance has a syntagmatic relationship with its object, be it the word *cake, biscuit* or *sandwich*. Similarly the determiner that precedes a head noun has a syntagmatic relationship with it.

The terms paradigmatic and syntagmatic can be used at many points in the process of describing English. Their contribution here is to demonstrate that linguistic items such as words can enter into two different kinds of relationship, and that both are part of the meaning of that item. Thus the meaning of *eat* in English is defined partly by its paradigmatic relationship with other verbs, including *consume* and *drink* and partly by its syntagmatic relationship with *beef, chicken, cakes* and *chocolate*, which can occur as its Object and with *me, Judy* and *everyone*, which can occur as its subject.

7.6.2 Diachronic and synchronic dimensions of study

In addition to looking at the dimensions in which linguistic items relate to each other, we can also look at language itself from different perspectives. One of the most important developments of twentieth-century linguistics was the recognition that we could study language from either of two viewpoints: synchronically or diachronically.

The history and tradition in linguistic study before the twentieth century was largely **diachronic**; that is, it took a historical and developmental view of language, with changes in the sound system, lexis and structure being the main object of study. In the early twentieth century there was a shift in this outlook, with linguists increasingly seeing the study of a language at a single point in history as their main object, and the history of how the language got to be that way as being of secondary interest. This **synchronic** approach was based on the idea that theoretically treating language as stable at a single point in time and space was the best way of explaining the regularities and patterns in the language, with historical shifts being ironed out. There was also the view that speakers at any one period of a language's history would not be particularly aware of, or concerned about, the historical development of the language, and would treat it as though it were the stable system described in the synchronic approach.

In recent decades there has been a refocusing on the changes that happen across time, and diachronic study, which often focuses on fairly recent changes, has been recognised as having an equal, but different, value to synchronic study. What has not changed is the recognition that it is very difficult, if not theoretically impossible, to do both kinds of study at once.

This book takes a largely synchronic view of language, making the convenient assumption that English is a stable system that works pretty well without major changes during a speaker's lifetime. However should students wish to study aspects of diachronic change (for example in youth culture and vocabulary), the descriptive terminology and categories introduced here will serve the purpose.

7.7 Language system and use

So far this chapter has emphasised the **systematic** aspects of language, because this book is largely concerned with the regular patterns that make up the English language. However most students and researchers will ultimately want to apply the analytical tools they have used to study language to real situations, for example when considering the way in which children or second-language learners learn English, the use that creative writers make of the resources of English, the ways in which conversations can be studied, the manipulation of people by the power of language and so on.

There are a number of established terms that can help us to think about the relationship between the 'codified' core of the language, as described here, and the way in which we actually use (and abuse) it. Despite insisting on the importance of internal relationships between linguistic units, I do not wish to claim that language exists independently of human society and life. We therefore need to consider how the system of language links with life. The rest of this chapter introduces concepts and distinctions which help us to consider the vital interface between our language and everyday experiences.

7.7.1 Langue and parole, competence and performance

The first distinction we shall consider is between **langue** and **parole**. These French terms, first proposed by Saussure, refer to the language as a complete system (langue) and its use in real situations (parole) respectively. Langue, then, is a somewhat idealised form of the language, where people do not hesitate, use incomplete sentences or make up new or surprising structures. Parole is where they do all of those things and more. One of the problems with this distinction is that it appears to suggest that there is something complete and perfect about langue, and something messy and imperfect about its use (parole).

In fact, as linguists have looked in detail at more and more contextualised examples of language, through fields such as dialectology, sociolinguistics, stylistics and pragmatics, it has become evident that what appear to be messy, creative or mistaken uses of the langue have their own regularities and patterning that simply differ from the idealised general language.

This presents a theoretical problem for linguistics but does not invalidate the langue–parole distinction for the purposes of this book. While the coded version of English presented here is not identical in every detail to the real versions that readers will encounter in their everyday lives, it does capture a version of English that at some level we all draw upon when using both subtly and also radically different varieties.

There is a similar distinction between **competence** and **performance**. This has arisen from the work of transformational-generative linguists and was first introduced by Chomsky. Competence, in this theory, refers to the language ability and knowledge that speakers of any language have available to them, and that are in some sense stored in the brain of the speaker. Performance is therefore, like parole, a poorer version of the internal language system; one in which the brain fails to retrieve the appropriate words and structures, breaks down half way through an utterance and so on. The distinction between these two sets of terms is one of emphasis. The

Saussurean distinction between langue and parole focuses on the social use of language, and draws upon the idea of commonality between speakers to theorise an idealised form of the language. The Chomskyan distinction reflects an underlying difference of theoretical outlook. The competence–performance distinction arises from a language theory that views language primarily as the cognitive ability of the individual speaker, rather than an abstract but socially based, self-defining and independent system that speakers draw upon.

7.7.2 Reference and sense

Another significant distinction that relates to the bridge between language and life is that between 'reference' and 'sense'. We have already hinted at this when discussing the importance of relationships between linguistic items in the language system.

As we have seen, structuralists have argued that language is not simply a naming system and they have focused on the interrelations between linguistic units as the most important aspect of language to be described. This distinction is sometimes called the distinction between **reference**, which connects language to the world, and **sense**, which connects linguistic items to each other.

Whilst sense has been crucial to all developments in language description in recent times, reference cannot be discounted entirely. The word *house*, for example, can be used specifically to refer to a particular house, as in *that house over there*, or it can refer to a class of houses, as in *terraced houses in Leeds*. It is also possible to discuss the range of all buildings that could be referred to in general by the word *house*, though the boundaries of that referential pool might be difficult to draw. Is, for example, a ramshackle hut in a refugee camp part of the pool of referents of the word *house*? Philosophers of language have raised these issues for many generations, and they remain of abiding interest. Nevertheless linguistic structuralism has also made us look at language from the perspective of its internal form and structure, and this has led to great developments in the description of all human languages, including English.

7.7.3 Sign, signifier and signified

There are many terms in linguistics that refer to very similar concepts, and they sometimes overlap each other in ways that are interesting for theories of language but can be confusing for students. For example you may come across the terms **'sign'**, 'signifier' and 'signified' in your studies. These are Saussurean terms that have gained great currency in fields related to linguistics, such as literary criticism and cultural studies, but also encapsulate ideas that are fundamental to the way that linguists see human language as working.

Their linguistic meaning is relatively simple and not unrelated to reference and sense, which we considered in the previous section. Saussure's contention was that the linguistic sign was not just the letters or the word you see on the page (or the sounds you hear). Instead he argued that the sign was made up of two parts; the signifier, which is the physical manifestation of the linguistic unit in sounds or words (or hand signals in British sign language), and the signified, which is the potential range of referents of the signifier in that language. He emphasised that you could not really separate the two, and that human language depends on this unifying of the arbitrary symbol with its referents. The usual way of representing the relationship between sign, signifier and signified is as a triangle, with the sign at the apex, as shown in Figure 7.2.

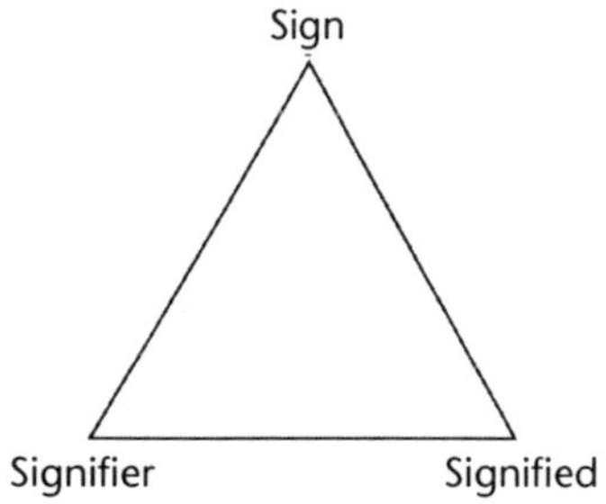

Figure 7.2 The relationship between sign, signifier and signified

7.7.4 Denotation and connotation

One of the abiding distinctions made by structuralism, and one that has had many repercussions in literary and cultural studies as well as linguistics, is that between 'denotation' and 'connotation'. As we saw in Chapter 6, these words are used in rather more specific and narrower senses in linguistics than in everyday usage, though the general meaning is also of interest to linguists.

Denotation is the central, codified meaning of a linguistic sign (such as a word) and is independent of its use in any particular situation. The **connotation** of a sign is attached to it by the habit of its use and thereby becomes part of its meaning, though it may be more readily cancelled out by a speaker than the denotation.

Thus when a British teenager says *That's really tight* to his or her parents, its denotation is that something is unfair, and its connotation identifies the speaker as a young British person with street credibility. The denotation would not change if the same sentence were uttered by the parents to the young person; it would still mean that something is unfair. What would change is the connotation, because the speaker would not be identified as a trendy young person. This challenge to the norm can be interpreted in a number of ways, for example the parent could be seen as inappropriately trying to be on the same wavelength as the young person.

7.7.5 The Sapir–Whorf effect

Often called the **Whorfian hypothesis**, the **Sapir–Whorf effect** refers to one inevitable consequence of the way in which human language operates in our lives. Linguistics has rejected the view that the world we live in is independent of our perception of it, and it explicitly denies the idea that language is a kind of naming system added on to the reality of our lives. The alternative view, which has been embraced by linguists, is that language is not just a reflection of a separate reality but is part of that reality, and as such has its own internal structure that is overlaid on the physical world to form our perceived reality.

The reason why I am avoiding the term 'Whorfian hypothesis' here is that it has often been associated with a very strong form of this argument; namely that our language completely structures the way in which we perceive the world, and that we have no way of escaping from this linguistically imposed reality. Most linguists now accept a weaker but nevertheless significant version of this view: that the languages we speak have an effect on how we perceive the world, that they divide up and name 'reality' in different ways, and that this is bound to have an effect, in the long term, on our categorisation of the world.

This tendency is not inescapable, as proven by the fact that language changes have both reflected and directed social and political changes in the world. That we are not trapped by the language we speak is also evidenced by multilingual speakers who can clearly cope with more than one linguistic version of reality, as well as being able to translate from one to the other.

Rather like the distinction between langue and parole, which is not as clear-cut as it seemed when first suggested, the Sapir–Whorf effect is a concept that helps us to understand how our experience of the world is partly created by language, without proposing that it completely dictates our reality.

7.8 Further reading

This chapter has dealt with topics that are covered in more detail in the companion books in the Perspectives on the English Language series. Clark (2006) provides a detailed introduction to cohesion, conversation analysis and other

discourse and pragmatic aspects of language, and Chapman (2006) introduces students to deixis, speech act theory and other contextual aspects of meaning, as well as theories of reference, questions of code and the bridge between language and the world.

There are many books on linguistic theory that cover some or all of the topics considered in this chapter. For a readable introduction the books by Lyons (1968, 1981) cover the fundamental issues raised here, though they are now getting quite old. What is striking about the recent titles in linguistic theory is that they each deal with very detailed areas of concern and few general introductions have been published in recent years. Instead there are a great many encyclopaedic volumes, that define and illustrate the kinds of distinction and areas of contextual study introduced in this chapter. Crystal (1987, 1995) and McArthur (1992) are among the most accessible of these.

For a definitive treatment of cohesion read Halliday and Hasan (1976). There are many books on discourse analysis, some of which are focused in scope and some are very broad-ranging. Students who wish to know how the multitude of discourse studies originated could read Sinclair and Coulthard (1975), Stubbs (1983), Coulthard, (1977) and Coulthard and Montgomery (1981). Hutchby and Wooffitt (1998) provide an introduction to conversation analysis, and you can read the original proposal on the cooperative principle in Grice (1975).

Bibliography

Allerton, D. J. (1981) *Valency and the English Verb* (London: Academic Press).

Aronoff, M. and Rees-Miller, J. (2003) *The Handbook of Linguistics* (Oxford: Blackwell).

Ballard, K. (2001) *The Frameworks of English* (Basingstoke: Macmillan).

Bauer, L. (1983) *English Word-Formation* (Cambridge: Cambridge University Press).

Bauer, L. (1990) *Introducing Linguistic Morphology*, 2nd edn (Edinburgh: Edinburgh University Press).

Bloor, T. and Bloor, M. (1995) *The Functional Analysis of English* (London: Edward Arnold).

Brazil, D. (1992) *The Communicative Value of Intonation in English* (Cambridge: Cambridge University Press).

Brazil, D. and Coulthard, M. (1980) *Discourse Intonation and Language Teaching* (Harlow: Longman).

Brown, K. and Miller, J. (1991) *Syntax: A Linguistic Introduction to Sentence Structure* (London: Routledge).

Burton-Roberts, N. (1997) *Analysing Sentences*, 2nd edn (Harlow: Addison Wesley Longman).

Carr, P. (1993) *Phonology* (Basingstoke: Macmillan).

Carter, R. and McCarthy, M. (2005) *The Cambridge Grammar of Spoken English* (Cambridge: Cambridge University Press).

Chapman, S. (2006) *Thinking About Language: Theories of English* (Basingstoke: Palgrave Macmillan).

Chomsky, N. (1957) *Syntactic Structures* (The Hague: Mouton).

Chomsky, N. (1965) *Aspects of the Theory of Syntax* (Cambridge, Mass.: MIT Press).

Clark, U. (2006, forthcoming) *Studying Language: English in Action* (Basingstoke: Palgrave Macmillan).

Collins (1996) *Collins Cobuild Learners' Dictionary.*

Collins, P. (1998) *English Grammar* (Melbourne: Addison Wesley Longman).

Coulthard, M. (1977) *Introduction to Discourse Analysis* (London: Longman).

Coulthard, M. and Montgomery, M. (1981) *Studies in Discourse Analysis* (London: Routledge).

Cowper, E. (1992) *A Concise Introduction to Syntactic Theory* (Chicago, Ill.: University of Chicago Press).

Cruse, A. (1986) *Lexical Semantics* (Cambridge: Cambridge University Press).

Cruse, A. (2000) *Meaning in Language* (Oxford: Oxford University Press).

Crystal, D. (1987) *The Cambridge Encyclopedia of Language* (Cambridge: Cambridge University Press).

Crystal, D. (1995) *The Cambridge Encyclopedia of the English Language* (Cambridge: Cambridge University Press).

de Saussure, F. (1974) *Course in General Linguistics* (Glasgow: Collins).

Duffy, C. A. (1993) *Mean Time* (London: Anvil Press Poetry).

Golding, W. (1956) *Pincher Martin* (London: Faber and Faber).

Greenbaum, S. (1996) *The Oxford English Grammar* (Oxford: Oxford University Press).

Grice, P. (1975) 'Logic and Conversation', in Cole, P. and Morgan, J. (eds), *Syntax and Semantics, vol.III: Speech Acts* (New York: Academic Press).

Halliday, M. A. K. (1985) *An Introduction to Functional Grammar* (London: Edward Arnold).

Halliday, M. A. K. and Hasan, R. (1976) *Cohesion in English* (London: Longman).

Harris, J. (1994) *English Sound Structure* (Oxford: Blackwell).

Henderson, K. (1995) *Sam and the Big Machines* (Harmondsworth: Puffin).

Hockett, C. (1958) *A Course in Modern Linguistics* (New York: Macmillan).

Hockett, C. (1960) 'The origin of speech', *Scientific American*, 203, pp. 88–96.

Hockett, C. (1965) 'Animal "Languages" and Human Language', in J. N. Spuhler (ed.), *The Evolution of Man's Capacity for Culture* (Detroit, Mich.: Wayne State University Press), pp. 32–9.

Horrocks, G. (1987) *Generative Grammar* (London: Longman).

Huddleston, R. (1988) *English Grammar* (Cambridge: Cambridge University Press).

Huddleston, R. and Pullum, G. (eds) (2002) *The Cambridge Grammar of the English Language* (Cambridge: Cambridge University Press).

Hutchby, I. and Wooffitt, R. (1998) *Conversation Analysis: Principles, Practices and Applications* (Cambridge: Polity Press).

Jaworski, A. and Coupland, N. (1999) *The Discourse Reader* (London: Routledge).

Jeffries, L. (1998) *Meaning in English* (Basingstoke: Macmillan).

Johnson, K. (1997) *Acoustic and Auditory Phonetics* (Oxford: Blackwell).

Jones, D. (1956) *The Pronunciation of English* (Cambridge: Cambridge University Press).

Kearns, K. (2000) *Semantics* (Basingstoke: Macmillan).

Kingsolver, B. (1998) *The Poisonwood Bible* (London: Faber and Faber)

Kuiper, K. and Scott Allan, W. (2004) *An Introduction to English Language*, 2nd edn (Basingstoke: Palgrave Macmillan).

Labov, W., Ash, S. and Boberg, C. (2005) *The Atlas of North American English* (New York: Mouton de Gruyter).

Ladefoged, P. (2001) *A Course in Phonetics*, 4th edn (Orlano: Harcourt Brace).

Ladefoged, P. (2000) *Vowels and Consonants* (Oxford: Blackwell).

Laver, J. (1994) *Principles of Phonetics* (Cambridge: Cambridge University Press).

Leech, G. (1971) *Meaning and the English Verb* (London: Longman).

Lobner, S. (2002) *Understanding Semantics* (London: Edward Arnold).

Louw, W. (1993) 'Irony in the Text or Insincerity in the Writer?', in M. Baker, G. Francis and E. Toginíni-Bonellí (eds) *Text and Technology* (Amsterdam: Benjamins), pp. 157–76.

Lyons, J. (1968) *Introduction to Theoretical Linguistics* (Cambridge: Cambridge University Press).

Lyons, J. (1977) *Semantics*, vols 1 and 2 (Cambridge: Cambridge University Press).

Lyons, J. (1981) *Language and Linguistics: An Introduction* (Cambridge: Cambridge University Press).

Maidment, J. and Garcia Lecumberri, M. (2000) *English Transcription Course* (London: Arnold).

Matthews, P. (1991) *Morphology* (Cambridge: Cambridge University Press).

McArthur, T. (1981) *Longman Lexicon of Contemporary English* (London: Longman).

McArthur, T. (1992) *The Oxford Companion to the English Language* (Oxford: Oxford University Press).

Nida, E. (1975) *Componential Analysis of Meaning* (The Hague: Mouton).

O'Grady, W., Dobrovolsky, M. and Katamba, F. (1996) *Contemporary Linguistics*, 3rd edn. (Harlow: Pearson Education).

Palmer, F. (1974) *The English Verb* (London: Longman).

Palmer, F. (1976) *Semantics* (Cambridge: Cambridge University Press).

Palmer, F. (1986) *Mood and Modality* (Cambridge: Cambridge University Press).

Pullman, P. (1990) *The Broken Bridge* (Basingstoke: Macmillan).

Quirk, R., Greenbaum, S., Leech, G. and Svartvik, J. (1985) *A Comprehensive Grammar of the English Language* (London: Longman).

Radford, A. (1988) *Transformational Grammar* (Cambridge: Cambridge University Press).

Roach, P. (2001) *English Phonetics and Phonology: A Practical Course* (Cambridge: Cambridge University Press).

Roca, I. and Johnson, W. (1999) *A Course in Phonology* (Oxford: Blackwell).

Sacks, H., Schegloff, E. and Jefferson, G. (1974) 'A Simplest Systematics for the Organisation of Turn-taking for Conversation', *Language*, 50, pp. 696–735.

Semino, E. (1997) *Language and World Creation in Poems and Other Texts* (London: Longman).

Simpson, P. (1993) *Language, Ideology and Point of View* (London: Routledge).

Sinclair, J. and Coulthard, M. (1975) *Towards an Analysis of Discourse* (Oxford: Oxford University Press).

Stubbs, M. (1983) *Discourse analysis: The Sociolinguistic Analysis of Natural Language* (Chicago: University of Chicago Press).

Summers, D. (1993) *Longman Language Activator* (London: Longman).

Websites

Macquarie University, phonetics site: www.ling.mq.edu.au/speech/phonetics/topics.html.

Phonetics and Linguistics Department, University College London: www.phon.ucl.ac.uk.

The internet grammar: www.ucl.ac.uk/internet-grammar/home.htm.

University of Pennsylvania, phonological atlas: www.ling.upenn.edu/phono_atlas/home.html.

Exercises and Questions

In the following exercises you can use abbreviations as follows:

A = Adverbial
Aj = adjective
AjP = adjective phrase
Aux = auxiliary verb
Av = adverb
AvP = adverb phrase
C = Complement
cj = conjunction
det = determiner
H = head (usually, but not only, of a noun phrase)
Lex = lexical verb
mod = modal
n = noun
NP = noun phrase
O = direct object
P = predicator
pass = passive
perf = perfective
postmod = postmodifier
PP = prepositional phrase
premod = premodifier
prep = preposition
prog = progressive
S = subject
sub cj = subordinating conjunction
VP = verb phrase

Chapter 1 Phonetics

The important thing to grasp from this chapter is where the articulators are situated and how they work to produce speech sounds. You should therefore use your tongue to find your alveolar ridge, your palate and your velum, and also make sure that you can turn voicing on and off, as described in Chapter 1. Specific tasks that will be useful to you as you work with speech sounds are as follows.

Exercise 1.1

Work out your own set of speech sounds, and note whether or not you use a postvocalic 'r' (rhotic accent) and the range of vowels you use, including the number and type of diphthongs.

Exercise 1.2

Draw up a set of words that illustrate all the possible consonant clusters in English syllables, based on the description given in Chapter 1. Remember that in English the syllable is made up of the following elements (with optional parts in brackets):

> (/s/) + (obstruent) + (sonorant) + verb + (any consonant except /w/, /j/ and /h/) + (obstruent) + (/s/).

Do not forget that it is not usual for a syllable in English to have both opening and closing consonant clusters of the most complex kind.

Exercise 1.3

Identify the number of syllables and the position of the main word stress in the following words. Note that some of the longer ones may have secondary stresses. Use a slash (/) to indicate a stress and a hypen for unstressed syllables.

1 angrily
2 connive
3 bangle
4 curiosity
5 surreptitious
6 roundabout
7 sausage
8 furious
9 arbitrary
10 animalistic
11 insidious
12 banana
13 complementary
14 agricultural
15 hardware
16 arrive
17 undisclosed
18 presumption
19 carousel
20 phenomenology

Chapter 2 Phonology

In Chapter 2 we considered the significant speech sounds and looked at some of the variants of the main sounds. It would be useful for you to make sure you are familiar with the main allophones of the English consonants, and you may wish to work out whether you (and others) use a glottal stop as an allophone of /t/, and if so, where and when this happens. The first exercise is a mini-project on this topic. The other general area of practice is the identification of utterance stress and recognition of intonation patterns. You can practice using different tones on individual words, and on the main stress in a short utterance, but you should also listen to people in your everyday life and try to spot the different tones in their conversation.

Exercise 2.1

Construct a set of words that have the /t/ phoneme in different positions. This should include single-syllable words with initial and final /t/ sounds, and also two-syllable words with /t/ in the middle.

Now put these words into a small number of sentences, preferably making up a continuous passage that makes some kind of sense. At this point you may find it convenient to change some of the words to fit the meaning.

Ask some informants (friends or family) to read the word list out loud to you, and then to read the passage. You may record this process if you wish, but if you are quick you should be able to tick the ones that are glottal on your sheet whilst they are reading. Do not tell your informants why you are doing this until they have read the texts. The word list is quite a formal text to read out, and it is likely that they will take more care over pronunciation in this reading than when they read the passage, where the meaning is more likely to occupy their conscious thoughts than the sounds.

If you are recording the readings, after the informants have finished their reading let the recording equipment continue for a few minutes whilst you chat informally to them about what you are doing (in general terms). This will give you an idea of the informal style of speech of each informant, and with luck there will be some /t/ phonemes in this section of the data.

Finally, work out the score for each informant and for the group as a whole. Did they use more glottal stops (proportionately) in the more formal readings? Were they using glottal stops more at the ends of syllables, medially, or initially? Indeed were there any examples of an initial glottal stop? You might like to think about why this might be a less common place for this allophone.

Exercise 2.2

Transcribe the following passage as a carefully pronounced version of a formal reading. You can check your transcription in the section that provides the answers to the exercises (but do not worry if you use a slightly different accent from the RP version I have supplied). Identify the places where a more casual reading would lead to cases of assimilation, elision or insertion, and change the transcription accordingly. Next check with the second transcription in the answers section. Note that if you want to transcribe on a personal computer you can download phonetic fonts from the website of University College, London www.phon.ucl.ac.uk).

> Sometimes we go for a walk on a Sunday. Gets us out of the city and it can be a laugh too. Last September we decided to do the canal walk. Partly because it's mostly flat so no one can moan about going uphill. What we do is take a train east for about five miles and then walk back into town on the tow path.
>
> Anyway, we'd been walking for about an hour and people were starting to suggest we stopped for a drink, when we first saw him.

Exercise 2.3

Identify the likely positioning of the main utterance stress in the following short utterances. Try pronouncing them with different tones. How many contrastively stressed versions can you invent?

1 Other people eat it with rice.
2 Sandra asked him to sing.
3 Can you lift the end up?
4 He wouldn't come to the party.
5 I'll get there about twelve.

Chapter 3 Word

Exercise 3.1

Chapter 3 introduced the structure of words, their morphology, and the word classes in English. Try finding examples of all of the following in the passage below:

- Free and bound morphemes
- Allomorphs
- Inflections
- Derivations
- Compounding
- Nouns
- Verbs
- Adjectives
- Adverbs
- Pronouns
- Determiners
- Prepositions
- Conjunctions
- Auxiliary verbs

> The shop smelt of musty old clothes and you had to push past nylon minidresses and moth-eaten fur coats to get to the men's section, which was much smaller than the women's and right at the back. The assistant looked as though she lived there, getting up every morning and deciding which of the clothes in the shop to wear. Today it was the purple taffeta dress with a thick grey cardigan and a beige felt hat. She was friendly: 'How old is your son? Seventeen? I get a lot of mothers in here. Is he like you in size?' There was a slight accent. German, maybe, or Polish. The assistant made her try on the jacket – it was an old one, she said, woollen rather than polyester, and double-breasted. Nicer than the James Bond style dinner jacket they'd seen in the window. She liked it, though it looked silly on her. Emily got the giggles when the assistant said 'Remember there will be no bust'. She didn't need reminding!

Chapter 4 Phrase

Exercise 4.1

Sort the following phrases into noun phrases, adjective phrases, verb phrases and adverb phrases. Then work out their internal structure.

1. the most enormous red balloon.
2. completely fantastic.
3. all my aunts on my mother's side.
4. might have taken.
5. dead gorgeous.
6. absolutely definitely.
7. has been seeing.
8. the cats that come into my garden.
9. was spilt.
10. afraid of the dark.

Chapter 5 Clause and Sentence

Here the task is to look beyond the small detail of phrase structure and see the bigger patterns at the clause and sentence levels. This skill, once acquired, is invaluable for a student of English language. When you have finished the exercise, look at any text in a newspaper, an advertisement and so on, and identify the clause structure in them. Remember, though, that many advertisements use a truncated clause structure or phrases, rather than full clauses.

Exercise 5.1 Simple clauses

Work out which of the seven basic clause structures is applicable to the following sentences, putting any optional adverbials into brackets:

1 Caroline bought Colin a new coat.
2 These strong-smelling onions will overpower the flavour of the meat.
3 One hundred and thirty singers performed at the Barbican.
4 That man in the blue Renault seems rather upset.
5 Surprisingly, Janine has become a really good doctor.
6 Everyone in the room paid the organisation three hundred pounds.
7 Next birthday my uncle in America is sending me a new computer.
8 The prime minister attended a meeting with European heads of state.
9 The children ran to the playground.
10 Robbie Williams records hit albums in the United States.
11 Luckily, you can't make me jealous any more.
12 After the concert all the musicians went to the pub.
13 The seven best places to visit in Thailand are on my itinerary.
14 That summer Ted Hughes wrote Sylvia Plath a poem.
15 Unfortunately the committee does not consider this your best work.
16 Ever afterward, Little Red Riding Hood would think of her adventure in the forest.
17 In the spring, after Easter, I always plan the summer bedding plant layout.
18 On balance, I would like some chocolates for Christmas.
19 This holiday has been absolutely wonderful.
20 None of the troops in the front line surrendered.

Exercise 5.2 Coordinated and subordinated clauses

Work out whether the sentences below are made up of coordinated clauses, or whether they contain subordinate clauses. Then work out the clause structure of each of the clauses in each sentence.

1 I'll come to your house about seven, or you can come and pick me up.
2 Although I feel sorry for her, she does make matters worse.
3 Being on time for meetings was Judy's great strength.
4 Pete cooked the cold vegetables that were left over from Sunday.

5 I'll clean the bathroom but you can make the beds.
6 Claire decided that she would apply for a new job.
7 The team won the match despite having three ill players.
8 The sun was shining as Jasper left home for the last time.
9 These hippos make a lot of noise and keep me awake.
10 The main problem was that no one would wash up.

Chapter 6 Semantics

Exercise 6.1

Study the passage below and pick out examples of the following sense relations and other semantic features:

1 A semantic field with three or more members.
2 An example of opposites – state the type of opposition.
3 An example of restricted collocates.
4 A superordinate and a hyponym.
5 A word that has multiple meanings (though not necessarily in this context). Is it homonymous or polysemous?

> It's not that the young ones don't care, exactly, but they don't seem to know how much work is involved in running a big choir. After all, the Ladies Committee has been raising money for over 50 years and we can't just throw away a tradition like that. I wouldn't mind, but they haven't got anything to replace it with. And it's getting more expensive every year, putting on big concerts with proper soloists and famous conductors. We could try reducing the costs of our concerts, but it would be like giving the prize to Huddersfield – there's always been a friendly rivalry between us you know.
>
> I know we ladies don't raise a lot with our coffee mornings and cake stalls, but every little helps and we're doing what we know best. Though we don't get the same standard of home cooking that we used to. I don't know what their mothers teach young girls these days. As often as not, it's a bought Swiss roll, from Ainsley's if you're lucky. I wouldn't mind, but they don't come and buy anything, either.
>
> Take last Autumn. We'd made it clear that the Society's funds were in serious trouble and that everyone was needed to sell at least ten of the tickets for the Grand Christmas Draw. Well! You'd have thought I was asking them to sell their souls the way some of them looked at me when I thrust a book of tickets into their hands just before we settled down to the first Messiah rehearsal of the season. I felt I had to say something at the break, though I know the committee don't approve of just anyone standing up and addressing the choir. I thought they should know how hard my husband always works at folding up the ticket-stubs in the week of the draw. If they don't want our efforts, I suggested, we would retire gracefully and see how they would manage to raise the £800!

It was a bit embarrassing, but I felt a little better after my outburst – and it certainly made the young ones sit up a bit. I noticed that quite a few of the young men especially came up to take extra tickets on the way out. I suppose their hearts are in the right place after all.

Would you like another curd tart with your tea?

Answers to the exercises

Exercise 1.3

1	angrily / - -	11	insidious - / - -
2	connive - /	12	banana - / -
3	bangle / -	13	complementary - - / -
4	curiosity - - / - -	14	agricultural - - / - -
5	surreptitious - - / -	15	hardware / -
6	roundabout / - -	16	arrive - /
7	sausage / -	17	undisclosed - - /
8	furious / - -	18	presumption - / -
9	arbitrary / - - -	19	carousel - - /
10	animalistic - - - / -	20	phenomenology - - - / - -

Exercise 2.2

sʌmtaɪmz wiː geʊ fə ə wɔːk ɒn ə sʌndeɪ gɛts əs aut əv ðə sɪtiː ən ɪt kən biː ə lɑːf tuː lɑːs sɛptɛmbə wiː dɪsaɪdɪd tə duː ðə kənæl wcːk pɑːtliː bɪkɒz ɪts məusliː flæt miːnɪŋ nəuwʌn kən məun əbaut gəuwɪŋ ʌphɪl wɒt wiː duː ɪz təɪk ə treɪn iːst fə əbaʊt faɪv maɪlz ən ðɛn wcːk bæk ɪntə taʊn ɒn ðə təʊpɑːθ ɛniːweɪ wiːd biːn wɔːkɪŋ fə əbaʊt ən aʊə ænd piːpel wɜː stɑːtɪŋ tə sədʒɛst wiː stɒpd fə ə drɪŋk wɛn wiː sɔː hɪm

Commentary

The above transcription is rather overcareful, and some of you might have already made some of the changes that are likely in any fluent reading of the passage, particularly, for example, adding the /r/ to the word *for*, even in non-rhotic accents. I have put spaces between the (orthographic) words to make it easier to read, though this does not represent the real-time stream of speech, as we observed earlier. Note that even in fairly formal readings, grammatical words such as *and*, *to* and *for* are likely to have a schwa vowel, and not a full stressed vowel.

Below is the more informal version, with as many assimilations, elisions and insertions as could be envisaged.

sʌmtaɪmz wiː geʊ fər ə wɔːk ɒn ə sʌndeɪ gɛts əs aut əð ðə sɪtiː n̩ɪk km̩ biː j ə lɑːf tuː lɑːs sɛptɛmbə wiː dɪsaɪdɪd tə duː ðə kənæw wcːk pɑːtliː bɪkɒz ɪts məusliː flæp miːnɪŋ nəuwʌn km̩ məun əbaut gəuwɪŋ ʌphɪl wɒp wiː duːw ɪz təɪk ə treɪn iːst fər əbaʊt faɪv maɪlz n̩ ðɛm wcːk bæk ɪntə taʊn ɒn ðə təʊpɑːθ ɛniːweɪ wiːb biːn wɔːkɪŋ fər əbaʊt ən aʊə əm piːpl̩ wɜː stɑːtɪn tə sədʒɛst wiː stɒpd fər ə drɪŋk wɛm wiː sɔːr ɪm

Commentary

Things to look out for here are the syllabic consonants, where even the unstressed schwa is elided, the assimilations, particularly to the bilabial place of articulation, and the insertion of semivowels between two vowels. One example of insertion is interesting because it depends on the dropping of initial /h/ between the words *saw* and *him*. Once the /h/ is missing there are two vowels next to each other, /ɔː/ and /ɪ/. These vowels need to be distinguished in the stream of speech and so an /r/ is inserted to perform this function. Of course a /w/ would do the same job if it were pronounced in the word *saw*, but not many speakers do pronounce final /w/ sounds and they are very difficult to hear anyway. In addition the movement from a back vowel to the bilabial position and then to a front vowel is very much harder than using an alveolar semi-vowel, /r/.

Exercise 2.3

1 Other people eat it with rice.
2 Sandra asked him to sing.
3 Can you lift the carpet?
4 He wouldn't come to the party.
5 I'll get there about twelve.

The underlined words are the final main clause elements in these utterances, and would be the neutral position for the main pitch movement in the intonation. The most neutral direction of the tone in each case is falling, although in question in number 3 there would probably be a rise on *carpet.*

The most likely contrastive placings of the utterance stress are as follows:

1 Other people eat it with rice (not my family or friends).
Other people eat it with rice. (not animals or birds).
Other people eat it with rice. (they don't stuff it with rice).
2 Sandra asked him to sing. (it wasn't Sheila).
Sandra asked him to sing. (she didn't tell him to).
Sandra asked him to sing. (she didn't ask anyone else).
3 Can you lift the carpet? (or are you not able to?)
Can you lift the carpet? (I don't want to do it.)
Can you lift the carpet? (Don't leave it down.)
4 He wouldn't come to the party (but she might).
He wouldn't come to the party (however much I argued).
He wouldn't come to the party (he just agreed to sit in another room).
5 I'll get there about twelve (don't know about the others).
I'll get there about twelve (but I may have to leave again quite soon).
I'll get there about twelve (but I won't be back here till later).

Commentary

Note that the contexts in brackets are not the only possibilities, but simply indicate a likely contrast that is implied by this particular version of the utterance. I have not taken contrastive stress to its extreme here, though it is sometimes possible for grammatical words, for instance articles, to be stressed in this way: He wouldn't come to <u>the</u> party (though he goes to all the others).

Exercise 3.1

The following are some of the words you could have picked under each heading:

- Free morphemes: *shop, slight, remind.*
- Bound morphemes: *-ing, -en, -ly.*
- Allomorphs: coats (/s/), *giggles* (/z/), *dresses* (/ɪz/).
- Inflections: clothes, *men's, looked, smaller.*
- Derivations: *woollen, musty.*
- Compounding: *moth-eaten, mini-dresses, double-breasted.*
- Nouns: *son, accent, jacket.*
- Verbs: *push, was, made.*
- Adjectives: *silly, old, German.*
- Adverbs: *there, here.*
- Pronouns: *she, he, it, her.*
- Determiners: *The, your, an.*
- Prepositions: *to, with, on.*
- Conjunction: *and.*
- Auxiliary verbs: *-'d, will.*

Exercise 4.1

(premod) (h)
1 NP: the most enormous red balloon.

(pre-mod) (h)
2 AjP: completely fantastic.

(pre-mod) (h) (post-mod PP)
3 NP: all my aunts on my mother's side.

(aux) (lex)
4 VP: might have taken.

(pre-mod) (adj)
5 AjP: dead gorgeous.

(pre-mod) (adv)
6 AvP: absolutely definitely.

(aux) (lex)
7 VP: has been seeing.

		(pre-mod)	(h)	(post-mod rel clause)
8	NP:	the	cats	that come into my garden.

		(aux)	(lex)
9	VP:	was	spilt.

		(h)	(post-mod PP)
10	AjP:	afraid	of the dark.

Exercise 5.1

	(subject)	(predicator)	(indirect object)	(direct object)
1	Caroline	bought	Colin	a new coat.

	(subject)	(predicator)	(direct object)
2	These strong-smelling onions	will overpower	the flavour of the meat.

	(subject)	(predicator)	(adverbial)
3	One hundred and thirty singers	performed	at the Barbican.

	(subject)	(predicator)	(complement)
4	That man in the blue Renault	seems	rather upset.

	(adverbial)	(subject)	(predicator)	(complement)
5	Surprisingly,	Janine	has become	a really good doctor.

	(subject)	(predicator)	(indirect object)	(direct object)
6	Everyone in the room	paid	the organisation	three hundred pounds.

	(adverbial)	(subject)	(predicator)	(indirect object)	(direct object)
7	Next birthday	my uncle in America	is sending	me	a new computer.

	(subject)	(predicator)	(direct object)	(adverbial)
8	The prime minister	attended	a meeting	with European heads of state.

Note that in number 8, the final prepositional phrase is structurally ambiguous. I have chosen to define it as an optional adverbial, which specifies who else was at the meeting, but it would also be possible, given its position after the noun phrase, *a meeting*, to define it as a postmodifier to the noun *meeting*. This would make a slight difference to the meaning, because the emphasis would be on the prime minister going into a meeting called by the heads of state, or at least into a meeting where they were already present. The above version is more neutral; they are all seen as attending the meeting together, and as having equal status.

	(subject)	(predicator)	(adverbial)
9	The children	ran	to the playground.

	(subject)	(predicator)	(direct object)	(adverbial)
10	Robbie Williams	records	hit albums	in the United States.

	(adverbial)	(subject)	(predicator)	(direct object)	(complement)	(adverbial)
11	Luckily	you	can't make	me	jealous	any more.

	(adverbial)	(subject)	(predicator)	(adverbial)
12	After the concert	all the musicians	went	to the pub.

	(subject)	(predicator)	(adverbial)
13	The seven best places to visit in Thailand	are	on my itinerary.

	(adverbial)	(subject)	(predicator)	(indirect object)	(direct object)
14	That summer	Ted Hughes	wrote	Sylvia Plath	a poem.

	(adverbial)	(subject)	(predicator)	(direct object)	(complement)
15	Unfortunately	the committee	does not consider	this	your best work.

	(adverbial)	(subject)	(predicator)	(adverbial)
16	Ever afterward	Little Red Riding Hood	would think	of her adventure in the forest.

It is worth noting here that it is not always easy to determine whether an adverbial is optional or obligatory. The fact that the verb *think* (number 16) can be intransitive (I'm thinking) probably makes this one optional, though the sentence would look odd without it. Note also that the inclusion of the prepositional phrase *in the forest* as part of this adverbial, rather than as a separate adverbial in its own right, reflects the fact that it was the adventure that happened in the forest, not the thinking. If you cannot understand this ambiguity, try reading the sentence out loud, giving the two prepositional phrases first separate and then joint intonation patterns. This should make the two meanings clear.

	(adverbial)	(adverbial)	(subject)	(adverbial)	(predicator)	(direct object)
17	In the spring,	after Easter,	I	always	plan	the summer bedding plant layout.

	(adverbial)	(subject)	(predicator)	(direct object)	(adverbial)
18	On balance,	I	would like	some chocolates	for Christmas.

	(subject)	(predicator)	(complement)
19	This holiday	has been	absolutely wonderful.

	(subject)	(predicator)
20	None of the troops in the front line	surrendered.

Exercise 5.2

The tables below demonstrate the relationship between the higher and lower levels of clause element, and the depth of the embedding of the subordinate clauses where relevant. The abbreviations are as follows: A = adverbial; C = complement; Cj = conjunction; N = noun phrase; O = direct object; P = predicator; S = subject.

clause S	 P	 A	 (A)	cj	clause S	 P	 O	 A
I'll	come	to your house	about seven,	or	you	can come and pick	me	up

The above sentence has two equal main clauses, coordinated by *or*. They have different clause structures, and the second clause has a coordinated predicator with two verbs, *come* and *pick*.

Adverbial clause Cj	 S	 P	 C	 A	 S	 P	 O	 C
Although	I	feel	sorry	for her,	she	does make	matters	worse.

Subject clause P	 A		P	C
Being	on time for meetings	was	Judy's great strength.	

S	P	O NP pre-mod	 head	post-mod clause (relative) S	 P	 A
Pete	cooked	the cold	vegetables	that	were left	from Sunday

clause S	 P	 O	cj	clause S	 P	 O
I	'll clean	the bathroom	but	you	can make	the beds

S	**P**	**O**			
		clause			
		cj	**S**	**P**	**A**
Claire	decided	that	she	would apply	for a new job

S	**P**	**O**	**A**		
			clause		
			cj	**P**	**P**
The team	won	the match	despite	having	three ill players.

S	**P**	**A**				
		clause				
		cj	**S**	**P**	**O**	**A**
The sun	was shining	as	Jasper	left	home	for the last time.

clause			**cj**	**clause**		
S	**P**	**O**		**P**	**O**	**C**
These hippos	make	a lot of noise	and	keep	me	awake

S	**P**	**C**		
		clause		
		cj	**S**	**P**
The main problem	was	that	no one	would wash up

The verb in the subordinate clause in the final table (*wash up*) is one of the many multiword verbs in English, often called 'phrasal verbs'. These are made up of a verb and one or more particles, which often resemble adverbs or prepositions but are not as behaviourally independent as these word classes. Thus although there is *wash up*, there is no *wash in, wash around* or *wash for*.

Exercise 6.1

1 A semantic field with three or more members:
choir, concert, soloists, conductors, Messiah,
mother, husband, girl, men.
2 An example of opposites – state the type of opposition: buy–sell (converses).
3 An example of restricted collocates: home cooking, friendly rivalry.

4 A superordinate and a hyponym: cake (superordinate); Swiss roll, curd tart (hyponyms).
5 A word that has multiple meanings (though not necessarily in this context). Is it homonymous or polysemous?: tea – here it is a drink, but it has other meanings, including the early evening meal taken by children and some families in Britain.

Appendix
Syntactic Tree Diagrams

A tree diagram is a way of showing the structure of a sentence. It can only work as a branching structure – the lines can never cross or go in two directions at once. The branches divide a higher level of structure into lower-level units (for example clauses into phrases) and are based on the function of the lower-level unit. This relationship is known as 'constituent structure':

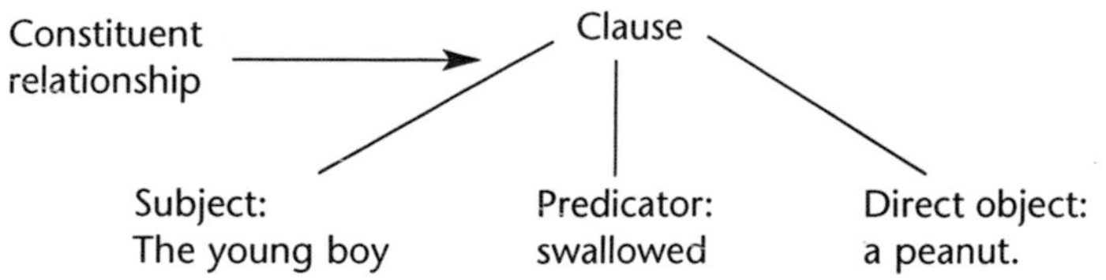

Non-branching lines are used to show the form–function relationship. This relationship is also called 'realisation'.

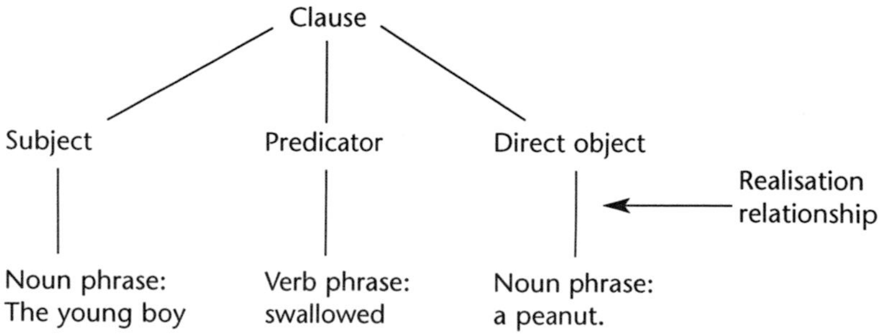

Tree diagrams work for all levels of structure, as follows.

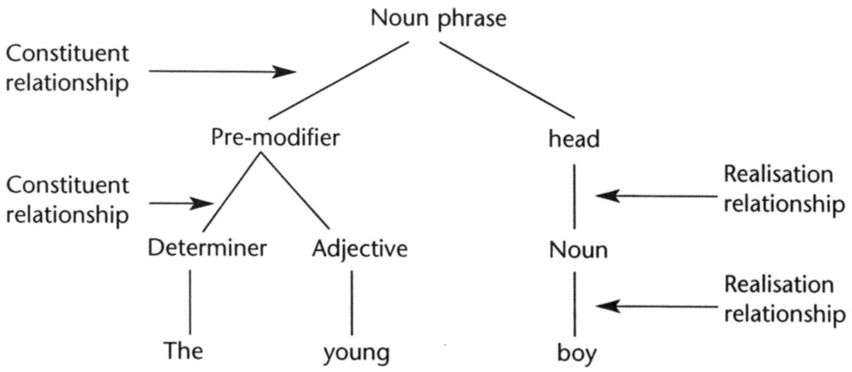

Note that the realisation relationship at the final level is between a word class label and an actual lexical item.

The following structure is for the same noun phrase, but this time with a postmodifier. Note that there is no verb here – it is only a noun phrase, and in normal circumstances would not function as an utterance on its own (that is, it would have to be part of a larger clause structure as a subject, an object or a complement):

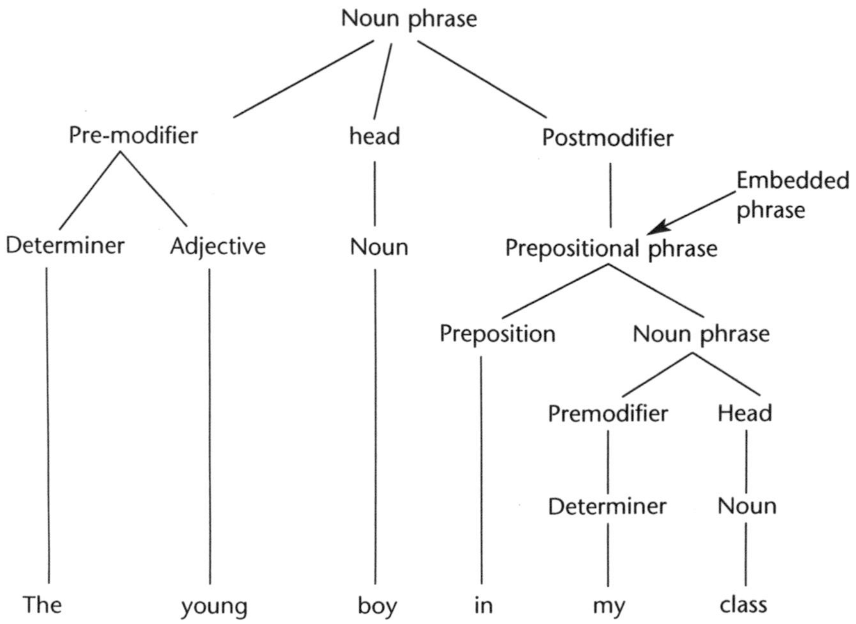

Note that once an embedded phrase has been included, the branching has to start again to show the structure.

The following example has phrases (but not clauses) embedded in each other.

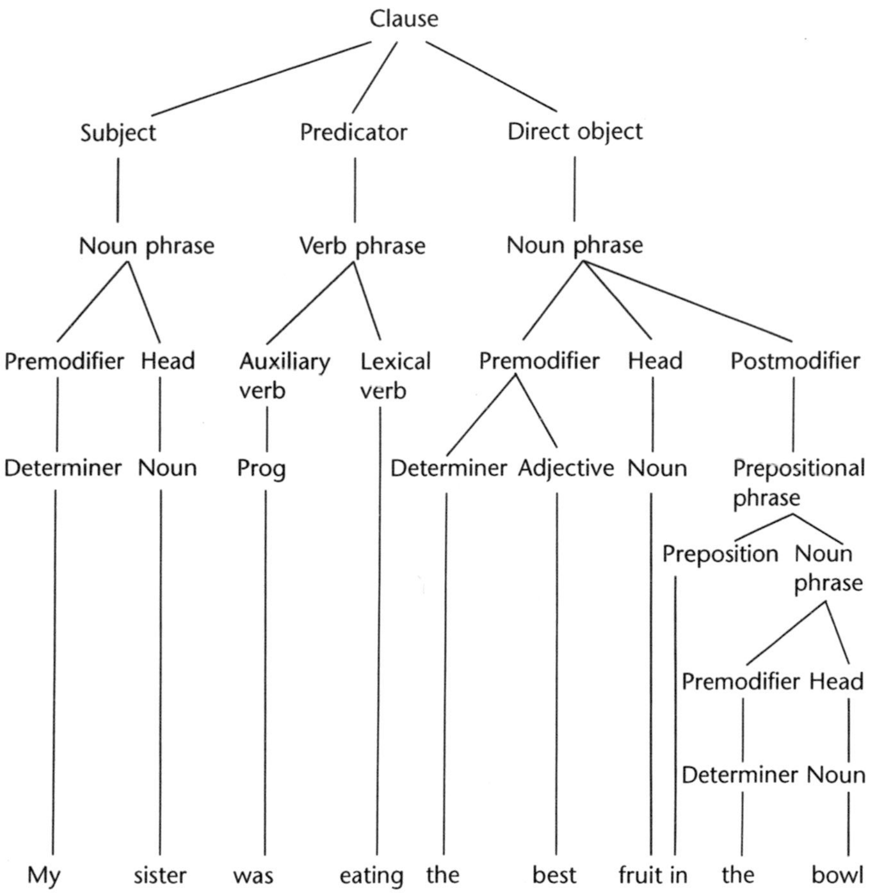

Although these tree diagrams might appear complicated at first glance, they do not contain anything we have not studied in this book. Try constructing your own, using very simple structures to start with and working from your notes on noun phrase and clause structure.

The next tree diagram is of a sentence with two coordinated clauses.

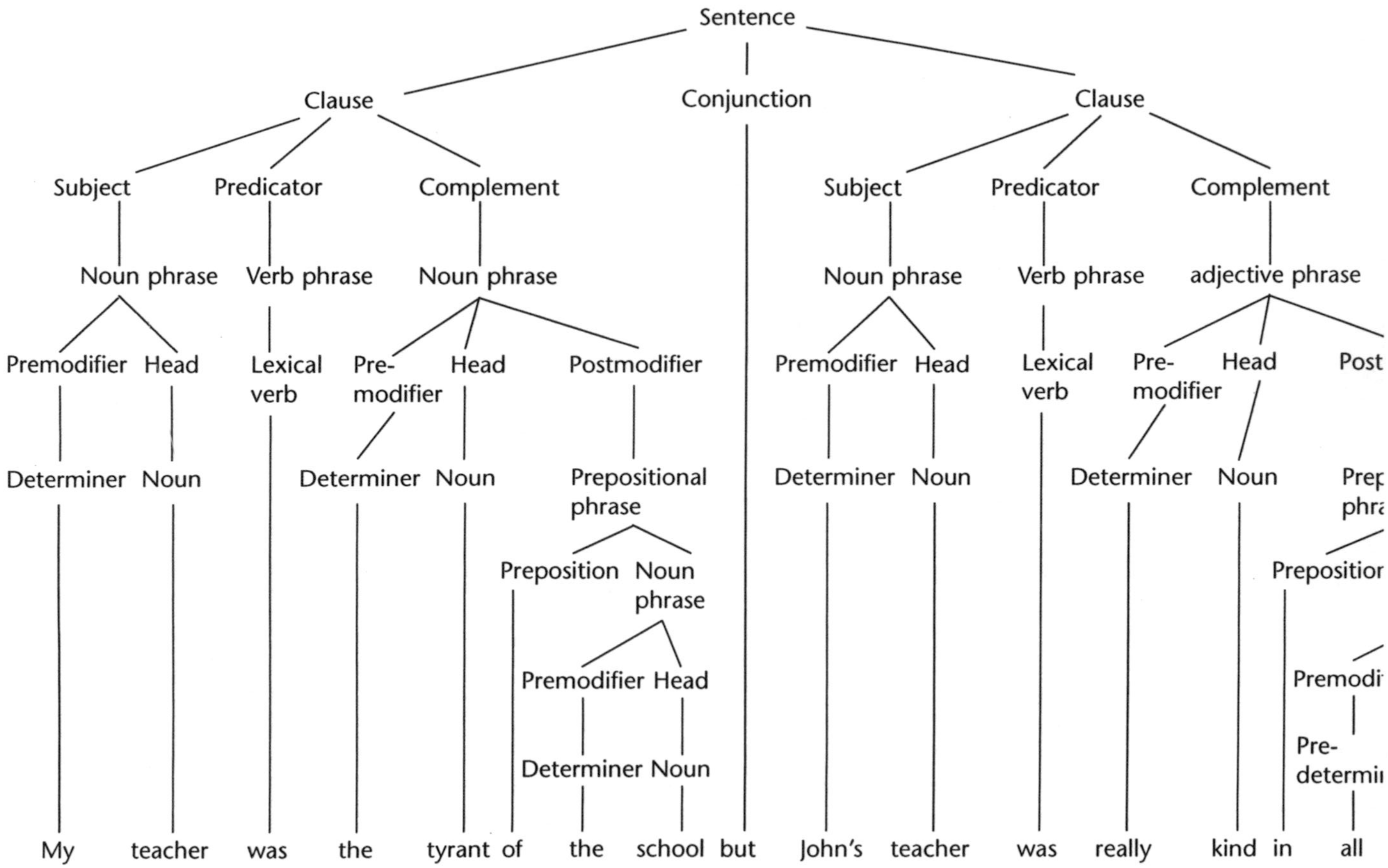

Sentence
Clause
Conjunction
Clause
Subject
Predicator
Complement
Noun phrase
Verb phrase
Noun phrase
Premodifier
Head
Lexical verb
Pre-modifier
Head
Postmodifier
Determiner
Noun
Determiner
Noun
Prepositional phrase
Preposition
Noun phrase
Premodifier
Head
Determiner
Noun
My teacher was the tyrant of the school but John's teacher was really kind in all
Subject
Predicator
Complement
Noun phrase
Verb phrase
adjective phrase
Premodifier
Head
Lexical verb
Pre-modifier
Head
Post
Determiner
Noun
Determiner
Noun
Prep
phra
Prepositior
Premodi
Pre-
determi

The following is an example of a sentence with subordinate clauses. It looks complicated, but if you just focus on individual phrases an you will begin to see how the tree diagram puts it all together.

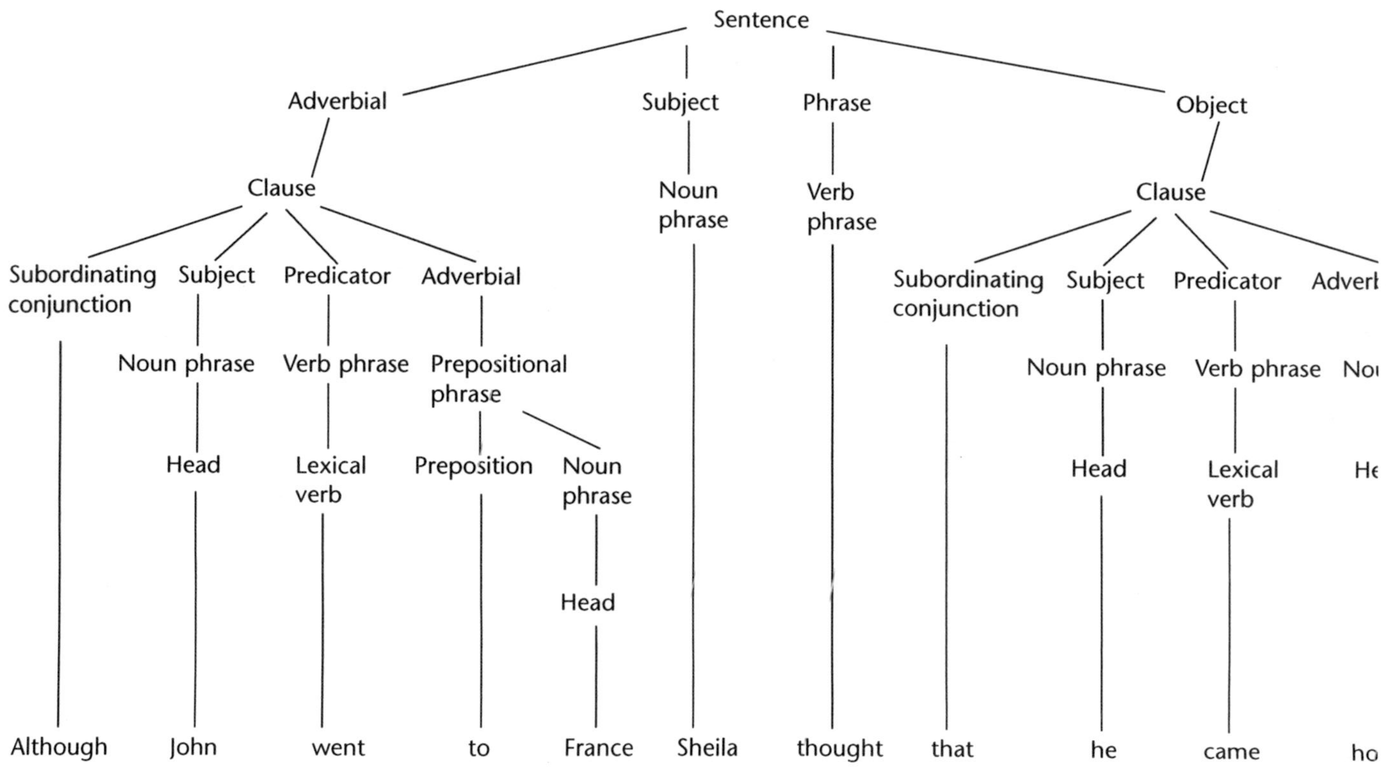

Glossary

This glossary defines all of the technical vocabulary you will meet in this book, but is not a substitute for reading the book! In many cases, the definition is a reminder of the full explanation given elsewhere, and readers may wish to refer to the fuller explanation too. These can be found by following the **bold** page numbers in the Index that indicate the main entry, rather than the first occurrence of the word or phrase.

The definitions in the glossary are kept as short as possible by using other terms which are also defined in the glossary, rather than trying to also break those terms down into their own definitions. This means that readers may occasionally have to follow a trail of definitions to understand the one they started with. This may seem onerous at first, but is a good way to become thoroughly conversant with linguistic terms. It also illustrates the basic circularity of what linguists are trying to do: explain language by using language.

* * *

acoustic phonetics The study of how speech is transmitted through soundwaves to the hearer. Based in physics, and not explored in this volume.

adjectival complement Phrases (e.g. *beautiful* ***as a butterfly***) and clauses (e.g. *hard* ***to understand***) which are integral to the adjective phrase and follow the head adjective.

adjective A lexical word class which fulfils the function of Complement or noun premodifier. Includes a class of gradable adjective (e.g. *big, small*) which has comparative and superlative inflections (e.g. *bigger, biggest*). Also includes adjectives of material (e.g. *wooden*), provenance (e.g. *Japanese*), colour (e.g. *red*) and many other 'general' adjectives.

adjective phrase A phrase which has an adjective as head word (e.g. *excited*). May contain a premodifying intensifier (e.g. ***very*** *excited*) and sometimes an adjective complement (e.g. *very excited* ***by the show***).

adjunct A term used in some descriptions of grammar for what we have called adverbial in this volume.

adverb A lexical word class which fulfils the function of Adverbial or adjective premodifier. It is a somewhat odd mixture of both words derived from adjectives (e.g. *slowly, softly*), which often indicate the manner in which an action is performed and words which designate the time/space context (e.g. *soon, near*). There is also a subgroup of adverbs, known as intensifiers.

adverb clause A subordinate clause which functions as an Adverbial (e.g. *Having eaten her tea*, she read the paper).

adverb phrase A phrase performing the same range of functions as an adverb. Usually made up of an adverb premodified by an intensifier (e.g. *very slowly*).

adverbial A clause element which is normally realised by an adverb phrase (e.g. *incredibly quickly*), a prepositional phrase (e.g. *on the buses*) or an adverb clause (*after having eaten his supper*) and provides some context to the process described by the clause. Many adverbials are not obligatory parts of the structure of their clauses, though a few are required for grammaticality, depending on the choice of verb.

affix A general term used for bound morphemes added to other (free) morphemes to make complex words. Not specific about the placing of the bound morpheme, which may occur before (prefix) or after (suffix) the free morpheme. Examples include *reconsider* and *consol**ation***.

affricate A manner of articulation of consonants which involves the complete closure of the articulators, like a plosive, but a much slower release of the closure, which allows the air to leak out, rather than 'exploding'. The result is a combination of the abruptness of a plosive at the beginning of the sound, and the longer noisy phase of a fricative at the end of the sound. In English, fricatives are /tʃ/ and /dʒ/, respectively found twice in *church* and *judge*.

allomorph The variant of a morpheme, usually determined by its (phonological) context or by its historical derviation. For example, the plural morpheme for nouns has a regular form where the end of the noun will influence its form (e.g. *dogs* /dɒgz/, *cats* /kæts/ and *horses* /hɔːsɪz/) and some nouns also have irregular forms due to their history, including no suffix at all (e.g. *fish*) and a change of vowel (e.g. *man* /mæn/ – *men* /mɛn/).

allophone The variant of a phoneme, usually determined by its phonetic context (complementary distribution), but also may be in free variation. The phoneme /l/ in English has at least two variants in most accents, the clear (alveolar) variant in initial position (e.g. *light*) and the dark version in final position (e.g. *pull*).

alveolar An adjective describing a place of articulation of consonants, where the blade of the tongue touches the alveolar ridge, just behind the teeth. The English alveolar consonants are /t d r s z l r/

alveolar ridge One of the articulators used in pronouncing consonants. A 'platform' behind the teeth and between the teeth and the palate.

alveolum Another, less common, word for alveolar ridge.

amplitude The width of soundwaves, correlating in general terms with the loudness of the sound. Important for perceived linguistic stress.

anaphoric reference The use of words and phrases to refer backwards in a text to something or someone who was introduced earlier. Pronouns are often used in this way (e.g. ***Mr Jones** came to tea. **He** wore a hat*).

anticipatory assimilation Also called regressive assimilation, this is the varying of phonetic realisation of a phoneme, depending on the following sound. This could result in the phrases *right pair* and *ripe pear* sounding identical: /raɪppɛə/ as the alveolar plosive at the end of *right* anticipates the bilabial plosive at the beginning of *pair*.

approximant A manner of articulation of consonants which is much less typically consonantal than plosives and other consonants, because the articulators are only brought towards each other, rather than making complete closure (plosives) or partial contact (fricatives). The approximants (also called semi-vowels), involve a movement of the tongue and other parts of the mouth towards and away from contact. Examples include /j/, often spelt as 'y' in English, as in *yacht*.

arbitrariness The fundamental insight of structuralist approaches to language is that the form and structure of human language is not intrinsically connected to the world it describes and manipulates. Thus, the word for any particular referent (e.g. dog) may vary radically in different languages (e.g. French *chien*, Spanish *perro*, English *dog*, German *hund*).

articles There are two articles in English, the definite article (*the*) and the indefinite article (*a/an*). They form part of the class of determiners, which usually introduce noun phrases (e.g. ***the** silk tie*).

articulatory phonetics The study of how human beings use the vocal organs (tongue, teeth, larynx etc) to articulate the sounds of speech.

arytenoid cartilage The place at which the vocal folds are attached to the larynx. The vocal folds can be drawn together (for voicing) or apart (for voiceless sounds and quiet breathing) at this point.

aspiration Audible exhalation during a sound (often a plosive consonant), which may form a distinctive characteristic of a phoneme or allophone.

assimilation The influencing of the nature of a phoneme by an adjacent phoneme. Can affect the voice, place or manner of articulation of the sound.

auditory phonetics The study of the reception of speech sounds by hearers. Based on physics and not covered in this book. Has overlapping interests with acoustic phonetics.

auxiliary verb A verb which occurs before the lexical verb, and carries general meanings, such as tense and person, as well as indicating the modality, the aspect (perfective, continuous or both) or the voice (active or passive) of a verb phrase. One of the grammatical classes of word. Auxiliary verbs in English are *have*, *be* and the modal verbs (e.g. *may*, *can*).

back vowels Those vowels which are articulated with the resonating cavity concentrated at the back of the mouth. English back vowels include /ɔː/ (e.g. *for*) and /uː/ (e.g. *too*).

base The base of a complex word is the free morpheme on which it is built. Thus, the base of the word *uncomfortable* is the free morpheme *comfort*, which has a prefix and a suffix added.

bilabial A place of articulation of consonants, which involves the use of both lips. English bilabial sounds are /p b m w/.

blade of the tongue This is the top of the outermost part of the tongue, which is the part closest to the alveolar ridge. It is therefore used in articulating alveolar sounds such as /d/. Not to be confused with the tip of the tongue.

bound morpheme A morpheme which cannot stand alone, but is necessarily attached to another morpheme, usually a free morpheme. Thus, the *-ed* of a past tense verb in English, such as *changed*, is a bound morpheme.

broad transcription The phonemically based system used for writing down speech sounds, concentrating on their contrastive potential for making meaning rather than their phonetic detail. Normally enclosed in slashes: e.g. *pyjamas* might be transcribed broadly as /pɪdʒɑːmez/. See also **narrow transcription**.

cardinal numbers Part of the class of enumerators which occur in the noun phrase, after determiners, and before the head noun (e.g. *the* ***ten*** *soldiers*). Indicates how many cases of the head noun are being referred to.

cardinal vowels The vowels represented by the extreme points on the vowel chart, which are normally not exactly those used in particular languages. They are reference points against which the precise articulation of vowels can be plotted.

case system Some languages (e.g. German, Russian) have different forms of nouns according to the function they are performing in the clause, either in relation to the verb (e.g. as Subject or Object) or in relation to other nouns. The nearest thing English has to grammatical case of this kind is the possessive morpheme which adds *'s* to the noun and the different pronoun forms which occur in Subject position (e.g. *I*) and Object position (e.g. *me*).

cataphoric reference The use of words and phrases to refer forwards in a text to something or someone who will be introduced in detail later. Pronouns can be used in this way: ***He*** *was never wrong. Jenny hated* ***her father*** *for that.* Less common than anaphoric reference, as it causes anticipation in the reader, which is useful in some narrative settings, but not always helpful in functional writing.

catenative verbs Lexical verbs such as *try, want* and *intend* which are followed by another lexical verb in infinitive form (e.g. *try to sing*).

central vowels Those vowels which are articulated with the resonating cavity in the centre of the mouth. They include /ə/ (schwa) and /ɜː/ in English.

centralising diphthongs Diphthongs which end on a central vowel such as schwa in English (e.g. /ɛə/ as in *hair* or *stare*).

citation form The form of a lexeme that is listed in reference works such as dictionaries. In English, usually the infinitive form for verbs (e.g. *put, sing, ride*).

clause The basic structure of syntax, being the simplest structure which can stand alone grammatically and has some semantic meaning without the necessity of referring to contextual information and/or shared knowledge. Has one of seven basic structures, with the option of additional Adverbials.

clause element The building-blocks of clause structure, there are five clause elements: Subject, Predicator, Object, Complement, Adverbial. Only the Adverbial can occur more than once in a single clause.

clear 'l' The lateral approximant when it is articulated at the alveolar ridge is known as clear 'l', in contrast to dark 'l', which is velar. Occurs at the beginning of English syllables (e.g. *lake*).

cleft sentence A structure which allows the producer to focus on any clause element (except the verb) by putting it into the focal position in a general structure such as 'It is the children thatI feel sorry for' or 'It was the children that I felt sorry for'.

closed Vowels articulated with the resonating cavity high up near the palate, so that the tongue is raised and the jaw relatively closed. Examples from English are /iː/ and /uː/.

coda The final consonants in a syllable, forming part of the rhyme with the nucleus (e.g. the final consonant in /stɪk/).

cohesion The interconnections between sentences in a text which prevent it from being a random sequence of unrelated statements. Cohesion is delivered in a number of ways, for example by referencing, substitution, ellipsis and lexical connections.

cohesive links The specific connections between parts of different sentences in a text which help to make it work as a unit.

co-hyponym Two or more word senses which share a superordinate (e.g. *cow* and *pig* both have the superordinate *animal* and are therefore co-hyponyms of each other).

collocation The relationship between word senses that are found together. When this co-occurrence is frequent, the relationship is implicit even when only one of a pair of collocates is present.

comparative The form of an adjective (or occasionally an adverb) which shows that the noun it is attached to has more of the property described by the adjective than some other referent (e.g. *Sheila is* ***taller*** *than me*).

competence Chomsky's term for the cognitive capacity of a native speaker to construct utterances in the language concerned. See also **performance**.

complement A clause element which follows only certain verbs, and has the same referent as either the Subject (after intensive verbs such as *be*) or the Object (after verbs of creation or production such as *make*).

complementaries Mutually exclusive opposites such as *dead* and *alive*, which form a semantic relation between word senses. If one is explicitly negated (*I am not* ***dead***), the other automatically applies (*I am* ***alive***).

complementary distribution The patterns of occurrence of some allophones, which are always found in different contexts from each other. Thus, aspirated plosives are found in English at the beginning of syllables and their unaspirated counterparts are found at the ends of syllables.

complementary opposite See **complementaries**.

complex sentence A sentence made up of a main clause and one or more subordinate clauses (e.g. *Jasper was very tired after staying out all night*).

compound sentence A sentence made up of two or more main clauses (e.g. *Jasper was tired but Serena was elated*).

compounding One of three forms of word formation (see also **derivation** and **inflection**) by combining two or more free morphemes to make a new word which usually has a more specialised meaning than the sum of its parts (e.g. *clockwork*).

conditional subordinator The word *if*, which introduces a subordinate clause as a potential (conditional) context for the main clause (e.g. ***If they don't arrive soon,*** *they'll miss the play*).

conjunction A grammatical class of words whose task if to join other grammatical units and structures together. These fall into two main groups; co-ordinating conjunctions (*and, but, or*) and subordinating conjunctions (*if, although, since,* etc.).

connotation Those meanings which attach to a word sense by virtue of their usage. Thus, the connotations of a word like *choo-choo* will be associated with being used by or to children, whereas the connotations of *My learned friend* are of being used in court.

consonant A speech sound which involves the cutting off or restricting of the egressive airstream in different ways and places, in order to make distinctive sound effects (e.g. /d/ and /k/).

consonant clusters The combinations of consonants that can occur at the beginning and end of syllables in any particular language (e.g. the initial consonant cluster in *stripe*: /straɪp/).

context A very broad-ranging word which can cover the immediate linguistic surroundings of a word or sound and also the situational setting in which language is used, including the relationships between participants and the place in which they find themselves.

contrastive stress The use of utterance stress in a non-neutral way to change the focus of a clause without changing the structure. Thus, the stressing of a non-final clause element will imply some kind of contrast (e.g. *THEY were never on time* implies that *WE were on time*).

conversation analysis The study of interaction between speakers, looking for patterning in the ways in which speakers take turns, respond to each other's turns etc.

converses Semantically opposite word senses which are mutually dependent on each other, such that if one exists or is happening, the other also must exist or be happening (e.g. *husband* and *wife*, *buy* and *sell*).

cooperative principle The overriding principle of human interaction, as postulated by philosopher Paul Grice. Although it is clear that not all human communication is in fact cooperative, his claim is that it all takes place against an expectation of cooperation and thus allows participants to judge instances of the principle, and its maxims, being flouted, typically giving rise to a conversational implicature.

coordinating conjunction See **conjunction**.

coordination The process of joining two grammatical units or structures of the same level (i.e. word, phrase or clause) together by the use of a coordinating conjunction (e.g. *fish and chips*).

countable noun A member of the noun word class which has singular and plural forms (e.g. *cup / cups*), and whose referents can thus be counted. See also **mass noun**.

creativity The design feature of human languages which allows for an infinite number of different sentences to be made up from a finite number of units and structures.

dark 'l' The lateral approximant when it is articulated at the velum is known as dark 'l', in contrast to clear 'l', which is alveolar. Occurs at the end of English syllables (e.g. *pool*).

definite article The definite article (*the*) forms part of the class of determiners, which usually introduce noun phrases (e.g. ***the** silk tie*). It indicates that there is a specific referent, as opposed to *any* referent of the noun. See also indefinite article.

deixis A referential property of some linguistic items, including the demonstrative adjectives, the pronouns, and some adverbs of time and space. This property allows the reference of the words concerned to shift according to context. A simple example is the 1st and 2nd person pronouns, *I* and *you*. The actual meaning of these pronouns depends on who is speaking and who they are talking to.

demonstrative adjective These form a sub-class of the determiner word class, with the members *this, these, that* and *those*. They have deictic meaning which shifts according to the location of the speaker and the referent. Thus the exact meaning of *This jumper* will change if the identity of the speaker and the jumper indicated also change.

denotation This is the opposite of connotation, which is meaning derived from a word's use. Denotation, by contrast, refers to the stable, conventional meaning of a lexeme.

dental A place of articulation of consonants involving the teeth. Usually, the tip of the tongue pushes up against the teeth from behind in this kind of speech sound. Not common in English, but occurs in Italian, and sounds similar to English alveolar sounds such as /d/ and /t/. See also **interdental.**

deontic/boulomaic modality Although not quite the same, the deontic and boulomaic functions of modality often occur in the same kinds of text, and overlap in certain ways. Deontic modality concerns the attitude of the speaker as to what ought to happen or be the case. Boulomaic modality refers to the speaker's wishes and hopes. Thus, *I think you should get a job* might have elements of both kinds of modality.

derivation One of three forms of word formation (see also **compounding** and **inflection**), which adds a bound morpheme to a free morpheme, to make a new word, usually in a different word class, and also with a significant, and not entirely predictable, change of meaning (e.g. *farm-er*). Although there is some patterning to the derviations that occur in English (e.g. *teach-er, bank-er*), they are not comprehensive (e.g. **nurs-er*).

design features The characteristics of human language which distinguish it from some other forms of communication, including animal communication systems and artificial languages, such as computer code. See also **arbitrariness, creativity, stimulus-freedom** and **duality of patterning.**

determiner The grammatical class of words which usually introduce noun phrases. Includes articles, demonstrative adjectives and possessive adjectives (e.g. *the corner, that shop, my house*).

devoicing The reduction in voicing of a consonant which is normally voiced.

diachronic dimension of study The study of language evolution and change. See also **synchronic.**

diacritics The small additions to phonetic symbols which indicate variants of the main sound. For example, devoicing is indicated by a small circle beneath the symbol: e.g. [d̥].

dialect A variety of a language which is spoken by people who inhabit a particular geographical area or who have similarities of social class.

diphthong A long vowel sound which is made up of two distinct vowels and the gliding movement between them (e.g. /eɪ/ as in *say* and /aʊ/ as in *how*).

direct object The most common kind of Object clause element in English, often indicating the goal of the verb, and usually taking the form of a noun phrase or a noun clause (e.g. *I ate* ***the tomato sandwich***). See also **indirect object**.

directional/reversive opposition A semantic relation between word senses whereby the meaning of one of the words implies the reversal of the process denoted by the other (e.g. *button/unbutton*).

discourse This term is used in different ways to indicate something 'larger' than sentence structure. Here it is used to suggest those considerations which lie beyond the scope of this book, such as conversational structure, pragmatic meaning etc. Thus, here it both indicates textual structures larger than the sentence, and also the need for contextual understanding for interpretation.

discourse intonation The form of intonation analysis favoured by discourse analysts that concentrates on meaning and impact of intonation structures in preference to the phonetic properties of pitch variation.

discovery procedure A method of investigating the units and structure of an unknown language by progressive questioning of informants.

displacement One of the design features of human language that focuses on the human ability to talk and write about things and events that are distant in time and space. Also called stimulus-freedom.

distal One of the terms used to describe deictic meaning. In this case, the meaning is distant or far away (either physically or psychologically) from the speaker (***that*** *cushion over* ***there***).

ditransitive verb Verbs which tend to require the presence of both a Direct and an Indirect Object (e.g. *send* and *put*).

duality of patterning One of the design features of human language which focuses on the double patterning (of sounds and meaningful units) which allow enormous numbers of words to be constructed out of a relatively small number of sounds (about 40 in English).

dummy operator The auxiliary verb *do* which has the same functions as other auxiliaries in forming questions (*who did you say?*), emphasising (*I DID go!*), and negation (*she didn't arrive*) but has no separate meaning of its own.

egressive pulmonary airstream mechanism A very fancy way of saying that we mainly speak on an outward breath! Try breathing in when you speak and you will find that it is hard to talk for very long.

elided/elision Used to describe sounds that are missed out in connected speech to make it flow more smoothly or quickly (e.g. *handbag*/hæmbæg/).

ellipsis/ elliptical The missing out of words which are entirely predictable from the context (e.g. *Shelley got up and (she) sent to the window*).

embedding See **subordination.**

enumerator The grammatical class of numbers, comprising the cardinal and ordinal numbers, which occur in the pre-modification of a noun, after determiners and before adjectives (e.g. *those* ***three*** *yellow dusters*).

epiglottis This flap of skin is found at the base of the tongue, covering the windpipe, so that food does not go down into the larynx.

epistemic modality Although often delivered by the same mechanisms as deontic and boulomaic modality, epistemic modality concerns not the speaker's wishes, but his or her attitude to the truth or likelihood of a particular occurrence (e.g. *She may not come to the party*).

etymology The history and derivation of a word.

falling tone A distinctive pitch pattern, beginning on the tonic syllable of a tone group,which indicates finality or new information.

fall–rise A distinctive pitch pattern, beginning on the tonic syllable of a tone group, which falls first and then rises. Normally refers to given information.

finite form One of the forms of a verb which can occur as the main verb in a clause and has to agree with the Subject in number and person. The finite forms include the present tense in the 1st , 2nd and plural persons (e.g. *play*), present tense in the 3rd person singular (e.g. *plays*) and the past tense, all persons (e.g. *played*).

flap A manner of articulation of consonants in which the tongue hits one of the other articulators (e.g. the alveolar ridge or the teeth) once. There are no flap consonants in most English accents, though the Scottish 'r' is sometimes realised as a flap.

form The physical shape or structure of a linguistic unit which may be used to identify which class of unit (e.g. adjective or noun) it belongs to. See also **function**.

free morpheme A morpheme which can occur without any affixes (e.g. *stair*).

free variation The possibility that some phonemes in some accents may vary between allophones irrespective of position.

frequency The speed of soundwaves in reaching the peak and trough of their amplitude. It is perceived largely as pitch and studied by acoustic phonetics which is not covered in this book.

fricative A manner of articulation of consonants when the airstream passes through a narrow space between articulators and produces a 'messy' or whistling noise (e.g. /f/ and /s/).

front vowels Those vowels articulated with the resonating cavity situated at the front of the mouth (e.g. /iː/, /ɛ/ and /æ/).

fronting The movement of a clause element to the beginning of the clause, to produce particular focal (often literary) effects (e.g. *Often have I thought that . . .*).

function In general, function refers to the part that a unit or structure plays in a higher structure. Thus, for example, we can talk about the function of a noun phrase as being the Subject of a clause.

functional linguistics The approach to linguistic description derived from the work of Halliday, amongst others, which places the function of linguistic units and structures at the heart of the description, thus bringing contextual factors of meaning into all aspects of linguistic analysis.

fusion Fusion occurs where two adjacent consonants are influenced by their proximity and change to become a single (different) consonant. This usually results in an affricate in English (e.g. In a phrase such as Would you? /wudjuː/ becomes /wʊdʒuː/).

General American The name for one of the most common accents of American English.

generative theory Those approaches to linguistics which have the label generative are normally concerned with the cognitive production of linguistic structures, and include Chomsky's transformational-generative grammar.

given information Information which is already shared by the participants in a conversation, or which is known to be part of the background information against which the conversation takes place.

glide The movement between vowels in a diphthong which sometimes results in a sound similar the to approximants.

glottal fricative The /h/ phoneme is a glottal fricative.

glottal stop The very well-known sound which is an allophone of /t/ in many British English accents. Transcribed as [ʔ].

glottis The combined vocal folds and surrounding mechanisms for moving them into position. Positioned within the larynx.

gradable adjective Adjectives which can be intensified by adverbials and often have comparative and superlative forms (e.g. *very hot, hotter, hottest*).

gradable antonyms Opposites (usually adjectives) which are not mutually exclusive, but have a range of possibilities between them (e.g. *hot-cold, high-low*).

grammatical words Those word classes (e.g. determiner, pronoun, conjunction) whose main function is to relate the lexical words to each other and make standard links to the context (e.g. through definiteness or situational reference). These classes have a limited and stable membership, unlike the lexical word classes which are open-ended and unstable.

Gricean maxims The four general 'rules' by which Paul Grice thought that conversation is generally regulated within his proposed overall 'co-operative principle'.

half-closed/half-open The height of the tongue (less than/more than half way towards completely open respectively) during the production of vowels. Half closed vowels in English include /ʊ/ as in *book*. Half open vowels include /ɛ/ as in *ten*.

hard palate The 'roof of the mouth' or bony dome above the tongue, not including the soft palate or velum.

head In grammatical structures, the head is usually the irreducible core of the structure (e.g. the main noun in a noun phrase). In intonation patterns, the head is the part between the first stressed syllable of a tone group and the beginning of the pitch movement on the nucleus.

hierarchy This term is used in linguistics to refer to categories which are 'nested' inside each other, with the result that the larger categories have a particular relationship of inclusion over the smaller categories. For example, hyponymy is a hierarchical category because the superordinate term (e.g. *bird*) is broader, and includes the hyponymous terms (e.g. *thrush* and *robin*).

homographs Two words which look the same written down but sound different and have different meanings (e.g. *moped*: /məʊpd/ /məʊpɛd/).

homonyms/homonymy Two words which share their written and spoken forms, but have radically different meanings to the extent that speakers do not consider them to be the 'same' word (e.g. *ring*: of bells v. circular shaped items).

homophones Two words which have different spellings, and different meanings, but sound the same (e.g. *row*: /rəʊ/ and /raʊ/).

hyponym/hyponymy The inclusive relationship between superordinate terms and those terms whose meaning is included in, but more specific than, the superordinate (e.g. *flower* is superordinate to *daisy*).

iambic rhythm The pattern of alternating unstressed plus stressed syllables which makes up much English speech, and is regularly used in English poetry.

ideational One of Halliday's three metafunctions, the ideational function of language is concerned with transference of semantic content from speaker to hearer. See also **interpersonal** and **textual**.

imperative The 2nd person form of the verb, used without an explicit Subject, whose function is to exhort the hearer to act in the way specified by the verb's semantics. In other words, it is used to give orders. Part of the grammatical system of mood. See also **indicative clause**.

indefinite article A member of the determiner class of words, the indefinite article (*a* or *an* in English) indicates that the following noun is in the singular, and is unspecific in its reference.

indicative clause In English, the verb phrase in a clause may be either imperative or indicative. This choice is often called 'mood' by grammarians. The indicative is used for making statements and asking questions, but not for giving orders. The subjunctive, which is another mood contrast available in other languages, is very rare in English.

indirect object A sub-type of the Object clause element, which is used only following certain verbs, usually indicating some kind of movement or transfer of the Object. The Indirect Object specifies the destination of the Object (e.g. *I sent* ***John*** *a card*).

infinitive form One of the non-finite forms of the verb, this form is used in subordinate clauses (***To dance*** *is her main ambition*), follows the modal verbs (e.g. *Judith might* ***write*** *it*), and also occurs after catenative verbs (e.g. *I want* ***to go***). The infinitive form may occur with or without a preceding particle, *to*, and is the citation form of the verb.

inflection One of three forms of word formation (see also **compounding** and **derivation**), which adds a bound morpheme to a free morpheme to make a new word in this case, not changing the word class, and usually changing the meaning in a regular and predictable way. Inflections in English include the plural form of the noun (e.g. *bus-es*) and the progressive form of the verb (e.g. *touch-ing*).

insertion The addition of a consonant, normally an approximant, in connected speech, between vowels belonging to different words, and therefore different syllables (e.g. the addition of /w/ in *you are* /juːwɑː/).

intensifier/intensifying adverbs A sub-class of adverbs which are used to indicate the extent to which an adjective, or another adverb is applicable (e.g. *really difficult, quite differently*).

intensive verb A sub-class of lexical verbs which are followed by Subject Complements and usually indicate an intrinsic connection between the Subject and the Complement (e.g. *Teresa* ***is*** *a good athlete. Simon* ***seems*** *well.*)

interdental A place of articulation of consonants whereby the tip of the tongue protrudes between the upper and lower teeth. English sounds /θ/ and /ð/ are interdental.

interpersonal One of Halliday's three metafunctions, the interpersonal function of language is concerned with the use of language to manage and influence the relationship between speaker and hearer. See also **ideational** and **textual**.

intonation The pitch patterns of language which add a further dimension of meaning to the spoken language.

intransitive verb A sub-class of verbs which do not require an Object to follow them (e.g. *Harry's granny* ***died***).

inversion See **fronting.**

IPA The International Phonetic Association.

IPA chart The chart detailing the transcription symbols of the International Phonetic Alphabet.

key In discourse-oriented accounts of intonation in English, key is used to describe the general pitch of the tone group in relation to the speaker's norm.

labiodental A place of articulation of consonants, with the upper teeth making contact with the lower lip (e.g. /f/ and /v/ in English).

language system/language use This distinction is important for approaches which aim to describe an 'idealised' form the of the language separately from the context of use. It is fundamental to a structuralist approach.

langue Saussure's term for the system of language which could be described by its internal structures and relationships, and was seen as the basis upon which everyday language use (parole) was built.

larynx The voice box, a structure in the throat which contains the vocal folds, muscles and ligaments which enable the vocal folds to be moved together and apart.

lateral A manner of articulation of consonants in which the blade of the tongue makes contact with the alveolar ridge, and the sides of the tongue are lowered, allowing air to escape (e.g. English /l/ and Welsh 'Ll').

lateral release The release of a plosive sound via the lowered sides of the tongue when it is followed by a syllabic /l/ (e.g. some pronunciations of *bottle* /bɒtl̩/).

length One of the distinctive differences between vowel sounds, though not phonologically significant in English.

level tone A non-varying nucleus pitch which normally indicates that the item is one of a list, or is not related to the text before and after it.

levels model of language One of the most enduring models of how language works, the levels of language are perceived as having units of increasing size (e.g. phoneme, morpheme, phrase, etc.) which fit inside each other. The flaws in the model are cause by recursion (where a 'higher' unit is embedded in a 'lower' unit) and the placing of semantics (meaning) which is not obviously a level at all.

lexeme The collection of different forms making up a single identifiable semantic unit (e.g. *like* – incorporating *like, likes, liking, liked*). Replaces *word* where the need is for greater precision.

lexical cohesion The effect of semantic connections (sense relations) between words in a text on its cohesion.

lexical semantics The study of word meaning.

lexical verb The verb word class, not including auxiliary verbs which are grammatical.

lexical words The four main semantic word classes, noun , verb, adjective and adverb, these have an extensive and changing membership and have more semantic content than grammatical words.

lexis Another word for vocabulary or the range of lexemes in a text or language.

lip-rounding The pushing forward (pursing) of the lips during the pronunciation of certain vowels (e.g. English /uː/, /ʊ/, /ɔː/ and /ɒ/).

manner (of articulation) The way in which the air is allowed to pass from the lungs out through the oral (and/or nasal) cavity. Includes plosive, fricative, nasal and approximant.

mass noun Nouns which are not countable and cannot therefore occur with the indefinite article or cardinal numbers, though they are grammatically singular (e.g. *air, sugar, fear*). Note that some mass nouns may also occur as count nouns.

meronymy The sense relation between lexical items which denote referents having a part–whole relationship (e.g. *body–leg, house-room*).

metafunctions Halliday's highest level of linguistic function, the ideational, interpersonal and textual metafunctions, under which all other linguistic functions may be subsumed.

minimal pairs Pairs (and sets) of words which differ in only one sound and are used to identify the set of phonemes in a given language (e.g. *bed-bid* to identify /ɛ/ and /ɪ/).

minor sentence A sentence which has no main verb phrase, and thus no usual clause structure (e.g. *Betraying her country*). Normally used in the spoken language, but also popular in poetry.

modal/modal auxiliary verb The grammatical word class consisting of a small number of verbs (e.g. *may, might*) which do not change their form, which require an infinitive form following them, and which indicate the speaker's view of what s/he is saying in relation to its truth, its likelihood or its desirability.

modality The expression of the speaker's view of what s/he is saying in relation to its truth, its likelihood or its desirability. Delivered by modal verbs (e.g. *will, would*), adverbs (*probably, certainly*), adjectives (*likely, possible*) amongst others.

morpheme The smallest unit of meaning, larger than the phoneme (which can make, but not carry meaning) and smaller than the word (which may be made up of more than one meaning). Morphemes may be free (*tree*) or bound (e.g. *farm-**er***).

morphology The study of the morphemic structure of words in a particular language or of word structure in general (morphological theory)

multisyllabic words Words with many (more than two) syllables (e.g. *tantamount*).

narrow transcription The phonetically based system used for writing down speech sounds, concentrating on their phonetic detail, rather than their contrastive (meaning-making) potential. Normally enclosed in square brackets: e.g. *cattle* might be transcribed narrowly as [kæʔl̩]. See also **broad transcription**.

nasal A manner of articulation of consonants in which the uvulum is drawn away from the back wall of the pharynx, allowing air to exit from the nasal as well as the oral cavity. This causes a distinctive resonance to occur in the nasal cavity (e.g. English /m/, /n/ and /ŋ/).

nasal cavity The space behind the nose, with an 'entrance' from the pharynx and exit through the nostrils.

nasal release The release of a plosive sound via the nasal cavity when it is followed by a syllabic /n/ (e.g. some pronunciations of *button* /bʌtn̩/).

nasalisation The addition of nasal resonance to any sound.

new information Information which is not shared by the participants in a conversation, and which is deemed to be the main semantic content of the utterance.

non-finite form The three forms of the verb in English which cannot on their own form the main verb in a clause, but may occur in subordinate clauses (e.g. *being a clown, . . .*) or as part of a complete verb phrase (e.g. *has been drawing*).

non-gradable adjective The very many members of the adjective class which cannot be preceded by an intensifier as they do not represent a range of any identifying feature (e.g. **highly Greek*).

non-restrictive relative clause A relative clause which provides more information about the referent of the noun phrase it occurs in, but is not instrumental in identifying that referent (e.g. *The young child,* ***who was in the field,*** *saw a wolf*).

non-rhotic An accent where /r/ is not pronounced after vowels.

noun A lexical word class which fulfils the functions of Subject, Object or Complement (and occasionally Adverbial too). It has plural and possessive inflections (e.g. *donkeys, donkey's, donkeys'*) and two important subclasses; mass nouns and count nouns.

noun clause A subordinate clause which takes the place of a noun phrase and thus functions as a Subject, an Object or a Complement (e.g. ***Trying to do yoga on a full stomach*** *is disastrous*).

noun phrase A structure based around a head noun with optional pre- and post-modification (e.g. *that sad old man in the corner*) and which functions as a Subject, an Object or a Complement.

noun phrases in apposition More than one noun phrase occupying the same clausal position (e.g. *Mr Oatridge, my milkman; Mary Poppins, our nanny*).

nucleus The beginning of the significant pitch movement in a tone group. Also, the vowel in syllable structure.

object A clause element normally realised by a noun phrase and following transitive and ditransitive verbs (e.g. *I painted* ***the fence****; Gregory sent his cousin* ***the letter***).

object complement A clause element, usually realised by a noun phrase or an adjective phrase, which has the same referent as the Object and occurs with certain kinds of verb, usually of creation or perception (e.g. *he thought her a* ***stuck-up prig****; she made me* ***furious***).

obstruent A term which encompasses both the plosive and the fricative manners of articulation of consonants, and refers to the partial or complete obstruction of the airflow.

oesophagus The pipe to the intestine, down which food is deflected by the epiglottis.

onset The opening consonant cluster in a syllable (e.g. /skr/ as in *scream*).

open Vowels articulated with the resonating cavity low down, away from the palate, so that the tongue is lowered and the jaw relatively open. Examples from English are /ɑː/ and /æ/.

open-endedness See **creativity.**

operator The first auxiliary verb in a verb phrase, which is used to negate, emphasise and ask questions. See also **dummy operator.**

oppositeness The sense relation which relates two word senses on the basis of their opposite values for a particular salient semantic feature, though they often share many of their other features of meaning (e.g. *hot–cold, alive–dead*).

oral cavity The mouth, which performs the function of a resonating chamber for the pronunciation of vowels and other sounds.

ordinal number Part of the class of enumerators, which occur in the noun phrase, after determiners, and before the head noun (e.g. *the* ***tenth*** *soldier*). Indicates which referent the head noun is referring to, in order.

orthographic Relating to the written form of the language.

palatal A place of articulation of consonants involving the body of the tongue rising toward the hard palate (e.g. /j/ in English).

palate See **hard palate**.

paradigmatic relationship Any linguistic relationship between items or structures which can occur in a particular point in the syntax but cannot co-occur. For example, all nouns are in a paradigmatic relationship because they can occur as the head of a noun phrase.

parole Saussure's term for everyday language use which was based upon the system of language (langue) which could be described by its internal structures and relationships.

participle Sometimes used to refer to the *-ing* and *-en* forms of the verb which are also known as the progressive and perfective forms respectively.

passive The passive form of the verb phrase causes the goal of the verb to become the grammatical subject, whilst the 'doer', the original Subject, becomes part of an Adverbial at best (e.g. *John kicked the dog / The dog was kicked by John*).

passive transformation The most well-known of the many suggested transformations in transformational-generative grammar. It produces passive structures from an underlying active deep structure.

perfective/perfective auxiliary The perfective form of the verb phrase is made up of the perfective auxiliary, have, and an –en participle following (e.g. *has left*).

performance Chomsky's term for the actual use of a speaker's competence. This may include errors or creative uses of the rules and units that make up the speaker's cognitive knowledge of the language. See also **competence**.

pharyngeal A place of articulation of consonants (in the pharynx) which is not used by English speech sounds.

pharynx The muscular tube leading down from the back of the tongue towards the larynx and the trachea. Air travels through the pharynx to reach both the oral and nasal cavities.

phoneme The smallest identifiable unit of speech, with a capacity to change meaning. The phoneme is identified by means of minimal pairs (e.g. *bit* /bɪt/ and *bid* /bɪd/).

phonetics The study of how human speech is produced, transmitted and received.

phonology The study of the speech sounds in a particular language.

phonotactics The patterns of combination possible in consonant clusters in a given language.

phrase A group of words which perform a single function at a higher level (e.g. in another phrase or clause). See also noun phrase, verb phrase, adjective phrase, adverb phrase and prepositional phrase.

place (of articulation) The place at which consonants are articulated and the airflow obstructed or squeezed to produce a speech sound. See also **VPM**.

plosive A manner of articulation in which there is a complete closure at some point between the glottis and the lips. The air pressure inside the closure builds up as the air flows out of the lungs, leading to an explosive release of the articulators and escape of the air. Examples from English include /p/ and /g/.

polysemy A sense relation between word senses which have the same form, and are related in meaning to the extent that we would think of them as belonging to the same lexeme. The polysemous senses, however, can enter into different sense relations from each other, including different opposites etc. An example in English is the range of meanings of the lexeme *wave*, including the wave of the hand and the waves in the sea.

possessive Nouns in English have an inflection to show possession. In writing it is *'s* and in speech variously /s/, /z/ and /ɪz/.

possessive adjective These words, which relate to the pronouns in English, are part of the determiner class because they precede the head noun in a noun phrase. They include *my, your, his, her, its, our* and *their*.

post-alveolar A place of articulation of consonants between the alveolar ridge and the hard palate. Examples from English include /ʃ/ and /ʒ/.

postmodifier The elements which follow a head noun in a noun phrase but are also part of the noun phrase. Usually either a prepositional phrase or a relative clause (e.g. *The desk* ***that I bought last week***).

pragmatic meaning Aspects of textual meaning that rely on context for their understanding.

predeterminer Small class of grammatical words which can precede the determiner in a noun phrase (e.g. ***some of*** *the children*).

predicator Clause element always realised by a verb phrase and obligatory in a full clause structure.

prefix Bound morpheme added to the beginning of a free morpheme base (e.g. ***dis****interested*).

pre-head Any unstressed syllables which occur before the head in a tone group.

premodifier The elements which precede the head noun in a noun phrase, but are also part of the noun phrase. Usually includes determiner and may also include predeterminer, adjectives and noun premodifiers.

preposition Largest class of grammatical words in English, usually used to relate the process and participants to the context in space and time (e.g. *in, on, under, over, round*, etc).

prepositional phrase A group of words made up of a noun phrase preceded by a preposition (e.g. *on the stairs*) and fulfilling the function of noun phrase postmodifier or adverbial clause element.

primary cardinal vowels Idealised forms of the most common vowels in human languages against which actual vowels may be mapped.

proclaiming tone A term from discourse approaches to intonation and referring to patterns which end in a falling tone and introduce new information.

progressive The progressive form of the verb phrase includes the progressive auxiliary, be, and an –ing form of the following verb (e.g. *is fighting*).

progressive assimilation Variation in the phonetic realisation of a phoneme in connected speech as a result of following another phoneme (e.g. careful pronunciation of *who's this?* /hu:zðɪs/ becomes /hu:zzɪs/)

pronoun A grammatical set of words which can refer to people or things which have already been mentioned or whose identity is evident in the context. They effectively replace more complex noun phrases. English pronouns include *he, she, us, them.*

proximal Used in the study of deixis, this refers to those words which place their referents close to the speaker – either psychologically or literally (e.g. ***this*** *car*).

pure vowels Vowels which involve only one placement of the tongue, and are thus not diphthongs.

rank-shifting Systemic-functional term for subordination or embedding, leading to recursion.

realisation The actual language used to fulfil a unit of structure. Thus, a noun phrase might be realised as *the old dog* and a {plural} morpheme might be realised as /-s/.

Received Pronunciation (RP) The accent of some southern British English accents and the upper classes. It is less common than it used to be and is changing and evolving like all accents.

recursion The application of grammatical rules more than once, so that theoretically there could be infinitely long structures. Alternatively, the embedding of higher level structures within lower level structures, causing a 'loop' in the structure which also leads to theoretically infinite structures.

reference Though it is less important than was thought in the past, the ability of language to make contact with non-linguistic aspects of the world is essential to its functioning well. This is reference. See also **sense**. Reference is also used to refer to textual reference, which is a kind of cohesive link.

referent A very useful term which indicates the real-world item or person that is being referred to.

referring tone A term from discourse approaches to intonation referring to patterns which end in a rising tone and indicate old or given information.

regressive assimilation See **anticipatory assimilation**.

relative clause A subordinate clause which functions as a post-modifier within the noun phrase and is usually introduced by a relative pronoun such as *that* or *which* (e.g. *The saucer* ***that I broke yesterday***).

restrictive relative clause A relative clause which is instrumental in identifying that referent (e.g. *The young child* ***who was in the field*** *saw a wolf*).

retroflex A manner of articulation of consonants, not used in English, in which the tip of the tongue curls back and flaps the back of the alveolar ridge. Occurs in languages of the Indian subcontinent, and thus is noticeable in some Indian accents of English too.

retrospective assimilation See **progressive assimilation**.

rhotic accent Accents of English in which the alveolar approximant, /r/ is pronounced after vowels. Typical of the West country of England (Cornwall, Devon and Somerset) and also common in the USA.

rise A distinctive pitch pattern, beginning on the tonic syllable of a tone group, which rises. Normally refers to given information.

rise-fall A distinctive pitch pattern, beginning on the tonic syllable of a tone group, which rises first and then falls. Normally refers to new information.

RP See **Received Pronunciation.**

Sapir–Whorf effect The tendency for speakers of a language to view the world through the words and structures that their language imposes on it.

schwa The only vowel with its own name, schwa is the unstressed central vowel in English and is transcribed as /ə/.

secondary cardinal vowels Idealised forms of the less common vowels in human languages, against which actual vowels may be mapped.

segmental Concerning the linear ordered units of the language such as phonemes or morphemes.

selectional restrictions The general semantic constraints on co-occurrence that are built into the semantics of a lexeme (e.g. the verb *believe* must have a human subject).

semantic features The components of meaning which can be identified as shared by a range of words, and thus make up a word's meaning.

semantic fields Groups of words with a shared set of semantic features, and thus shared core meaning (e.g. all words relating to *fires*: *coal, wood, flames, smoke,* etc.).

semantics The study of meaning, at word, clause or textual levels. Contrasts with pragmatics in not being context-dependent.

semi-vowel See **approximant.**

sense An individual (polysemous) meaning of a lexeme. Also refers to the interrelationship of words with one another; the mutuallydefining nature of all language.

sense relations The different relationships that a word sense enters into with other word senses. Includes synonymy, hyponymy, homonymy, oppositeness, etc.

sibilant A sub-class of the fricative manner of articulation where the tongue is grooved and the airflow whistles down a more focused route than in other fricatives (e.g. /s/ and /z/).

sign The Saussurean concept of a combined 'signified' (meaning) and 'signifier' (word) to produce the 'sign'.

sonorant Term referring to both the nasal and approximant manners of articulation of consonants which highlights their common feature of resonance.

stimulus-freedom See **displacement.**

stop Term referring to both the plosive and nasal manners of articulation of consonant which highlights their common feature of complete obstruction of the airflow through the oral cavity.

stress-timed language English is said to be stress-timed because there is a relatively regular 'pulse' of stressed syllables in English, however many unstressed syllables there are between them. See also **syllable-timed language**.

structuralist theory The approach to linguistic description, initiated by de Saussure, which emphasises the interrelatedness of linguistic units and structures.

subject A clause element, normally realised by a noun phrase, with which the verb phrase is obliged to agree in person and number where relevant.

subject complement A clause element, usually realised by a noun phrase or an adjective phrase, which has the same referent as the Subject and occurs with certain kinds of verb, usually intensive verbs (e.g. *Hugh was a dancer; Jenny is beautiful*).

subordination Related to recursion, this is where a unit or structure is embedded within a lower level of structure.

substitution One of the means by which texts become cohesive is to use substitution of, for example, pronouns, for other nouns, making a link between the noun and the pronoun (***Mr Jones** was furious. **He'd** been queuing for hours*).

suffix Bound morpheme added to the end of a free morpheme base (e.g. *correct-**ion***).

superlative An inflected form of adjective (or adverb) in which the quality ascribed by the adjective is at its most intense or extreme (e.g. *cleverest, stupidest*). May also be conveyed by an intensifier (e.g. *most exciting, most predictable*).

superordinate The more inclusive term in a relationship of hyponymy (e.g. *tree* is superordinate to *oak*).

suprasegmental Describes those aspects of phonology which are not featured in the segments (phonemes), but are 'overlaid' on top of them. Intonation and utterance stress are two examples.

syllabic consonant A consonant (usually a sonorant) which can take the place of a vowel at the centre of a syllable (e.g. bottle [bɒtl̩]).

syllable The phonological segment larger than a phoneme which has a vowel as its irreducible core and may also have opening and closing consonant clusters.

syllable-timed language Languages (e.g. Spanish) which give approximately the same length of time to each syllable. See also **stress-timed language**.

synchronic dimension of study The study of a language system at a single point in history, as it is used and experienced by the speakers. See also **diachronic study**.

synonymy A sense relation of identity, where the meaning of two word senses is the same in every way. True synonymy is very rare, but English has many partial synonyms.

syntagmatic relationship Any linguistic relationship between items or structures which can co-occur in different syntactic roles. For example, animate nouns are in a syntagmatic relationship with verbs needing animate Subjects (e.g. *breathe, live*).

syntax The study of structures in a language, made up of words, phrases and clauses.

systematicness One of the features of human language postulated by the structuralist approach to linguistics.

tail The syllables (stressed and unstressed) which follow the nucleus in a tone group and continue the pitch movement (tone) begun on the nucleus.

text There are many possible meanings of this term, but in the current book it is used for any stretch of language, whether spoken or written.

textual One of Halliday's Three metafunctions, the textual function of language is to construct the relationships between different parts of the text. See also **ideational** and **interpersonal.**

tone The significant meaningful moving pitch in a tone group. May be a fall, a rise, a rise–fall, a fall–rise or a level tone. Begins on the nucleus and is continued throughout the tail.

tone group The basic unit of intonation, in which there is one main pitch movement, starting on the nucleus, and continuing through the tail. Before the nucleus, there is the head and the pre-head. The tone group is most neutrally associated with the clause, but may be shortened or extended to achieve different effects.

tonic syllable See **nucleus.**

trachea The windpipe. The route for the egressive pulmonary airstream to leave the lungs and enter the larynx.

transcription The process of writing down speech, either in phonetic/phonemic form or in order to analyse other features, such as the turn-taking in a conversation.

transformation A kind of rule suggested by Chomsky which would make the grammatical description of a language simpler by taking regular syntactic relationships and deriving one type of structure (e.g. the passive) from another (e.g. the active), reducing the need for the grammar to produce all such sentences individually.

transformational-generative grammar Chomsky's particular version of a generative grammar, introducing transformations as a significant feature of the rules.

transition relevance place (TRP) Those places in a conversational turn where the speaker and hearer are aware that a turn change might take place. These include, for example, the ends of clauses and sentences.

transitive verb Lexical verbs which require an Object to complete them (e.g. *I ate an apple*). Some transitive verbs may also occur without an Object, though the conceptual object is usually clear (e.g. *I ate* presumes some kind of food).

trill The repeated flapping of the tip of the tongue or another articulator (e.g. the uvulum), producing a speech sound. Not used in English.

turn A speaker's contribution to a conversation without anyone else speaking.

turn-taking The pattern of changing turns in a conversation.

unexploded plosive A plosive sound in which the closure of the articulators is not followed by the release of the air pressure behind this closure. This can happen before another plosive or before silence.

unstressed syllables Those syllables which do not carry word stress and often have the schwa vowel at their centre.

utterance stress The extra emphasis given to certain syllables in context, often reflecting their focal importance in the structure, but possible used in contrastive ways too.

uvular A manner of articulation of consonants in which the uvulum moves towards the root of the tongue.

uvulum The very back of the palate, beyond the velum (soft palate). The uvulum hangs down at the back of the throat and is used in speech sounds in some languages, but not English.

variety A useful term to refer to any particular version of a language, whether geographically or socially based or connected with a specific group of people (e.g. in a working situation).

velar A manner of articulation of consonants in which the back of the tongue is raised towards it and may cause a complete closure (e.g. /k/, /g/). The velum may also be lowered away from the back wall of the pharynx, to cause nasal resonance.

velarised 'l' The pronunciation of a lateral approximant near the back of the mouth, although there may also be alveolar contact too.

velum/soft palate The part of the palate which is only fleshy, having no bone above the flesh. This is able to be moved up and down, and is used in velar sounds.

verb A lexical word class which specifies the process or state being described and links the participants in the action to each other.

verb phrase The phrase which contains a main verb preceded by up to four auxiliary verbs. Its function is as Predicator in the clause.

vocal folds Also popularly known as vocal cords, these are actually quite wide bands of muscle which extend vertically into the larynx as well as horizontally across the top of the trachea. Their horizontal stretching causes the voicing that makes up a lot of speech as well as singing. At rest, the vocal folds are apart, and when pulled together they vibrate.

vocalised 'l' Some accents of British English have a fully vocalised 'l' in syllable final position (e.g. *pool*), where other versions have a dark (velarised) 'l'. The effect is like a /w/, with only a little lateral escape of air to distinguish it.

voice/voiced/voicing The vibration of the vocal folds, to create a louder sound which has an identifiable pitch.

vowel The essential sounds in a syllable, which are made by the airflow resonating around the oral cavity, rather than being interrupted in the manner of the consonants.

vowel chart Now part of the IPA chart, the vowel chart was created by Daniel Jones, to indicate the height of the tongue at the back and front of the mouth in pronouncing different vowel sounds.

VPM The basis of classification of consonant speech sounds, made up of the voice, place and manner of articulation.

Whorfian hypothesis See **Sapir–Whorf effect.**

word senses The different, but related meanings of lexemes which form semantic relationships (sense relations) with other word senses.

word stress The prominent syllable in English words, usually only one, though long words may have secondary stresses too.

zero derivation The formation of a new word by simply changing its word class, rather than adding a derivational morpheme (e.g. *to paper a wall* – noun becomes verb).

Index

Breinigsville, PA USA
30 September 2010

246446BV00002B/36/P

9 781403 912626